OWLS
SHEFFIELD WEDNESDAY
THROUGH THE MODERN ERA

TOM WHITWORTH

First published by Pitch Publishing, 2016

Pitch Publishing
A2 Yeoman Gate
Yeoman Way
Worthing
Sussex
BN13 3QZ
www.pitchpublishing.co.uk
info@pitchpublishing.co.uk

ISBN 978-1-78531-219-9

Typesetting and origination by Pitch Publishing
Printed by Bell & Bain, Glasgow, Scotland

Contents

Act III: Return?

For our Mum and Dad

Introduction

This is a story of Sheffield Wednesday, a football club formed in the north of England, in Yorkshire, in 1867.

Cast of Key Characters

The Football Club
Sheffield Wednesday

The City
Sheffield – *Former industrial powerhouse. City of hills. Population: 500,000-plus. Home to it all*

The Stadium
Hillsborough – *Capacity: 39,000-plus. Home to the club since 1889. Scene, in 1989, of the worst disaster in British football history*

The Directors and Executives
Dave Allen – *Casino owner. Chairman (2003–07)*
Dejphon Chansiri – *Businessman from Bangkok, Thailand. Owner of Sheffield Wednesday (2015–)*
Sir Charles Clegg – *Father of the game. Football Association chairman and president (1890–1937). Sheffield Wednesday chairman (1915–31)*
Bob Grierson – *Finance director (1990–2010)*
Milan Mandarić – *Serbian-American serial football club owner. Wednesday owner (2010–15)*

Sir Dave Richards – *Sheffield Wednesday chairman (1990–2000).
Premier League chairman (1999–2013)*
Lee Strafford – *Co-founder and former CEO of PlusNet.
Wednesday chairman (2008–10)*
Kaven Walker – *Wednesday chief executive (2005–08)*
Howard Wilkinson – *Experienced football man. Sheffielder.
Wednesday player (1962–66). Wednesday manager (1983–88)
and chairman (2010)*

The Managers

Ron Atkinson – *Charismatic 'Big Ron'*
Carlos Carvalhal – *Well-travelled Portuguese who arrived at
Hillsborough in the summer of 2015*
Trevor Francis – *Player then manager who took on baton from
Ron Atkinson (1991–95)*
Paul Jewell – *Lasted less than a year in the job in 2000/01 as
Wednesday adjusted to life in the second tier following relegation
from Premier League*
Dave Jones – *Former Wolves and Cardiff boss. Oversaw promotion
from League 1 in 2012*
Brian Laws – *Likeable leader of Wednesday team (2006–09)*
Gary Megson – *283 appearances in a Wednesday shirt in the
1980s. Boss (2011–12). Son of club legend Don Megson*
David Pleat – *Experienced and knowledgeable figure in the game.
Manager (1995–97)*
Paul Sturrock – *Straight-talking Scottish manager. Guided club to
play-off success at Cardiff, 2005*
Danny Wilson – *League Cup-winning midfielder with club in
1991. Later, Wednesday manager (1998–2000)*

The Players

Andy Booth – *110 per cent Yorkshireman, centre-forward: 34
goals (1996–2001)*
Chris Brunt – *Belting left-footed winger destined for Premier
League. Sold on for millions in 2007*

CAST OF KEY CHARACTERS

Paolo Di Canio – *Volatile Italian maestro forward talent (1997–99)*

Derek Dooley – *Original goal machine: 63 goals in 61 games for the club over two seasons (1951–53). Later manager of club. Sacked Christmas Eve 1973*

Fernando Forestieri – *Shining light Italian forward of 2015/16 season*

Steve MacLean – *Striker. Scorer of key penalty at 2005 League 1 play-off final*

Gerald Sibon – *Sometimes good, often frustrating giant Dutch forward (1999–2002)*

Chris Waddle – Le Magicien *on the wing and crowd hero (1992–96)*

Des Walker – *Defender (1993–2001). Chant, 'You'll never beat Des Walker'*

The Others

The Fans – *Ever-present since 1867. 'We're all Wednesday, aren't we?'*

Daniel Gordon – *Documentary-maker and Wednesday fan*

Mark Lewis – *Lawyer. Represented Wednesday fans facing libel action from own club (2006–08)*

Nigel Short – *Supporter. Subject to libel action by own football club (2006–08)*

Wednesdayite – *Supporters' group (formerly the Owls Trust)*

Tom Whitworth – *Author and Wednesday fan*

[W]e've always dwelled on the past too much. Even when I went to my first match in 1944, the fans were harping on about the team that won the league in 1903 and 1904. You should never look back.

**– Lord Hattersley. Former Labour MP
Sheffield Wednesday fan (2011)**

Prologue

Relegation

*S*HEFFIELD. *30 April 2000. Out of the house and down the leafy street. Your dad and you joining the blue and white train of fans making their way down Wadsley Lane to the ground. Past the pub on the left and the newsagent. Hillsborough Park on your right. Then over the tram tracks.*

Buy the programme on the corner of Leppings Lane. A quick look at the table – Sheffield Wednesday, second bottom of the Premier League. Five points from salvation. Only four games to go. Grim faces all around you. Everyone seems to know it: we are going down. Dropping from the top table.

The Sky TV cameras are here today. Wednesday–Leeds. Our opponents, our aspirational neighbours from up the road. ('Got a Harvey Nics, you know.') Their players, David O'Leary's 'Babies', are chasing a Champions League place. All season O'Leary's been doing everyone's head in, bleating on about his youngsters. Their quality and their promise. Kewell, Bridges, Bakke... And four of them – Smith, Harte, Woodgate and Bowyer – aren't even playing today.

The ascent of O'Leary's 'Babies' is Wednesday's descent, you think as you walk.

For Wednesday, it's been the bad signings and the mis-investment – the money down the bloody drain.

Perpetual decline. The imminent drop. This awful season.

OWLS

* * * *

This year, the gates at Hillsborough, at Wednesday's home, have been okay: 25,000 on average or thereabouts, inflated by followings from across the Pennines and the north-east. But there won't be as many as that here today.

Big club Wednesday? People have had enough. It feels like the end of days.

As you make your way round to the North Stand, someone with a radio is telling people in earshot that Bradford are winning. 'Not good for us, that.' Wednesday will be six points behind now. No chance of staying up.

You pass through the turnstile and up the curved concrete walkway of the stand. Walk along the tight concourse and up the steps to the seats. Up there on top of the play.

'C'mon Wednesday!'

Forty seconds in and it's 1-0 to Leeds. Hopkin. Fuck's sake. Wednesday's done already.

'They used to throw the cushions on to the pitch from here, you know,' your dad tells you. No cushions today to throw at this lot, though. Shower of shite.

Then it's half-time. Programme out. Dad down the steps for the teas.

* * * *

Where does the blame for all this lie?

'Not the players' fault, is it?' they say. But some of them haven't been bothered, *you think. And some don't look good enough at all.*

'Whose then?'

Us? The fans?

No.

The manager, then? (Before he was sacked a few months ago.)

Or maybe it's those out of the picture: the directors who have been guiding the club. The custodians. Dave Richards, Mr Chairman, is good and gone now. He's the Premier League's chairman now: their top man. He left us right in it, they say. Left us with the debt that has been built up over the years, which now strangles the club.

Wherever the blame lies, definitely we're a long way from the good old days. Days like Wembley '91: Atkinson's men lifting the League Cup.

RELEGATION

And we're a long way from Wembley '93, too: Chrissy Waddle and two more cup finals. Five years after that was Di Canio pushing the referee, then buggering off to West Ham. Can't blame him, though. The decline properly set in by then.

Our club is meant to be a thing of good. Meant to be there for you, just as you are there for it, giving you happiness and memorable times. But it tests you, our club. Puts you right through it.

* * * *

Second half. Dad back with the drinks. Boothy tries, flying in. Quinny never stops running. And Walker's strong at the back, but the rest look all at sea. Not much sweat from the rest of them, all looking out of their depth in a failing side. O'Leary's 'Babies' running rings around them.

Fifty-three minutes and it's 2-0. Bridges.

Fifteen minutes later, it's Kewell in miles of space outside the area. His left boot sends it high and over Pressman, dipping in off the bar. 3-0. And Wednesday are done. All around you people are on their feet, streaming out.

They've seen enough.

The last minutes tick by. You look over the players, over green-and-white field to the refurbished sleek South Stand. The gabled roof and the clock with its golden finial top. The seats in the middle for the important people: the directors and the politicians and their hangers-on. The executive boxes. The rows of empty blue seats getting emptier.

In years to come, you'll realise what it represents, that stand – the spending and the losses, the bad decisions and the debt. And the years of going nowhere-ness that is to come.

* * * *

Final whistle and you and your dad have had enough, too. You get up out of your seats, walk down the steps, along the concourse and down the walkway. Then back home up the hill with only a few words said between you. Your club. Meant to be a thing of good.

You think of what is to come. The hopes and the let-downs. The wins and the defeats. The away days and the home days. The shouts, the cheers and the hugs. The 'cretins' and the 'scum'. The mistruths and the half-truths. The relegations and the bloody suing the fans.

OWLS

The blue and the white and the grey.
You're 14. Your team, about to be relegated from the Premier League.
How the fuck did this happen?

Act I
Fall

Factory Demolition, Carbrook Street (1989) [John Darwell]

1

Sheffield, Some Years Ago...

IT began on 4 September 1867 in the Adelphi Hotel, on the corner of Arundel and Sycamore Street, in Sheffield city centre, where the Crucible Theatre now stands. The gentlemen had gathered there to consider adding a new sporting arm to their cricket club.

The club had been around for over 50 years, formed to give the skilled craftsmen of the Steel City – those 'little mesters' whose expertly produced cutlery and tools gave Sheffield its global renown – something to do on their spare afternoons away from the filth of the workshops and the factories. But cricket was for the summer and during the dark winter months the members had no sport to play. It was thought another option, association football, might keep them together. So that night in the Adelphi Hotel it was agreed: The Wednesday Football Club would be formed.

The Wednesday – who, it was decided, would play in blue and white (though initially in hoops not stripes) – joined Sheffield FC, the world's oldest football club founded in 1857, and Hallam FC, founded a few years later, on the growing local footballing landscape. The new club soon took a steady footing and built up their following as they shifted around the various venues of London Road, Myrtle Road, Sheaf House and Bramall Lane.

Acceptance to the Football League came in 1892; the expansion of the league allowing The Wednesday to join the original founders from the north – Everton, Preston North End, Notts County and Blackburn Rovers. And as the club took to that higher stage, crowds at Olive Grove, the club's new ground and first 'real' home, averaged around 10,000 (by now, the cricketing side of the club had separated from its footballing brother: part of the reason, the football side reckoned, was that the football club earned the money while the cricket club spent it).

Following the decision to expand the busying nearby railway lines that led into Sheffield Midland station, it wasn't long before Wednesday were forced to leave their Olive Grove home. A ballot of supporters showed a site out at Carbrook in the city's industrial east end, where day and night the vast and glowing steelworks forged away, to be the preferred option.

But the move fell through when another bidder for the site got in there first. Never mind; as Wednesday's then chairman, the industrialist George Senior, declared, 'I breathe sulphur all the week, and I'm sure not goin' to Carbrook to suck it in.' So the outpost of Owlerton, a couple of miles outside the city centre, was chosen instead.

At the time, there wasn't much going on at Owlerton: an army barracks, a handful of basic roads, a park. Ordnance Survey maps show a few houses, a school and lots of meadowland. The rattle of the electric tramways had yet to reach that far out of town and the area wasn't even yet part of the Sheffield boundary. Nevertheless, Wednesday were determined to make the site work and in 1899, helped by the proceeds from a new share issue, fetched up there with the main grandstand from Olive Grove, transplanted across town brick by brick and rebuilt at the new ground.

Despite the difficulties reaching Owlerton, the crowds still came. As the city's economy, spurred on by its steel production, grew, so too did demand for more houses. A thriving community with a football club at its heart developed and in 1902/03 and 1903/04 The Wednesday – now sporting the club's new nickname, the Owls (in reference to the new Owlerton home) – won a pair of First Division titles. Three years later, they won the FA Cup.

Two men involved in the funding of the move to Owlerton were the brothers William and Charles Clegg. Both had played for the club in previous years, and even for England in the country's first international match, in 1872. Each would go on to play pivotal roles in the game both nationally and locally.

The brothers' father was William Clegg, a distinguished solicitor who had gained notoriety after the Great Sheffield Flood of 1864 when he had helped families bring their claims against the Sheffield Waterworks Company, following the collapse of the defective Dale Dyke Dam out in Bradfield in the north-west of the city. The floodwaters swept through Loxley and Malin Bridge, through town and out to the Don Valley. Some 238 Sheffielders died, many drowning while sleeping in their homes. The Clegg sons became lawyers, too; Charles also becoming chairman of the Football Association and, in 1915, chairman of The Wednesday.

A teetotal non-smoking Methodist, Charles Clegg abhorred gambling and violence, and pursued always a path of honest rightfulness in the club's boardroom. At Wednesday, explains David Conn in his book *The Beautiful Game*, Clegg 'insisted on rigorously above-board dealings', taking close care over the club's finances, refusing to spend money the club did not have; not willing to plunge the club into financial difficulty. 'Nobody gets lost on a straight road,' was his famous mantra.

Under Clegg, on that straight road, Wednesday picked up another couple of First Division titles in 1928/29 and 1929/30 (by which point The Wednesday had been renamed Sheffield Wednesday and Owlerton re-christened as Hillsborough), and in 1935 won the FA Cup, the deadly wing pairing of Mark Hooper and Ellis Rimmer getting three of Wednesday's four goals against West Bromwich Albion. Captured on film was the team's welcome home from Wembley: an open-top coach creeping and weaving through the packed, waving Sheffield crowds.

After Charles Clegg passed away in 1937, a memorial brass plaque dedicated to him was unveiled in the Hillsborough boardroom. Many years later, when the plaque had for some reason been discarded by the club, the Sheffield and Hallamshire Football Association would rescue it – supposedly, as one story goes, from a skip.

* * * *

After the Second World War and the break in the nation's regular footballing programme, emerging for Wednesday was the original goal-machine centre-forward, Derek Dooley. Over two brilliant seasons for Wednesday, the local lad, one-man powerhouse battering ram, would notch 63 goals in 61 games for the club he supported. Tragically, his promise was cut short when, on one icy afternoon at Preston North End, having chased down a through ball, he collided with the advancing goalkeeper and broke his leg. As Dooley lay in his hospital bed, gangrene set in from an infected cut on the back of his leg. The leg had to be removed and his career was over. 'I might as well snuff it,' said Dooley later, 'because I've not got a lot to live for.'

For Wednesday, that decade, the 1950s, were the yo-yo years – three promotions to the top division and three relegations. To arrest the unstable situation the club turned to a new manager, Harry Catterick, a dour disciplinarian brought in from lowly Rochdale, who managed to build a formidable side with a group of promising players. Using the experience of the future England centre-back Peter Swan, alongside the talented youth of goalkeeper Ron Springett, full-back Don Megson and forward Johnny Fantham, the new manager forged a stern yet attacking unit that saw Wednesday entertain and succeed. In his first season in the job, Catterick led his men to the Second Division title. Two years later, in 1960/61, they finished second to the great double-winning Tottenham Hotspur side.

The 1960s were something of a boom time for the club and the city. In the Don Valley to the east and Stocksbridge in the north, the steel factories were forging and hammering away at a great pace, sending millions of tons of the highest-grade specialist metals and the most robust machine tools and cutlery out across the world. Order books were full and employment levels were high.

The city's landscape was transforming too.

In 1961 Park Hill and Hyde Park flats, the concrete 'streets in the sky' which sat above the train station, replaced the nearby slums to provide high-rise living with panoramic views of the city from their Brutalist concrete grid frames. The sleek concrete-and-glass University Arts Tower, and white modernist Hallam Tower Hotel in well-to-do Fulwood would open in 1965. They, along with new measures like 'operation clean air' – which since 1956 had sought to control fuel usage and reduce smoke levels in the city – would help further shed the city's grimy and smoggy industrial image. While the Tinsley viaduct, running over the River Don – the city's main river which cooled the furnaces of the vast steelworks that lined its banks – and past the imposing power station cooling towers, brought the M1 to the city, serving to better link Sheffield to the economic power of the south. Sheffield, proclaimed the book *Sheffield: Emerging City* optimistically, was moving 'into a richer future'.

Wednesday's contribution to this emergence was a ground-breaking development that would give its Hillsborough stadium the status of being one of the best in the country.

Opened in 1961 the North Stand, a cantilevered masterpiece – the first of its kind to run the full length of the pitch – was designed by Sheffield engineers and constructed using metals forged in the city. It held 8,000 spectators, its curved concrete walkways taking fans up to the top half of the stand, while its girders stretched backwards like a claw to support the acre-sized roof, providing all with an unobstructed view of the play. From the outside it looked like a spaceship.

However, such development came, at least in the eyes of Owls manager Harry Catterick, at the expense of his playing budget. Even though the £150,000 cost of the new stand had been funded by a share issue (the proceeds never destined for new football players) the Wednesday boss began to feel restricted and aggrieved. His side that had returned to, and gone on to compete well in, the First Division had cost only £17,000 to assemble, a fraction of the £250,000 the Tottenham 1961 double-winning team had been brought together for, and Catterick wanted more cash for players so that he could achieve more with his team.

But club secretary Eric Taylor, emulating the beliefs of Charles Clegg decades before, could not and would not risk jeopardising the club's financial health by investing heavily in both the club's infrastructure and the team. So Catterick, realising that while he was Wednesday's manager he would never have the riches some of his rivals had, left the club before the 1960/61 season had even finished. At Everton, where he was given the budget he desired, he would go on to win a pair of First Division championships while, post-Catterick, Wednesday's fortunes would wane.

A betting scandal in 1964 saw the Wednesday captain Peter Swan, along with his then teammates David Layne and Tony Kay, sentenced to a few months in prison and banned from the game for life after they had been found to have bet on a Wednesday defeat at Ipswich a few years earlier. The scandal reached all levels of the game in England but the Owls trio were the highest-profile culprits and their careers were all but finished because of their actions.

Then, in 1966, there was the heartbreak of an FA Cup final defeat to Catterick's Everton. The Wednesday lads, in their whiter-than-white change kit, took a 2-0 lead over the Merseysiders. But Everton were to pull it back to win 3-2 and take the trophy. Afterwards, captain Don Megson led his team on an unsmiling losers' lap of the pitch; an enduring metaphor, perhaps, for the fortunes of the club in years to come.

After Wembley came the spectacle of the World Cup, hosted by England. Sheffield and Wednesday played their part: Hillsborough staged four games; over 40,000 were there for the West Germany–Uruguay quarter-final. Yet whatever good feeling remained from Catterick's days, or from the cup final, or even from the World Cup, would be gone by the end of the decade as Wednesday were relegated from the First Division.

* * * *

A few years of hanging around at the wrong end of the Second Division led to the promotion of Derek Dooley from his role in the club's development office to first-team manager: he was back again in a prominent role at Wednesday following the ending of his playing career on that icy Preston pitch two decades before. However, with little money to spend and serious injury problems, Dooley had a hopeless task and struggled to turn the club around. On Christmas Eve 1973, he was sacked by the club. A cruel blow for one of the club's greatest ever players; his second major hurt in football.

The backdrop to these footballing dramas was the contraction of the city's steel and engineering industries. Increasing competition from overseas devastated orders, while roller-coasting inflation rates compounded the problem, which in turn produced turbulent unemployment levels in the city. Partly because of these economic factors, and partly because the team was so bad at the time, crowds at Hillsborough were down (at times even below 10,000). During some of the more lowly attended midweek games of that time, the heartbeat sound of drop-hammer on metal coming from nearby steelworks on nightshift could be heard over the quietened Hillsborough crowd.

In 1974/75, after winning only five games all season, Wednesday were relegated to the Third Division.

Around this time, the Hillsborough-born Bert McGee took over as chairman of the club. Recently, Wednesday had developed a habit of making losses and being overdrawn with the bank (since 1966, the club had lost money nearly every year) and McGee, a bluff, strong, industry man who had risen from apprentice to chairman of the tool-making company Presto, sought to reverse the trend of losses, instituting a necessary policy of financial prudence and living within your means. As McGee explained of the club's attempts to address its financial problems, 'We stopped spending and started earning, kept a tight control on all overheads, instituted rigorous, sensible housekeeping, appointed sound management, and let them get on with it.'

After sacking the club's manager Len Ashurst, McGee brought in someone who would be able to get the best out of what was a lowly paid and, in terms of footballing ability, limited group of players: Jack Charlton.

Charlton, World Cup winner in 1966, armfuls of trophies with Leeds United before a few successful years managing Middlesbrough, was ready for his next challenge in the game.

Under him, Wednesday's decline levelled off before curving upwards. In 1977/78 he kept Wednesday up in the Third Division, progress consolidated the year after, and then the following year brought success. The 4-0 Terry Curran-inspired demolition of Sheffield United at Hillsborough on Boxing Day 1979, in front of 49,309 humiliated hated city rivals, spurred the club on to promotion. Happy days.

Less happy was from January 1980 onwards, when almost 100,000 steelworkers up and down the country went on strike for 13 cold weeks over pay rises and potential job losses in their industry. In Sheffield there was picketing of the vast Hadfields East Hecla Works in the Don Valley. One day saw 2,000 pickets (their numbers swelled by supporters from the National Union of Mine Workers) confront 2,000 police. The South Yorkshire force was well-drilled and ready for such a dispute: arrests were made and snatch squads used to get the ringleaders. The industrial battle ended with pay rises for the workers in the short term, but job losses and plant closures in the long.

Politically, at the time the city was renowned for its council-led radicalism and alternative socialist ideas. Its leader, David Blunkett, went against the Thatcher grain by doing things like keeping bus fares low – freedom of movement for a few pence a trip – and business rates high.

Sheffield would be called 'The Socialist Republic of South Yorkshire'; on May Day the red flag could be seen flying over the Town Hall; and as the academic Paul Lawless would observe, 'Hardly any retail, commercial or industrial development took place in the city in the first half of the 1980s.'

Meanwhile, Jack Charlton's Wednesday side, now in the Second Division and with an increasingly local and youthful feel (the promising Mel Sterland, John Pearson and Mark Smith supplementing the older heads), crept closer and closer towards the First Division. In 1981/82 they fell just short of promotion and in the years that followed finished fourth and sixth.

Thanks to Bert McGee's tight control of the finances, Charlton would spend little over a net £500,000 (the sales of players offset by the purchases) during his six seasons with the club. During the same period, about the same amount was spent on upgrading the club's infrastructure (the focus of much of this spending being the club's Hillsborough home). Partly because of the club's approach to spending in these two key areas, Wednesday moved to a position of profitability, or at worst one of posting limited, manageable losses, which spiked after the club became established in the Second Division. Live within your means was McGee's way, and Charlton accepted that.

After 1982/83, however, when Wednesday had finished sixth in the table and reached an FA Cup semi-final (losing to Brighton at Arsenal's Highbury), Jackie decided it was time to move on. He had picked the club up, dusted it off, reversed the slide and taken it back up close to the top. But for Wednesday, that was their lot. Charlton believed he had taken them as far as he could.

Taking on the baton, to finish the job Charlton had started, was the Sheffielder Howard Wilkinson.

Back in the 1960s, local lad and Owls supporter Wilkinson (who grew up in the Netherthorpe area, not far from Hillsborough) had played for the club, making a handful of first-team appearances before moving down the levels with Brighton and Boston United. Thanks to his work at Notts County, where on a limited budget he had taken the club to the First Division and kept them there, he was now a growing name in management.

At Wednesday, Wilkinson instilled great levels of fitness in his players. A qualified PE teacher, he ordered notorious gruelling runs in the green north Sheffield hills on the edge of the Peak District that meant his players would be able to outlast most opponents. The 'Wilkinson Way', a direct and effective pressing style underpinned by the excellent levels of fitness, and the principle of 'get a goal and don't let them back', worked well for the team. Wilkinson had Mick Lyons blocking at the back, tough-tackling Gary Megson battling away in the middle (Megson, son of Don, captain of the club through the 1960s, was also a passionate Wednesday supporter) and Imre Varadi knocking in the goals up front. Wilkinson's team of triers weren't pretty to watch, the ball ping-ponging around the place, but it worked.

After only one season, it was job done: Gary Shelton's overhead goal at Newcastle in April, followed up by a couple more wins, secured promotion back to the First Division. After 14 years away from the top tier, Wilkinson had finished the job Jack Charlton had started and the Owls were back.

For 1983/84, that first season back, the 'Wilkinson Way' remained and Wednesday comfortably settled down to life in the top division, taking some fine scalps along the way – Liverpool at 'fortress' Anfield (they'd lost there only twice the season before) and Manchester United at Old Trafford. The Owls reached as high as second during the course of the season, eventually taking eighth place.

From March 1984, the season had as its backdrop the miners' strike: a year-long struggle between the nation's colliers and the Margaret Thatcher regime and her police army.

Of Britain's 170 working coalmines in 1983, around a third were in Yorkshire, over half of those in South Yorkshire. But Thatcher said that over two-thirds of the mines were not profitable so the closures would be made. In response over 140,000 miners would come out on strike, over 54,000 of those in Yorkshire.

At Orgreave, a coking plant six miles from Sheffield city centre, there would be a violent pitched battle between at least 5,000 miners and 5,000 South Yorkshire Police practised from the steel strike in 1980 and bussed-in coppers from other forces. Coppers without numbers on their chests and coppers waving their overtime-swelled pay packets at, and laughing in the faces of the striking miners.

The police lines were pushed by the pickets and stones were thrown. Dogs chased the miners, the police lines opened and the horses charged. Then the snatch squads waded in along with the truncheons and the boots. Civil war.

Later, in court in Sheffield the Orgreave 'rioters' went on trial for their alleged part in the violence. When it was found that police evidence had been fabricated, though, with statements dictated and coordinated identical paragraphs produced and at least one forged signature identified, the prosecution's case broke down. The lawyer Michael Mansfield called it the 'biggest frame-up ever' as nearly 100 miners were cleared and no charges were brought against the South Yorkshire Police.

When the strike was over, the pit closures came – scores of them, every year. By 1990, 11 mines had gone in South Yorkshire alone and by the mid-2010s only one would remain.

* * * *

Through 1985/86, Wednesday improved further under Howard Wilkinson. Fifth spot in the First Division was achieved and, were it not for the ban on British clubs playing in Europe following the Heysel disaster and defeat to Everton in another FA Cup semi-final, there may have been a European place and a Wembley cup final for the club.

Bert McGee's tight housekeeping continued to keep the club's finances under control. Wages were relatively modest (Manchester United finished one place above the Owls that season and had a wage bill twice as large, as did West Ham United who also finished above the Owls), as was net spending on player transfers (between 1982/83 and 1986/87 less than £400,000 would be outlaid by the club in total). Meanwhile, over the same period Hillsborough would receive only limited investment too, with around £1.5m spent on construction at the club's home (of which at least £600,000 was provided as grants with about £1m spent on the new roof for the Kop end). But the club had been profitable – decent six-figure surpluses had been posted in 1985/86 and in 1986/87 – and generally Wednesday covered what it owed to others. The club didn't need or want to hammer the overdraft, or take on significant loans.

For thousands of people in the region, this approach mirrored the reality of life. The aftermath of the miners' strike had led to thousands of job losses across South Yorkshire. Meanwhile, the city's metal and engineering industries were finding ever-increasing competition from abroad. In 1987 unemployment across the region stood at 16.3 per cent – with the structural decline of the region's industries seeing the reduction of 'working-class affluence' – which, naturally perhaps, meant that for many doing things like going to Hillsborough or Bramall Lane was more of a struggle.

Such struggles, however, conflicted with Wednesday manager Howard Wilkinson's desire to spend on his overachieving squad. He believed that he was getting just about as much as he could from his players and that in order to progress – or indeed simply avoid falling behind other clubs – his team required substantial investment. Yet because of the level of wages Wednesday were offering at the time, Wilkinson found it difficult to attract the calibre of players he sought. So his band of honest triers began to drift down the table, finishing 13th in 1986/87 and 11th the year after.

In private, Wilkinson had attempted to persuade Bert McGee to change his approach to spending, but had gotten nowhere. He respected his chairman too much to go public with his thoughts, and so much like Harry Catterick had done back in 1961, he packed up and left for greener grasses; on this occasion 30 minutes up the M1 to Leeds United, then a struggling Second Division club.

The Leeds hierarchy wanted promotion and top-level success. They had to return to the days of Don Revie, of championships and cup finals. Howard Wilkinson, they believed, was the man to take them there.

Wilkinson thought about what he wanted to achieve; thought whether he could leave the club he had supported as a child, played for as a young man and was now managing successfully. He thought about the assurances Leeds were making about finances and their commitment to the plan of getting back to the top. In the end, he accepted their offer.

He said an emotional goodbye to his staff and his players; then, as he sat alone in the Hillsborough boot room underneath the South Stand, he wept into a blue towel, damning the board and the tightfistedness that had caused his departure. By 1992, his efficient and well-funded Leeds side would be First Division champions.

Wilkinson had wanted to take his assistant Peter Eustace with him to Leeds, but Eustace was a Wednesday fan himself and also a former player for the club (a classy passing midfielder who had started the 1966 FA Cup Final), so couldn't resist the offer to take over as Owls manager. He didn't take well to management though and after less than 20 dreadful, largely winless games, was sacked.

Someone better was required. A bigger figure in the game: Ron Atkinson. Flash 'Big Ron' had managed West Bromwich Albion and Manchester United, winning two FA Cups for the latter. After he returned from a short-lived spell with Atletico Madrid (he lasted only three months in Spain), Wednesday, hoping he would be the man to set the club on a positive course, somehow managed to tempt him to Sheffield.

An excellent man-manager who could inspire players, Atkinson immediately injected a spark into the Wednesday team, creating a relaxed and happy playing atmosphere; reviving a Wilkinson-esque work ethic while encouraging an attacking, passing approach which led at times to a beautiful fluidity. The 'Atkinson Way' suggested a new purpose for the club.

Under the new manager, results through 1988/89 improved and relegation looked as though it would be averted. And with a few new arrivals, like the young defensive midfielder Carlton Palmer, added to the likes of the emerging Barnsley lad David Hirst (a Wilkinson signing who was blossoming into a powerful and brilliantly effective striker), Atkinson was building a team that looked to have a good future.

Things looked well.

Then came the Hillsborough disaster.

2

Hillsborough

On 15 April 1989 a football match to decide a semi-final round of the FA Cup competition was to be played between the Liverpool and Nottingham Forest Clubs. The neutral venue chosen was Hillsborough Football Stadium, Sheffield Wednesday's ground. Only six minutes into the game, play was stopped when it was realised that spectators on the terraces behind the Liverpool goal had been severely crushed. In the result, 95 [the figure would rise to 96] died and over 400 received hospital treatment.

– Lord Justice Taylor's Interim Report into The Hillsborough Stadium Disaster (1989)

SINCE the 1960s Hillsborough and Sheffield Wednesday had regularly hosted one of the Football Association's showcase Cup semi-finals. Since the mid-1970s, however, when the club's costs were tightly controlled by chairman Bert McGee, expenditure on the stadium had been modest – around £450,000 spent on infrastructure improvements in the six seasons between 1975/76 and 1980/81. Many parts of the stadium were out of date.

In 1981 Hillsborough had hosted the Tottenham Hotspur–Wolverhampton Wanderers semi-final tie. That day, Tottenham fans standing on the Leppings Lane lower terrace had experienced severe crushing, some of them requiring medical treatment for broken arms and legs. Afterwards, when it was suggested to McGee that there could have been fatalities, he replied, 'Bollocks, no one would have been killed.'

It would be several years before Hillsborough again hosted an FA Cup semi-final, during which time a series of compartmentalising fences were introduced on to the Leppings Lane terrace (which served to pen supporters into separate areas of the terrace), and a crush barrier (there to take on pressure from people standing behind it and helping to prevent a build-up in pressure diagonally across the terrace), was removed.

Despite being notified of the changes made to the stand, Sheffield City Council, whose responsibility it was to issue an up-to-date safety certificate for the stadium, did not update the original document, which had been issued back in 1979. An update would have reflected changes to the maximum capacity of the ground after, for instance, works on the ground that had involved the introduction of the fences on the Leppings Lane terrace (which now took up space where people would once have stood). Across town at Bramall Lane, Sheffield United had no valid safety certificate either.

When Hillsborough next hosted an FA Cup semi-final in 1987 – the Leeds United and Coventry City tie – Leeds fans standing on the Leppings Lane terrace also experienced crushing.

Despite this, in 1988 Hillsborough would again host a semi-final, this time between Liverpool and Nottingham Forest. Like those Tottenham and Leeds fans had been before them, the Liverpool fans would be housed behind the goal in the Leppings Lane end and in the North Stand along the side of the pitch. In all the Liverpool fans had only 23 turnstiles through which they could enter their areas of the ground. The Nottingham Forest fans, given the Kop and South Stand, had 60.

Before the match, a crush built up on the Leppings Lane terrace, the area becoming 'packed solid' with Liverpool fans unable to move. Injuries would later be reported. One letter of complaint sent to the FA would refer to the Leppings Lane terrace as a 'death trap'.

Nevertheless, the following year Hillsborough would again be selected to host an FA Cup semi-final. The tie again would be between Liverpool and Nottingham Forest. The same arrangements for allocations as per the previous year would apply: Liverpool at the Leppings Lane end and in the North Stand; Forest the South Stand and Kop.

* * * *

On 15 April 1989, a clear and bright spring day, the fans of both clubs had been enjoying their journeys to Sheffield for the game, up the M1 from Nottingham or over the Pennines from Liverpool. In the build-up to kick-off a positive atmosphere had been building around Hillsborough as the 'good-humoured' and 'very compliant' supporters, as one police officer on duty would later describe them, made their way into the ground.

At the Leppings Lane end, electric counters monitored the number of Liverpool fans moving through the turnstiles. Worryingly, though, as they weren't able to let people in fast enough – only *seven* were available for the 10,100 people heading for the lower terrace – a crowd was building up dangerously outside. Kick-off approached but word from the stadium's small police control, that day housing Chief Superintendent David Duckenfield, a man only recently appointed as match commander, was that there would be no delay to the game.

Of the Liverpool fans now entering the Leppings Lane terrace, most headed straight down the middle entrance tunnel and into the middle pens, which by now were already full. Unlike the previous year when those pens were full, the tunnel had not been blocked off and fans directed left or right to the other side entrances, from which they could enter the more sparsely populated pens. Those already inside the full middle pens were now experiencing an immense crush. Due to the high fences that had been introduced several years before, however, they were unable to move over into space at the sides.

Back outside at the turnstiles, with the compressed crowd getting larger due to the slow rate at which people were being admitted through to the stand, the scene, according to one police officer on duty that day, was 'mayhem'. Frantic officers radioed through to request an exit gate at the back be opened to allow people in and relieve some of the pressure outside. Eventually, Chief Superintendent Duckenfield would order one gate to be opened. He would later say that the Liverpool fans had forced it open. They hadn't.

With the gate now open, people streamed in, many of them straight down the middle tunnel to the middle pens, the added pressure of people now transferred from outside to in. In the pens, hundreds of bodies were stuck. Air was short and in the crush people were screaming and crying. People were dying.

* * * *

Four minutes into the game, Peter Beardsley went close to scoring for Liverpool, hitting the bar with his shot. Those who were able to do so moved forwards for a better view. Previously, the crush barrier that had been removed from the terrace in 1986 would have relieved some of the pressure from the surge which resulted from that movement. But the barrier wasn't there now and, probably as a result of that surge, a corroded crush barrier further down the terrace broke. Many people fell and, as a subsequent report into the disaster would tell, 'The dead, the dying and the desperate became interwoven in the slump at the front of the pens.'

At the front of the terrace, two police officers opened a gate in the fence, letting people out on to the grass. Another officer ran on to the pitch to stop the game. Liverpool fans who had made it out worked with the police to pull down with their hands the wire fence to free others.

That afternoon, 94 Liverpool fans – 94 football fans, many of whom were under the age of 20 – lost their lives. A few days later, 14-year-old Lee Nicol died in hospital and in 1993 the life support of Tony Bland, a young man in his early 20s, would be removed: the 95th and 96th victims of the disaster.

Hillsborough, Sheffield. 15 April 1989. The darkest day.

* * * *

'Everyone has an opinion on Hillsborough,' says the documentary-maker and Sheffield Wednesday supporter Daniel Gordon, taking a break from the edit of his upcoming film about the disaster. 'It's such a huge story. And I guess as a Wednesday fan, as a football fan, and also because it is my ground – it's the place I go to as a fan – I felt a duty to tell the story.'

Gordon's film, *Hillsborough*, is a deeply moving two-hour journey which not only delves right into the events of that day, but also addresses the disgrace of the fall-out and decades-long search for justice that the families of the victims subsequently had to endure.

In the documentary there are parents speaking of the last time they ever saw their sons or daughters alive; people who were in the pens who believed that they were close to death; and ordinary, lower-ranking police officers who had been on duty that day and, amid the chaos, worked with fans to save lives.

'Speaking about it is a hard thing for people to do,' says Gordon of the interviews he carried out for the film. 'For most of the people you're talking to, it was the worst day of their lives. You only have to talk to any survivor who was in that pen to understand what they went through. In the end, some people spoke because they wanted to; some because they needed to. Most spoke in far greater depth than I thought they would. Many of the interviews were two-plus hours long.'

Along with the build-up to the disaster and the events of the day itself, the documentary also covers its shameful aftermath, when the shocking, blame-shifting and smearing campaign against the Liverpool fans began to occur.

From the start, drunkenness was cited by some as a cause for the crush (the coroner even ordered the unprecedented taking of blood-alcohol levels from all of the dead, including the younger victims), as was ticketless-ness and hooliganism. Added to this was Chief Superintendent Duckenfield's lie that the exit gate through which the Liverpool fans had streamed into the Leppings Lane stand had been forced, rather than being opened by police, as in fact had been ordered.

Talks were also held between the police, the local Conservative MP Irvine Patnick and the Sheffield-based Whites Press Agency, leading to a press release that referenced Liverpool fans kicking, punching and even urinating on police officers who had been trying to help the injured. *The Sun* took the release and ran a story under the infamous banner 'The Truth'. The *Sheffield Star* had run its story from the release the previous evening.

'I've now seen every frame that was shot on the day,' explains Gordon, 'and how the myth of drunken fans being the cause has survived is totally beyond me. To most people who have followed the Hillsborough story with a relatively open mind, it doesn't come as a surprise to find out the police got together and decided what their story was.

'What does surprise me about being in Sheffield and being a Wednesday fan, though, and knowing what type of city Sheffield is and how brutalised by the police and the Thatcher government Sheffield was in the 80s, is how many football fans in the city still think, "Actually the police were right and it was the fans' fault." I really can't see how proper football fans who know what it was like to be a fan in the 80s can still actually run with that.'

In time, details of the almost unbelievable lengths to which the police went in order to present its own version of events that day would be revealed. For instance, how over 150 police statements taken in the aftermath had subsequently been altered, with lines unfavourable to South Yorkshire Police removed and/or comments added to pin the blame on the Liverpool supporters themselves.

Subsequent reports into the tragedy from Lord Justice Taylor (published in August 1989 and January 1990 respectively) would dismiss any claims of it being the Liverpool supporters that were responsible for the disaster. Instead, Taylor outlined how 'the chief factor [in the disaster] was police failure to handle the crowd', and castigated Sheffield City Council, which was at the time led by the Wednesday supporter and future MP, Clive Betts, for failing to update the ground's safety certificate, even after the alterations which had been made through the preceding years – the council, according to Taylor, having demonstrated 'a serious breach of duty'. Sheffield Wednesday, meanwhile, were condemned for failing to ensure that the ground was safe. 'The Leppings Lane end was unsatisfactory and ill-suited to admit the number invited [to it]', Taylor noted.

In March 1990, almost a year after that fateful day and after giving over 20 years of service to the club, Bert McGee would step down as Wednesday chairman, though not before requesting help from the FA to obtain financial compensation for the club's likely loss of future semi-finals and the associated revenues from them. The FA did not respond to his request.

As for the rest of his board, despite what had happened at the ground while the club was under their guidance, no other directors would think it necessary to leave their post. In Daniel Gordon's view, 'Those board members should have taken responsibility and resigned. It was on their watch but they just carried on.'

'The disaster,' he says, 'was primarily caused because of a ground that's not fit to host a semi-final with such a number of people coming into it. And a police force that for whatever reason responded inappropriately. I still don't think that the club or Wednesday fans have fully grasped that yet, though.

'We allowed people into a ground that wasn't fit for purpose and 96 people died there. And our club is tarnished forever because of that.'

Despite Lord Taylor's findings, however, the smears against the Liverpool fans had already done the damage. It would be years and years before the families of the victims and the other Liverpool supporters who had been at Hillsborough that day could find any justice for what happened.

But it *would*, one day, be found.

3

A Terrific Goal

BEFORE Bert McGee had left the club in March 1990, following years of prudence and financial care while at the helm of the club, he had set Wednesday off on a transformative new course that would represent in general a whole new approach to spending.

Through Peter Eustace's brief spell as manager, the Wednesday fans' frustrations at the underinvestment in the team had become increasingly vocalised, with chants of 'McGee out' and 'sack the board' heard more and more often at home games.

Ron Atkinson's subsequent appointment and the support provided to him in the transfer market represented, however, a drastic change in approach; one which was now deemed necessary if the club were to be able to compete in the First Division, or even simply to avoid standing still or falling backwards.

To illustrate, in 1987/88, Howard Wilkinson's last season with the club, Wednesday's wage bill had been £1.4m per year. Twelve months later, now under Atkinson, it had risen to £1.7m as new arrivals Carlton Palmer, David Bennett and Steve Whitton freshened up his side. By the end of 1989/90 this figure would rise further still, to £2.2m, following the arrivals of striker Dalian Atkinson (£450,000), defenders Peter Shirtliff (£500,000), Phil King (£400,000), the immaculate Swedish right-back Roland

Nilsson (a bargain £375,000), and the classy Mancunian midfielder John Sheridan (£500,000 from Nottingham Forest reserves).

While this spending would help increase the club's debt (comprising predominantly bank lending) to a chunkier £1.6m by the end of the season, up from barely anything the year before, the club didn't seem to mind. As Wednesday's then club secretary Graham Mackrell would write, such spending reflected 'the cost of attracting quality management and players to the club'.

In late 1989, two new directors – Dave Richards, whose background was engineering, and the accountant Bob Grierson – had joined the club. By March 1990, when McGee departed, it was Richards who moved up in his place to chairman. It was from then on that the loosening of Wednesday's purse strings, which had begun under McGee as he supported his manager Ron Atkinson, would be advanced at an even greater pace.

* * * *

New chairman Richards was the son of a steelworker. In the early 1960s, before joining the company Three Star Engineering, he had completed an engineering apprenticeship. Then at Three Star, he had quickly risen through the ranks: first to general manager, then to director of the company.

He had once spoken of how, as a child, he had stood on Hillsborough's Kop with his father and watched Derek Dooley and Albert Quixall. Disconcertingly, though, as he would later admit to one of his Wednesday managers, in his strong Sheffield accent, 'What I knew about football you could write on the back of your hand.'

Under his and new finance director Bob Grierson's guide, Wednesday would transform from a club that didn't spend all that much to one that, relatively speaking, did, incurring years of losses as the club further increased its wage bill and spend on players; and gradually, eventually to racking up a mountain of debt.

Richards and Grierson were close and, as secretary Graham Mackrell would explain, 'not afraid of large numbers, or overdrafts, or interest on loans'. The consequences of losing money and taking out loans and overdrafts as you chased better results on the pitch seemed now to be tomorrow's problem. Spend to spur on the growth of the club and improve the team was the way. Speculate to accumulate.

* * * *

To date, under Ron Atkinson's leadership, Wednesday had been saved from relegation in 1988/89, revitalised and, despite a worrying run of defeats at the opening of the 1989/90 season, looked to have some promise for the future. Through that season form would improve and by spring the Owls would sit comfortably in 13th place in the table. With six games of the season to go, they'd be okay, people believed. Certainly, nobody expected the collapse that would come: the five losses from the last six games and, with them, relegation from the top division.

But, incredibly, it did come and Wednesday were down.

The shock of relegation posed a difficult question for the new chairman Dave Richards and his board. Support Atkinson and keep the players together? Keep on paying First Division wages in the Second Division, and gamble and borrow whatever was necessary to get the club back to the top table at the first attempt? Or should they disband a talented side (in spite of the relegation, they were a good group), cut the club's cloth appropriately and cash in on some of the talent?

The way Atkinson saw it, as it was the players who had got the club relegated it should be the same players who put the blip right. Happily for him, the board agreed and the former approach won out: for 1990/91 Wednesday would gamble, stay together and push for a return.

* * * *

Ahead of the season, striker Dalian Atkinson was the only key player to leave the club; the proceeds from his sale to Real Sociedad funding the signing of his replacement, Charlton's Paul Williams. Top players like John Sheridan and Roland Nilsson might also have left the club – they had clauses in their contracts that would have allowed them to go – but they didn't, so, along with Wednesday's other coveted stars, David Hirst, Nigel Worthington and Carlton Palmer, they stayed.

For the opening day game 6,000 Wednesdayites, some say more, were down at Ipswich to witness the delight of the Owls in motion. Full-backs Phil King and Nilsson bombed on by the wide midfielders Worthington and Danny Wilson. John Sheridan, working beside his engine sidekick Carlton Palmer, sprayed brilliant passes from the middle of the pitch. And Williams and Hirst combined beautifully for a 2-0 win and 'Yellows, Yellows, Yellows' roared the travelling support (yellow being the colour of the away strip worn that day by the team). A week later, when Hull were demolished 5-1 at Hillsborough – with four of the goals coming from Hirst – already there were signs of just how special the season might be.

On the wall of his office in Sheffield, Atkinson's assistant Richie Barker had stuck a graph that would chart the season's results. The progress graph would keep the group focused, showing on average just below two points a game – 90 by the end of the campaign – should take Wednesday up. Pleasingly enough, coming out of a points-filled autumn and winter, Wednesday would sit third in the promotion places; Barker's graph showing 54 points against a required 58. The Owls, just about, were on course.

If that wasn't positive enough, Wednesday had even managed to get themselves into their first cup final for 25 years. The 3-1 win in the second leg of the semi-final against Chelsea was the highlight of the run, setting up a meeting in April with Manchester United at Wembley.

* * * *

For the club's biggest game since the FA Cup Final of 1966 against Everton, the Wednesday squad arrived a few days early in London to prepare. In Hyde Park, it was trees for goalposts for a light training session. In the hotel, a party for birthday boy Trevor Francis. After that, more serious training out on the pitches at Bisham Abbey, where the master plan to beat United was hatched. By the Sunday afternoon of the final, Atkinson had his players relaxed and ready to go.

Along Wembley Way that day, the thousands who had come down from Sheffield created a sea of blue and white as they greeted the team bus as it slowly made its way to the stadium. Later, once inside, the team would walk out to a deafening noise from the Wednesdayites in the stands – a noise that would continue relentlessly throughout the match. On the pitch, the lads would equal the fans' performance. It was a glorious game.

Ron Atkinson's men that day in the final at Wembley: Turner, Nilsson, Pearson, Shirtliff, King, Harkes, Wilson, Sheridan, Worthington, Williams and Hirst.

For 90 minutes Manchester United's Mark Hughes found the unmoving and impenetrable wall of the Owls captain Nigel Pearson. Roland Nilsson and John Harkes combined brilliantly to thwart the young and dangerous winger Lee Sharpe (to the extent his teammates eventually gave up passing to him), while up front David Hirst harried and hassled all game, running himself into the ground and causing an endless nuisance to the United defenders, Gary Pallister and Steve Bruce.

The goal would come on 37 minutes.

For all of that season, the excellent John Sheridan had been able to show his creative elegance in the middle of the Wednesday midfield. And in the final, not long before half-time, when Pallister's headed clearance landed in front of his stride, his moment came. Striking the ball hard from the edge of the area, he sent it flying towards goal, hitting the post with a dull clunk on the way to landing in the United net. 'A terrific goal... by Sheridan' rang the warm voice of the TV commentator Brian Moore, as pandemonium took over among the Wednesday players and the Wednesday fans in the stands; 1-0 to the Owls, at Wembley, in the League Cup Final, against the mighty Manchester United.

United attempted the comeback but remained stumped as Wednesday resiliently held out. The minutes ticked by and the Owls held on magnificently to take the trophy, the club's first for over 50 years.

'WE WON THE CUP' read the front of the *Star* that Monday.

'A very good day,' the excellent Roland Nilsson would recall with some understatement.

* * * *

After that success, although the players' partying went on long into the night (probably as long as the fans'), there was still a job to be finished in the league. Six games remained. Eighteen points to play for. A place in the top three required for promotion. And as Wednesday already sat up there, all they had to do was stay put.

The 3-1 win over Bristol City at Hillsborough with a game to spare would seal it. Mission accomplished. Job done. Wednesday, at the first attempt, were back in the First Division.

It had taken only a year but after the shock of relegation the season before, the Owls were back (and had won a major trophy too). Thank you Mr Atkinson – a figure now loved by all at the club. And thank you Mr Chairman – Mr Dave Richards. The side had been kept together. The gamble had been taken as they pushed for the return and it had paid off. Yes, it had come at a cost – a modest loss of £1.7m would be posted for that season – but who minded?

Three weeks after the Bristol promotion game, an open-top bus took the Wednesday team through the streets of Hillsborough, past the waving fans stood on the pavements below, then into town where it crawled through the crowds. Once inside the Town Hall, the players made their way up to the balcony before emerging above the cheering blue and white masses. Happy days.

The needle was soon to come off that happy record, though, as not long after, manager Ron Atkinson landed a devastating blow to the fans, leaving the club.

* * * *

'For years and years, I had privately considered [Aston] Villa to be my ultimate destiny as a manager,' Atkinson would later write in his autobiography. And when Villa came calling in the summer of 1991, the temptation to join his boyhood team proved too great for him to resist.

When, a year earlier, Villa had first come calling for him, Atkinson had been persuaded by his Wednesday chairman to stay. 'Give us one more year and then move to Villa next summer,' Dave Richards had told him. He did – and gave the Owls their brilliant promotion and cup-winning year. Now, it was different. Now, following that successful year, he was ready for his 'ultimate destiny', Villa.

At first, it had seemed Richards again had persuaded Atkinson to stay. To stick with the club, take Wednesday on even further and in the process become the highest-paid manager in the country. On that celebratory bus ride into town, however, Atkinson seemed to look uneasy; like he knew something was not quite right. He couldn't turn down Villa now, could he? Not again.

Within a week he would change his mind and would be gone.

The departure was 'of course a disappointment', Richards would write, 'particularly in light of the manner in which the manager committed his loyalty to the club, only to change his mind a few days later'. But that didn't comfort the Wednesday fans who felt betrayed and abandoned by their messianic leader. He had let them down and to them Atkinson was now Judas.

He was gone. The Owls would have to move on.

* * * *

For his replacement, Wednesday would look inwards, promoting the intelligent veteran forward of the 1990/91 promotion team, Trevor Francis, to the main job.

Experienced from campaigns with Brian Clough's Nottingham Forest and Sampdoria in Italy – where the values of a good diet, good living and proper preparations for matches had been instilled in him, prolonging his playing career into his 38th year – Francis was the preferred, and perhaps logical choice to succeed Atkinson. Certainly, following an earlier brief spell as boss of Queens Park Rangers, he now felt ready for the step up from player to become Wednesday's new manager.

Before the 1991/92 season, the club again spent relatively heavily on player transfers and wages, with Francis, as Atkinson had enjoyed before him, receiving good financial support from his board. Not only had the board wanted a quick return to the First Division for the club, they wanted them to stay there and be able to compete towards the top of it.

Funds of £1.2m, then, were provided for Rangers and England goalkeeper Chris Woods, then £750,000 for Oldham's up-and-coming defender (and later makeshift striker) Paul Warhurst. Later in the season, those sums would be followed by the £800,000 purchase of the Nottingham Forest striker Nigel Jemson and

£575,000 for the young Leyton Orient forward Chris Bart-Williams.

By a quirk of the scheduling of the 1991/92 season's fixtures, the opening game would pit young apprentice against old master, Wednesday against Villa, new boy Francis against Judas Atkinson.

For the showdown August return of Atkinson passions were high, with the anger of the large crowd of fans that had gathered behind the South Stand on full, worked-up show. There was shouting, jeering and booing as the Villa bus made its way to the ground.

On the day, Wednesday would lose 3-2 to Villa. The Owls were swashbuckling in attack but ropey in defence and exposed at the higher level, as a 2-0 lead was squandered. But no matter – because after that kick up the arse, they would tighten up and improve and life under Francis would look good.

By Christmas, Francis's Owls had won over half of their games, playing confidently and adventurously, albeit now with more defensive care. And despite a few heavy defeats in the New Year to Leeds (6-1) and Arsenal (7-1) they otherwise looked strong and were progressing well, ultimately finding themselves third in the table, close in behind the two title contenders Leeds and Manchester United.

A further sign of this progress had been seen in January 1992 with the almost-signing of a certain controversial Frenchman, Eric Cantona.

Cantona had been looking to restart his career, having been handed a two-month ban in his home country for throwing the ball at a referee, before calling each member of the disciplinary panel punishing him an 'idiot'. That month, he arrived in Sheffield for a week-long trial with Wednesday.

Icy conditions in the city had meant that the only viewing Francis managed to get of the volatile-yet-exceptional Frenchman was inside on artificial surfaces (both in training and during an indoor six-a-side match at the newly built Sheffield Arena against the visiting American side the Baltimore Blast), but not on real grass.

Supposedly, the trial had come about as a favour to Francis's former agent, Dennis Roach. Roach knew Gérard Houllier, then assistant manager with the French national team, and following

Cantona's ban in his home country, the French were keen for him to get back playing games in readiness for the upcoming European Championship in Sweden.

A meeting was set up in France between Wednesday and Cantona's representatives, with club secretary Graham Mackrell travelling to Paris to help arrange a trial. There he met with Roach, Houllier and two of Cantona's representatives at the Cacharel fashion house, a discreet yet glamorous Parisian location that in every way was a long way from South Yorkshire and Sheffield.

Cantona's performance in the Sheffield Arena game gave a glimpse of what might have been for the team and the club had he actually signed; as did the photographs of him leaning over the side-hoardings, strutting around the pitch (that chest-puffed-out pose which would become familiar to football fans across the country), enjoying a pint in his hotel bar in Sheffield or posing, arms in the air, on the Hillsborough pitch in a Wednesday kit.

The move, of course, never came off.

'Sincerely, I loved those few days in Sheffield,' Cantona would later say. He had expected to be playing at Luton the weekend after the Arena game. He wanted to be a Wednesday player. But after being asked to extend his trial for a few more days so that, as the story goes, he could show his stuff on grass, he refused, said *adieu* and buggered off to Leeds and Howard Wilkinson (his triumphs with Manchester United to come).

Bizarrely, Francis would later say this of the story, 'It was never a consideration of mine to bring Eric Cantona to the club... never, ever a consideration.' He said that the club would not have been able to pay his wages (despite their less tight-fisted approach to spending). Strange, though, considering how Mackrell had been required to travel to Paris to arrange the trial in the first place.

Cantona or no Cantona, though, Wednesday, challenging for the top places in the First Division, certainly now seemed a bigger draw in terms of the players they could (or at least nearly) attract to the club.

And though by the end of 1991/92 it would be Howard Wilkinson's (and Cantona's) Leeds that would take the championship title, for Francis's Wednesday their third place finish – the club's highest league placing for over 30 years – was a fine achievement, especially considering they had just returned from the Second Division. In just a couple of years, the club had climbed quickly and well.

Some may have been concerned about how in making such strides Wednesday's debt had increased from just under a million pounds the year before to £3.3m, following a net £2.6m outlay on players that season (one of the highest outlays in the division, about the same as Manchester United). Others, though, would have said to progress you spend and to accumulate you spend.

* * * *

Around the same time, such a policy would be adopted by others in Sheffield too; notably the City Council. With the contraction of the city's steel industry (at least in terms of the number of people employed in it), the consequent rise in unemployment and resulting acres of closed-down and empty factories in the east end of Sheffield, the council in the late 1980s and early 90s had been eager to regenerate the city.

One part of their strategy was to grow the service sector (soon to employ over 150,000 people in Sheffield), a plan perhaps best symbolised by the giant new £450m Meadowhall shopping centre, built on sprawling and derelict former steelworks sites (previously these metal skeleton and brick rubble settings had been filmed for the post-nuclear-bomb-hit, apocalyptic city that was featured in the television drama *Threads* – a perfectly bleak wilderness in which the blast survivors could wander helplessly after the nuclear shit had hit the fan).

Another potential 'trigger' for development was the attempt to turn the city into a hub of leisure and sport activities. This had seen the construction – with borrowed funds – of several major facilities that would be used for the 1991 Universiade, otherwise known as the World Student Games. It was thought that hosting such an event would further help regenerate the city's old industrial image.

Yet it came at a price. The construction bill for the 25,000-capacity stadium at Don Valley, the nearby 8,000-seater arena and other venues came in at £147m, while a further £10.5m would be lost staging the event itself. The stadium turned out to be a £29m unviable white elephant and two decades later would be flattened. Meanwhile the £25m annual repayment and interest bill for the total Games venues' construction costs is expected to burden the city's residents and ratepayers until at least 2024.

Of the total £140m initially borrowed for the event and its infrastructure, it is likely over £300m will be paid back by the city.

Spend to accumulate. Borrow and progress.

* * * *

Back at Sheffield Wednesday, beyond the club's own financial strutting, just out of view and in the background another issue was lingering.

After he had joined the board in October 1989, Dave Richards had become aware of a series of potentially irregular payments made over the past several years by the club to its employees (including both the playing and football-management staff). The payments and loans had been made in addition to normal salary payments and had occurred under Bert McGee's chairmanship. When he learned of the payments, Richards tasked the club's accountants with finding out exactly what amounts had been paid, and to whom they had been made.

The accountants' investigation found how since at least 1985 loans totalling over £250,000 had been made to various players (this at a time when a *year*'s wage for the majority of club players was £30,000 to £40,000). How there may been instances of undeclared payments to players, or instances of the non-payment of tax on such things as the £3,000 of carpeting paid over by the club to a retailer on behalf of one employee. Wednesday would subsequently be required by the Inland Revenue to make a payment to cover nearly £700,000 in unpaid taxes.

The situation would be discussed in a board meeting held at Hillsborough in July 1992, the minutes from which referencing the employee payments, the subsequent payment to the Revenue and, most revealingly, the discussions held by the Wednesday board surrounding what action would or would not be taken against those who had made and received the payments.

Also discussed was how whether in taking such action against such individuals, Wednesday would then be leaving themselves open to punishment from the Football Association or the Football League, were either party to have found out about it.

Present at that board meeting, under the South Stand at Hillsborough, in its dark, wood-panelled boardroom, were chairman Dave Richards, finance director Bob Grierson, other directors Keith Addy, Cliff Woodward, Geoff Hulley and Joe Ashton (then MP for Bassetlaw), along with Owls manager Trevor Francis and club secretary Graham Mackrell. During the meeting, the group heard legal counsel outlining the risks associated with pursuing those who might have been involved in making the payments.

One point made was how, if any action were to be taken against those who had apparently been involved, some other people – say, a member or members of the club's board or top management – might then have to join the original culprits as co-defendants in the case. Another was how difficult and time-consuming it would be for the club to properly investigate each of the payments, to find the related documentation and chase up old members of staff and so on.

The final point covered the worry of how the FA and Football League might react were they to find out about the whole thing (which was more likely if action was taken against an individual or individuals). Wednesday might even have faced expulsion from the lucrative new Premier League; its first kick only a month away at the time of that meeting.

After hearing the legal advice, Richards and his board decided that they would keep the whole thing quiet. 'It was decided,' the board minutes of that day would read, 'that it would be in the best interests of the club and of its shareholders not to pursue the matter further.'

All of this would not be revealed until 2006, however, when the journalist Dan King investigated it for the *Mail on Sunday* newspaper. As King would note in one of the articles he would write about the story – his key source: the actual minutes of that July 1992 board meeting, Richards had 'advocated a policy that effectively covered up an estimated £1.25m worth of undeclared payments to players and other members of staff'.

Richards would subsequently claim that he did notify the FA about the situation (as required by the FA's rules at the time), apparently phoning its then chief executive Graham Kelly to tell him what had gone on (an odd move, perhaps, considering the decisions made in the Hillsborough board meeting). When queried about this by King, however, Kelly would deny that such a phone call ever took place.

Following publication of King's *Mail on Sunday* articles, Richards would be asked by the FA to explain the matter. Weeks would drag on, with no public explanation given by Richards, nor anyone at the FA, including its chairman, the Sheffielder Geoff Thompson. Eventually the FA would release the following discharging statement, '[Dave] Richards did inform the FA and the League of the payments, made prior to his involvement at the club. The FA was advised of these payments at the time, was therefore aware of potential breaches of the rules, and did not take any action. The evidence conclusively proves that David Richards acted entirely appropriately in regard to this matter.'

When in 1992/93 the glitz of the Premier League arrived – its £304m five-year broadcasting deal handing Wednesday an extra £1m in television revenues that first year alone (a significant sum at a time when the club's revenue that season would be £7.5m) – Wednesday were happily a confirmed, and not demoted, member of that league.

Ahead of that new season, the extra cash would enable Wednesday to spend £850,000 on the Crystal Palace striker Mark Bright (a deal which included the outgoing £500,000-rated Paul Williams), increase its wage bill by £1m on the previous year to £4.7m, and turn down £3m-plus offers from Manchester United for their top striker, David Hirst (as they had done at least twice earlier in 1992). Most notably, too, Wednesday would manage to come away from a perfect Mediterranean port-city in the south of France with a new £1m superstar signing. A signing that would, almost, spur the club on to glory.

Almost.

4

Le Magicien

Past the beaches and the villas the road winds along
the coast, hugging the blinding blue sea below. Up
to Cité radieuse, Le Corbusier's concrete tower of
flats, and up to the roof for perfect views over the
gleaming water. Park Hill on sea.

Back down the road to the Stade Vélodrome, the
arcing roof rising to the sky. Olympique Marseille.
Droit au but – *Straight to the goal their motto.*

The Vélodrome – once home to the gangling Geordie,
the English winger. For three years here he supplied the
bullets. Had the tricks and had the skills: the dropped
shoulders and the step-overs. And they loved him.
Le Magicien, *they called him.*

Back into town and to the old port. The cafés and bars
and the white bobbing forest of sailing-boat masts.
Into the bar for pints on the Med. A glance up at the
end of the bar. And there he is.

'You Are the Best', it says on the scarf, up high
and out of reach.

'You Are the Best – Chris Waddle'.
Le Magicien.

IT was in Marseille, the gem city in the south of France, in the late 1980s and early 90s that the winger from the north-east of England had dazzled. When Olympique's Marseille's eccentric owner, Bernard Tapie, had signed him from Tottenham Hotspur, Waddle had cost the French club £4.5m, a fortune at the time. But it was worth it.

Waddle was brought in to supply the likes of Jean-Pierre Papin, the prolific French striker, and helped bring the club title after title, trophy after trophy. Yes, he'd skied a penalty for his country in the World Cup semi-final of 1990 – Turin, 'World in Motion', 'Nessun Dorma' and all that – and from then on would bafflingly hardly feature in Graham Taylor's England side. But in Marseille and in France, Waddle was loved; his talents recognised and appreciated.

By late 1991, having exited the European Cup at the second-round stage (and having lost the previous year's final), Bernard Tapie decided his Marseille team needed a revamp. Waddle, now 31, would be one of those who would be moved on.

With the cash of the new Premier League coming along, and thanks to Sheffield Wednesday's stock in the transfer market seemingly being on the rise, a player of Waddle's quality in the blue and white would, it was thought, be an ideal fit. Certainly Trevor Francis wanted him, so he and club secretary Graham Mackrell travelled down to France to do the deal.

Reportedly, Wednesday offered Tapie and Marseille £1m for the player, along with offering Waddle himself £4,000 per week in wages, a figure that would make him one of the highest-paid players in the soon-to-kick-off Premier League. Newcastle, Leeds and Monaco were also interested, but Waddle had liked what he'd heard from Francis and was keen on joining Wednesday. So the deal was done. *Le Magicien* was coming to Sheffield.

At his unveiling at a press conference at the Hallam Tower Hotel in Fulwood, Waddle said, 'I wanted to sign for Wednesday. I like the way they play football. I have a lot of respect for the manager and for the club.' He added, optimistically, 'They are on the verge of something big.'

A few weeks later, Waddle would make his first appearance for his new club in a pre-season friendly at West Bromwich Albion. With his untucked shirt and spiky hairdo, Waddle showed that day exactly what he would bring to Francis's team. That extra dynamic. The tricks and the dinks. The fast switching of the play. Always searching for an opening in the defence. With Waddle in place, Wednesday were ready to push on in the new season.

* * * *

Frustratingly, however, 1992/93 would get off to a stuttering start both for Wednesday and their new main man Waddle. The Owls won only five of the opening 20 league games, with Waddle, after coming off with a twisted knee on the opening day at Everton, missing a handful of those matches.

Thankfully, though, as the season progressed, and with Waddle back in the team and into his groove, Wednesday would manage to rediscover their good form from the previous year and the season turned around. And after a mini UEFA Cup adventure, which took in games against Spora Luxembourg and German club Kaiserslautern, Wednesday, fantastically, had managed to forge their way through the rounds of both the FA Cup and League Cup.

By the spring, they found themselves at Wembley for an FA Cup semi-final. The opponents: Sheffield United. It was the first of what would be four visits to the old stadium over the next seven weeks – and was a game that would see *Le Magicien* tear the Blades apart.

For that sunny Saturday in April 1993 the Steel City emptied for Wembley, the stadium's surrounds becoming Sheffield as 75,000 fans converged on the capital for the biggest clash ever between the two city clubs. Originally Leeds United's Elland Road had been chosen as the venue, but thanks to overwhelming demand for tickets and great pressure from both sets of supporters, the FA allowed the tie to be switched to London (a move which handed Wednesday the advantage; their passing game being much more suited to the Wembley carpet than the Blades').

That afternoon it was a party atmosphere in which thousands and thousands of blue, white and red balloons floated around the ground. Both teams made their way out to the field backed by a proper deafening steel-city roar. And Sheffield, in London, was ready.

For Wednesday, it started brilliantly. Sixty-two seconds in they won a free kick, the Blades' John Pemberton bringing down the Owls' Mark Bright. Contemplating which of them would take it, John Sheridan and Chrissy Waddle stood over the ball. It was 30 yards out; Waddle thought he'd have a go. 'Get out of the way,' he said to Sheridan.

A run-up from Waddle and… *hit*. Sheffield United's keeper Alan Kelly dived. His hand reached close. But the missile flew past him and into his net. Waddle, arms aloft, ran off to celebrate, as delirious as the manic Owls in the Wembley stands; 1-0 to Wednesday.

The game went on and the Blades could not control the Owls' star winger. Again and again he opened up United's defence. '[T] hey sought him here and they sought him there,' reported the *Guardian*. 'To no avail.'

Only Kelly in the Blades net prevented the whitewash. Thanks to him, and Alan Cork's equaliser against the run of play, the Blades somehow managed to stay in the game. It wasn't until the second half of extra time that Mark Bright thankfully headed in the winner to send Wednesday to the final of the FA Cup.

Following the joy of that semi-final would be boring bloody Arsenal in the final of the League Cup, the other cup competition; the Owls having earned their place after they had knocked out Blackburn Rovers 6-3 in the two-legged semi-final.

Cup final one, at Wembley, saw George Graham's well-drilled and tactically disciplined Arsenal side stifle Trevor Francis's Wednesday from the start. Steve Morrow, sitting deep in midfield, prevented John Sheridan from supplying Waddle out wide, which in turn served to starve Wednesday's strike force of that day, Mark Bright and Paul Warhurst. The rest of the Wednesday team, ceaselessly pressed and thwarted by the London side, never even got playing.

The American John Harkes had put Wednesday ahead, sending a cleared ball back past David Seaman in the Arsenal goal. But Paul Merson's volley and Morrow's header won it 2-1 for George Graham's dominant men. Arsenal had won the League Cup. The trophy, won in 1991 by Wednesday, would not be coming back to Sheffield.

* * * *

The defeat, while a great disappointment for Wednesday and its supporters, was only round one, though. After the semi-final win against the Blades, the Owls would get another go at glory, again against Arsenal, this time in the FA Cup Final.

Cup final two, saw on another bright day, the two teams take to the Wembley field for the second time that season, the prospect again in store of Wednesday's flowing football versus the stifling defensiveness of Arsenal's.

Not surprisingly, Arsenal were as smothering as they had been before in the League Cup Final. Sheridan again was contained for large parts of the game, this time by Paul Davis, which again prevented Wednesday from getting playing. Arsenal manager George Graham was criticised for setting his team out in a cagey and 'negative' way, but it had brought home one trophy already that season and at this rate looked as though it would bring another and 20 minutes in, Ian Wright headed the Gunners in front.

Wednesday, though, weren't rattled and fought back through David Hirst; Harkes's header across goal finding the Wednesday striker unmarked to blast in. The game finished 1-1 and a replay would be required five days later.

In contrast to the sunshine of the previous Saturday, the replay on the Thursday evening was played in miserable pouring rain in front of a depleted Wembley crowd; a fourth trip to the national stadium in less than two months understandably too great a stretch for many of the Wednesday fans. Plus, a crash on the M1 had made many who did travel down to support the Owls late for the start of the game.

Thirty-four minutes in and it was here we go again as Wright once more gave Arsenal the lead, lifting the ball over the advancing Chris Woods into the Wednesday goal. But again the Owls weren't ready to give it up. Waddle was far freer than he had been in the previous games against the Gunners and got to work tormenting the full-backs, Lee Dixon and Nigel Winterburn. Earlier, even before Wright's strike, his cross to Harkes may have put Wednesday ahead, had the American managed to connect. As the rain continued to pour, there was hope.

With 20 minutes to go, Waddle stepped up with the equaliser himself; his effort deflecting off Dixon and past Seaman for 1-1. Wednesday then had their chances to win it; Bright and Hirst both could have done so. But they didn't, so extra time would be needed.

As the deadlock remained and the game laboured on, Arsenal won a corner. Paul Merson lofted the ball into the box as Andy Linighan rose above Mark Bright to meet it. As it moved towards the goal, the expressions on the faces of the Wednesday players were a mix of helplessness and knowing dread. The wet ball slipped through the hands of Chris Woods and landed in the net. It was two minutes from the end of extra time. Two minutes before penalties. And Arsenal had won it. Won the FA Cup.

On one side of Wembley, it was complete heartbreak. It was tears from the Wednesday fans in the stands, tears in the pubs and living rooms back in Sheffield – and tears on the Wembley pitch. The hero Waddle sat on the grass, his head bowed, distraught. 'That season had promised everything,' surmised Daniel Gordon in his book, *A Quarter of Wednesday*, but, after defeat in two cup finals, 'had delivered nothing.'

For the Wednesday manager, Trevor Francis, the memory of that season and those two cup-final defeats remains vivid. 'When I look back on the number of occasions that we went to Wembley, it was surreal,' he recalls. 'A club like Sheffield Wednesday and all of a sudden we were at Wembley four times in six weeks. But it was so disappointing that we didn't win one of the trophies. The replay is one that I still don't forget. We had our moments where we could have won it and were seconds away from going to penalties. But they scored that very, very late goal and that was it. That ranks as one of the biggest disappointments of my career.'

Yet despite the pain of the double Wembley final defeats, Francis's team still was a marvellous one. Maybe the players hadn't brought home a trophy that year, but the genuine feeling for many was that the future was looking bright. There would always be next year, and the year after that.

* * * *

Always next year. Providing, that is, that the £4.7m wage bill, increased by £1.1m from the previous year to help improve the team, along with the £6.5m of debt that had been building up in the club, didn't get too far out of hand. Providing, too, that the players who would be brought in next would improve the side and not worsen it. And providing that those in charge at the top of the club – the chairman and his board of directors – did only what was best for the club and its fans. Providing, providing.

Ahead of 1993/94, Francis adopted an interesting approach to building upon the previous year's fine yet trophy-less campaign. Rather than tweak the team as he had the previous summer – most notably by adding the dazzle of Chris Waddle – he opted now for revolution, as he effectively set about dismantling the cup finals side. The process took place over two summers: in 1993, when more delicate changes were made; and a year later, when the changes made were more drastic.

Francis's dilemma was that his squad included some players who were over or approaching the age of 30 (and supposedly now in the dangerous period of their career, when fatigue and reduced sharpness might play an increasing part). Among those players were Waddle and captain Nigel Pearson. 'We'd had three very, very good years,' explains Francis. 'But there were a number of players who were starting to look a little bit aged and I felt that one or two changes needed to be made to freshen it up. There was no pressure at all from the board to do it, but it was something I felt that needed to happen.'

Out of the club that summer, then, went the veterans Viv Anderson (defence, almost 37 years old) and Danny Wilson (midfield, 31), who both moved to Barnsley to take the manager and assistant manager jobs respectively. Peter Shirtliff (defence, 32) was also sold to Wolves for £250,000. More puzzling was the sale of the 25-year-old industrious midfielder John Harkes (a player who had complemented the flair and creativeness of Waddle and John Sheridan) to Derby County for £800,000. Meanwhile Paul Warhurst, scorer of 17 goals during the season just gone as a converted striker would soon be on his way to Blackburn Rovers. A reluctant sale for Francis, £2.75m was at least a good fee for Warhurst.

In place of those departing five players came three new faces for a combined fee of £6m.

First in was the England centre-half Des Walker for £2.75m from Sampdoria. Walker had previously starred for Brian Clough's Nottingham Forest, and for his country at Italia 90, which later helped him earn a big move to Serie A. But in Italy his confidence and form had dropped and after one disappointing season he had eyed a move back to England. Other big clubs had been sniffing – Walker was still a coveted top-class talent – but Wednesday won the day.

Initially, it was thought that Nigel Pearson would be partnering Walker in the Wednesday defence – a potentially excellent pairing. However, injuries would limit Pearson's appearances through the upcoming season, meaning that more often than not Francis would turn to the younger Andy Pearce, another capture that summer for £500,000 from Coventry City, to fill the gap.

Following Walker and Pearce into Hillsborough was QPR's promising England winger Andy Sinton. A skilful wide-man, Sinton had played ten times for his country and was seen by Francis as a preferred left-wing option to the reliable Nigel Worthington (who on and off for the past four seasons had operated in brilliant overlapping-and-dropping-back tandem with Phil King), and a better complement to the flair of Chris Waddle on the opposite side of the pitch. The £2.75m it cost to bring Sinton to the club equalled Walker's fee.

So far, Francis's evolution of the team had seemed positive. Significant experience had been lost, but that experience had, it was believed, been replaced by quality, expensive recruits.

At the beginning of 1993/94, their impact was decent: Sinton bagged three goals in his first six games while the Walker–Pearce partnership appeared reasonably strong, if not watertight. Sadly, though, things didn't start all that impressively for the whole team.

Wednesday had actually been made third favourites for the title before the season began but it would take seven games before the first win would come (a hangover from the cup finals heartbreak, some questioned). By Christmas, form improved, with some of the ground that had been lost to the top teams early on in the season gradually made up. Still, as Wednesday sat low in the table and often struggled to recreate the stylish form of the previous season, hopes of titles and European places were now a mile away.

There were some positive glimpses. Later in the year, a 5-0 win at Hillsborough against West Ham United (inspired by Waddle, who set up three of the goals himself and scored another) showed what they were still capable of. But such a performance was more the exception than the rule that season.

Injuries in the camp hadn't helped matters. Sinton would miss around a third of the games; Waddle over half; John Sheridan and David Hirst almost all of the season – the roots of Hirst's injury problems to be found in the ankle-breaking challenge from Arsenal's Steve Bould the previous season; the incident setting a miserable pattern of injury, comeback, then setback or new injury through the rest of Hirst's career.

After the 5-0 West Ham game, Wednesday pushed on for a seventh-place finish come the end of the season. It was decent, but not quite how it had been meant to be. After the almost-success of Wembley the season before, then the big spending on the two England internationals Walker and Sinton that followed, the club had meant to kick on – but alas, did not.

Although chairman Dave Richards didn't seem to mind that much. '[A]nother successful and progressive year for Sheffield

Wednesday,' he surmised. '[W]e again finished seventh, which was lower than we might have wished... [But] we are up there among the elite... showing we belong there.'

The summer of 1994 would see more player upheaval at the club. Phase two of Trevor Francis's revolution saw the moving on of more of the older heads and tired legs, replacing them with newer models. 'It had got a little bit stale,' explains Francis today. 'And we had one or two ageing players at that point. I wasn't looking to change everything. But we needed a little bit more energy and youthfulness in the squad.'

So out of the door went Carlton Palmer, Wednesday's engine in midfield sent up the road to Howard Wilkinson and Leeds for £2.75m, along with Nigel Worthington, who was sold to Leeds for a tribunal-set fee of £325,000 (Francis had rated the out-of-contract Northern Irishman at £1.3m). Nigel Pearson would also be sold, apparently against his wishes, to Middlesbrough for £500,000, while Phil King was reunited with Ron Atkinson at Aston Villa for £250,000.

Those were the players Francis could just about accept losing. But one he didn't want to let go was his exceptional Swedish right-back, Roland Nilsson.

Nilsson was one of the finest sights ever in a Wednesday shirt. A defender calm and confident on the ball and always effective in the tackle, in late 1993 he had asked to be released by the club so that he and his family could move back home to Sweden. His contract had been due to expire the following summer, but he wanted to leave before then. There was a brief stand-off between manager and player, but eventually Francis relented and a compromise was agreed that would see Nilsson finish out the 1993/94 season in Sheffield, before moving on to his hometown club Helsingborgs for nothing.

Nilsson would be greatly missed. After his last game against Manchester City at Hillsborough, he was lifted on to the shoulders of his manager and a teammate as the crowd gave him a moving send-off.

Into the club that summer came four new replacements: Peter Atherton, a tough and 'honest' defender/midfielder, signed for £800,000 from Coventry City. He would go on to serve the club sturdily and professionally for years; Ian Taylor, a midfielder similar in style to Palmer – hardworking and tough up and down the pitch – arrived from Port Vale for £1m; and to replace Nigel Worthington, Ian Nolan from Tranmere. Negotiations had begun with an offer from Francis of £750,000 which was refused. He went back, and back, until he got his man for £1.5m. Defensively Nolan was solid enough. But going forward, he was pedestrian and painfully one-footed.

Finally, replacing Roland Nilsson was the attack-minded right-sider Dan Petrescu, signed for £1.3m from the Italian side Genoa. He had been a fine performer in the Gheorghe Hagi-inspired Romanian side that had reached the quarter-final of that summer's World Cup in the USA.

To many, the new boys represented a shift from great experience to still unproven promise. But Francis was happy with the business he had done and ahead of the new season was positive, saying, 'I do believe that the present group are the best we have had here.'

The season began dreadfully, however, 'the best [group] we have had here' won only one of their first eight games.

Four games into that poor run, Francis moved to make another signing: the tall, blond, Swedish international midfielder, Klas Ingesson, joined from PSV Eindhoven for £800,000. He didn't feature much, though, and just over a year after joining the club, having played only 21 times, he would be sold on for a profit to the Italian club Bari.

Some better moments for Francis's men would come; a 1-0 win over Manchester United at Hillsborough and a draw down at Arsenal. But still they could not stop from slipping towards the bottom reaches of the table.

To help arrest the situation, Taylor, less than six months after being brought to the club, was moved on to Aston Villa in a swap deal for the forward Guy Whittingham. Whittingham made an immediate impact, notching four goals in his first two games and helping Wednesday win twice over Christmas to relieve some of the pressure. But this still wasn't quite good enough and the rumours were that Francis was losing his influence over the squad.

One telling development that season was the emergence of the 'mole' in the Wednesday dressing room, which saw one player feeding his, and apparently some of his teammates', disaffections with the manager to a national newspaper. Appearing in the *News of the World*, the unnamed 'mole' would criticise Francis's tactics and man-management style, claiming that the players had lost confidence in him and that several wanted to leave the club.

Francis fought back and dismissed the claims as nonsense. 'The mood has always been good and it's now better than ever,' he told another newspaper. And as he adds today, 'Overall it was a good dressing room. It was fine.'

But from the outside looking in, it didn't appear fine and after Christmas Wednesday stuttered on, looking anxiously down at the four relegation places below.

Mole or no mole, lost dressing room or not, the disappointing reality of the season had not been anticipated. Nor would it be accepted by the board. This was the season when Francis's improved team should have pushed on, but they hadn't.

Relegation would be avoided – just – on the last day. A 4-1 win over Ipswich made extra sure of it, giving Wednesday a 13th-place finish. Yet though they had just got there, there had been a real danger that the Owls could have gone down, had their result and others gone against them.

For Francis, after such a disappointing season, the writing, it seemed, was on the wall.

'During the last three or four months it seemed to be almost a *fait accompli* situation that I would be leaving,' Francis recalls. 'And I think it was widely leaked to the press that there would be a change at the end of the season. Certain members of the media seemed to be aware of that.

'But when I asked the chairman and the board if there was any substance to it, I was assured that everything was fine.'

But it wasn't.

'[L]ast season has to go down as a disappointment... a source of dismay and concern,' chairman Dave Richards would go on to write in the accounts for 1994/95.

Perhaps ominously for Francis, during the season Richards had taken the unorthodox step of sitting on the Kop – where he had said he had once stood as a boy, watching Dooley, Albert Quixall and co. – in order to be among the fans, and be able to gauge their feelings on the issue; their views on the man. '[H]e'll have to go,' was the consensus. And that's what would happen. Still, the big boot didn't come quick for Francis. As he recalls, 'As we worked towards the end of the season, I had to remain as professional as possible and see it through. After the Ipswich game I invited some close friends and staff into my office for a few glasses of wine. One or two directors even came in. It was like an end-of-season party, but also a sort of thank-you, going-away party.

'But, strangely, after the season had finished, a week passed and there was just silence. Nothing at all. So I started to think, "Have I misread the situation? Surely I haven't."'

Unfortunately for Francis, he hadn't.

'It was Saturday morning and the build-up for the FA Cup Final was about to start and I was about to put my feet up to watch that. I had a call from somebody at the club telling me that the chairman would like to see me down at Hillsborough. And I knew then that I'd not misread the situation at all.

'I went down and they informed me that they were going to make a change. The board felt that because of the club's lowly position, and it was a poorish season in their eyes, a change had to be made. I said, "Okay, I have to accept that. But did you have to do it today, on FA Cup Final day?" They said that a member of the board felt it was the most appropriate day to do it on. It would receive minimal publicity because everyone would have their eye on the FA Cup Final.

'I was hugely disappointed with that. It could have been done in a better way than it was. Having played for the club and then had four years as manager, it could have ended in better circumstances. But it was their decision. I didn't agree with it. I think it was the wrong decision to sack me. I would like to have been given the chance to change things a little and make changes to the team. But I accepted it of course.'

And the dressing room mole: 'I knew who he was,' says Francis. 'I didn't want to say at the time, and am not going to say now, but put it this way, he wouldn't have been there the following season if I'd have still been there.'

But Francis wouldn't be there. The decision had been taken. His contract would be ended a year early and Wednesday, now, looked for a new manager.

5

Imports and Fading Stars

W ITH Trevor Francis gone, the thoughts of Dave Richards and the rest of the Wednesday hierarchy now turned to who would be best to lead the club into the 1995/96 season.

Chris Waddle, then 34 and still playing for the club, was linked with the job. Many believed he was about to be offered the role of player-manager; the fans would have loved that. Also rumoured to be in line were Bobby Robson, fresh from winning the Portuguese title with Porto; the managerially inexperienced former Owls man Danny Wilson, who had been developing a promising side at Barnsley; and Ron Atkinson, now at Coventry City having moved on from his beloved Aston Villa, but rumoured to be on for a controversial return to Hillsborough following his walk-out in 1991. It was strongly suggested that the club had approached Atkinson. In the end, it went to a surprise choice, Luton Town's David Pleat.

Pleat, who had previously managed Tottenham Hotspur and Leicester City, was now enjoying a second spell as Luton boss. Even before Francis had been sacked, Pleat had heard on the grapevine that the Wednesday job might be coming up.

'I had a phone call,' recalls Pleat, sitting in the foyer of a Salford hotel one wintry afternoon, 'asking me, "If Sheffield Wednesday became available, would I be interested?" "Yes," I said. "I'd like another crack at the Premiership."

'Time went by, then, at the end of the season, they phoned me again, saying they were going to change the manager. "Would I still be interested? Would I like to meet them?" – "Yes," I said.

'I met the board in Sheffield. They all asked me questions and were happy with what I said. I think they'd already decided they wanted to take me on; Dave Richards had already made up his mind. So I was offered the job straight away and I accepted.'

A short wrangle with Luton over compensation – with a £150,000 payment being agreed – and Pleat was Wednesday's new manager. Although Pleat hadn't managed in the top flight for three years, he did have pedigree at the highest level. With Tottenham, Leicester and Luton he had delivered thoughtful and imaginative attacking football along with strong league finishes and cup runs. An experienced and vastly knowledgeable man, Pleat – Richards and his board presumably had believed – was a manager capable of progressing the club following the blip of the past few years. He joined up in June 1995 and got to work for his return to top-level management.

He used the £2.5m that had been received from Nottingham Forest for Chris Bart-Williams to bring in midfielder Mark Pembridge, a comfortable operator who cost £900,000 from Derby County, along with the inventive Belgian international forward Marc Degryse – £1.5m from Anderlecht. ('I was ready to leave Belgium,' remembers Degryse of the move. 'And Sheffield Wednesday were interested. I had a meeting with David Pleat and said, "OK, I will go to the Premier League." I was almost 30 and it was the best thing for me to do. So I came over to Sheffield and signed for three years.')

The summer included a mini European adventure in the Intertoto Cup, a competition offering a place in that season's UEFA Cup. Three seasons on from the club's two-round UEFA Cup foray against Spora Luxembourg and Kaiserslautern, Wednesday in the Intertoto took in trips to Switzerland, where under-strength they lost 1-0 to Basle, and Germany, a 1-1 draw with Karlsruhe. Meanwhile 'home' wins at Rotherham's Millmoor (works at Hillsborough prevented Wednesday from playing there that summer) were taken against Polish side Górnik Zabrze (3-2) and AGF Aarhus of Denmark (3-1).

Pleat's first real opponents as Wednesday boss for the 1995/96 opener were Liverpool at Anfield. Though that day Liverpool's new £8.5m man Stan Collymore's long-range strike gave his new club the 1-0 win, other early results for the Owls that season, along with the style of play produced by Pleat's side, would give encouragement for the new era; Wednesday were playing well as they picked up points over the next few games.

A spanner in the works was not far off for the new manager, however.

Much of the early-season positivity had been fuelled by the success of both the team's newly adopted 3-5-2 formation and the player used at right wing-back, the Romanian Dan Petrescu. After Roland Nilsson had left the club, back at the end of 1994/95, there had been concerns over how such a perfect operator at right-back might be replaced, but these concerns had been alleviated to some extent when Trevor Francis brought in Petrescu, who had shown glimpses of being a similarly gifted player, especially when going forward.

And, in those opening weeks of 1995/96, Petrescu had executed his role as attacking defender brilliantly – dangerous and creative on the right, with the freedom to advance far up the field. 'He was a great wing-back,' recalls Pleat. 'A terrific player. Brilliant at coming inside against his opposite number. One of the best I'd seen in that position.'

But then came that spanner in the works. 'Chelsea had already spoken to him about moving down there,' explains Pleat, '[and it] undermined me completely. I wanted to keep him but Dan wanted to go there. His mind was set on Chelsea and it was as simple as that. And before that his agent, Bacarli, had even insisted that if we didn't double Petrescu's money he wouldn't try a leg. He came to Middlewood [the club's training ground] to tell me that! Then we had a terrible row with Chelsea, who tried to deflate the fee. He had a medical and we were told there was something up and that he wouldn't be able to play a full season.'

Nine games into 1995/96, then, Petrescu, so far one of Wednesday's best performers of the season, left for Chelsea for

£2.5m. 'That was a big blow,' says Pleat. 'He was a great loss to the club.'

A cheeky tribute to this episode would appear in the fanzine *A View from the East Bank*, courtesy of the artist Pete McKee. Through the years McKee – who in the early 1990s had started designing T-shirts to sell outside Hillsborough – could be relied on to provide a humorous take on goings-on at Wednesday, first in the pages of the fanzine before later, the *Sheffield Telegraph*.

To cope with the loss of Petrescu, Pleat moved Ian Nolan over to the right and brought the youngster Lee Briscoe in on the left. But things weren't the same after that. Wednesday's dynamic had changed for the worse.

Now players like the club's new Belgian forward, Marc Degryse, were looked to even more for inspiration.

Back in his home league, the striker-converted-to-midfielder Degryse had shown himself to be an acute and accomplished passing creator who was capable of regularly finding the net. Through contacts in Belgium, Pleat had been alerted to Degryse's talents and after bringing him to Sheffield decided that his best role would be sitting just behind the front pairing of David Hirst and Mark Bright, acting as a conduit between them and the midfield – roaming around the pitch, finding and feeding and bringing others into the play.

By mid-December, Degryse had notched eight goals from his deep position, including two in the stylish 6-2 demolition of Leeds at Hillsborough.

'I enjoyed Sheffield,' remembers Degryse. 'The city has a tradition as an old industry city and we enjoyed our life there, no problem.'

For Degryse, though, despite games like the 6-2 Leeds rout, there were problems with how the team was playing.

'A lot of continental players were coming over,' explains Degryse. 'I was one of them. David wanted the team to play a little more continental football: to play from the goalkeeper to the full-backs to the midfield; through the feet to each other. But I don't think the team was ready to play like that. I saw that half of the team was ready to play that way, but the other half were only able to play typical English football – direct to the striker, kick and rush. That was a little bit of a problem. Everyone had their qualities but some were not as capable of that. It was frustrating.' As the season progressed, Wednesday's form fell flat.

In an attempt to boost his team, Pleat, as Francis had before him, got spending again, using the Petrescu fee and another few million pounds freed by the board to bring in two exciting young Yugoslavs from the famous Red Star Belgrade side: Dejan Stefanovic and Darko Kovacevic. The first was a cultured defender; the second, a prolific striker brilliant in the air and a fine finisher. Both had been attracting interest from a host of other European clubs. 'Mick Mills [Wednesday's chief scout at the time] came back from watching them in one game and told me we should sign them up,' remembers Pleat. 'He told me they were very good players.' Pleat went out to Belgrade to see for himself and bought them for a combined £4.5m.

Work permit issues delayed the Yugoslavs making their debuts: Home Office clearance didn't come until around Christmas 1995 even though they'd been signed a couple of months before. When they were cleared to play, Pleat was careful to ease the youngsters into his team: Kovacevic was given a few minutes off the bench against Southampton, before starting at Nottingham Forest on Boxing Day; Stefanovic coming off the bench to get an hour in Nottingham. On New Year's Day, at home to Bolton, both started and both impressed. Stefanovic cut a strong pose at left-back and provided an outlet from defence that went beyond the standard up-field hoof of his English team counterparts, while Kovacevic scored twice: the first goal a glancing header running in; the second, a strong confident strike. They'd do well in England, in Sheffield, many believed.

Some issues emerged, however. They were young men in a new city far from their homes and their families, speaking only basic English, which made things like understanding training ground instructions and conducting general interactions with teammates a challenge. Stefanovic had English lessons every day, but it was an uphill battle and the pair were left to get on with it. 'I was 22 years old,' explains Kovacevic today, 'and I missed home and my family.' And as Pleat remembers, 'We got them a flat, bought them a car, then pretty much left them to it. But,' he admits, 'they found it difficult. They were only kids and I don't think we did enough for them. You've got to look after them, night and day. Make sure they're happy. Make sure they've got everything they need. Make sure they're learning the language. We could have done more for them.'

In the end, the success of each player's integration and career in English football would vary significantly. Stefanovic would find himself in and out of the Wednesday side due – according to Pleat – to his sometimes erratic play and early language difficulties. And while he would eventually settle and turn into an excellent defender for the club when he did play, he would make only 72 appearances in a Wednesday shirt before moving on to Holland and Vitesse Arnhem, later returning to England with Portsmouth. Kovacevic, meanwhile, would see his season end with a series of substitute appearances and a transfer away from the club, moving to the Spanish team Real Sociedad for £2.5m; the same figure Wednesday had paid for him to leave Red Star a year before. 'You never know what happens in football,' explains Kovacevic. 'The offer came to play in the Spanish league and I took it.'

'It was a shame he didn't settle in Sheffield,' reflects Pleat.

Kovacevic would do well in Spain. So well in fact that within a year he would earn a £12m move to the Italian giants Juventus. Coy Wednesday had inserted a sell-on clause with Sociedad so would be due a further £2.1m from the sale. It is unclear, though, whether the club ever actually received that money – it is understood that even a number of years later it had still not been received by Wednesday, nor apparently pursued that desperately.

For the Owls and for Pleat, the remainder of 1995/96 was a disappointment as the team drifted worryingly towards the relegation places. After reasonably bright beginnings, certainly before the sale of Petrescu (not long after which, the new 3-5-2 formation was dropped for the more familiar 4-4-2), the Owls continued to stutter and slink along to the end of the season. Pleat brought in the dreadlocked winger Regi Blinker for £275,000 from Dutch club Feyenoord, and defender Jon Newsome for £1.6m from Norwich City in the hope of adding vibrancy to a flailing attack and sureness to his worryingly leaky defence (the transfers were funded by the sales of Andy Pearce to Wimbledon for £600,000 and Andy Sinton to Tottenham for £1.5m respectively). But not once for the remainder of the season did Wednesday reach above halfway in the table.

On the final day of 1995/96 Wednesday drew 1-1 at West Ham, meaning they would stay up. And although Pleat's men finished in 15th place, the margin of safety was only a few points. All in all, it had been another disappointing year for the club. As Pleat reflects simply, 'That first season was a damn difficult one.'

Challengingly for Pleat too, and making his first season with the club extra 'damn difficult', had been the task handed to him by the club's board when he had taken over. This task: to further dismantle the supposedly ageing squad and revitalise it in the hope of finally moving it on from the memories of Wembley 1993.

'When I came in,' remembers Pleat, 'it was explained to me that we had got to move some of these players out. They'd had their glory but they were on their way down. The board thought I was the right man to do it.

'I'd taken over a team of fading stars. Waddle. Sheridan. Hirst. Players who had been very good but were now in their twilight. They all thought they should be in the team, but the team wasn't doing well with those players in it. The club had relied on the old guard too long. And they should have turned more over before I got there.

'But they hadn't, so by the time I got there I was left with too many to turn over, to move on and replace. So that first year was really dramatic for me as I made some of those changes. It was a very difficult time.'

Initially, Pleat had offered fan hero Waddle the chance to become a player-coach. 'We did ask if he'd wanted to,' says Pleat. 'That was a semi-political suggestion from Dave Richards, but I was happy to embrace it because I liked him, Waddle.' But Waddle declined and while often used in the team in the first half of the season, he would finish it more as an impact substitute, not trusted by Pleat to complete the 90 minutes. 'He [Waddle] still thought he had a lot to offer,' says Pleat. 'But he didn't. He had a little bit to offer. He'd still got the football brain but had lost that bit of athleticism and a bit of pace. His legs had gone.'

It was a similar story for John Sheridan, the winning-goal man from the 1991 League Cup Final. Sheridan had begun the season in the team alongside Waddle, before being sent out on loan to First Division Birmingham City. And his and Pleat's relationship was less than harmonious.

'John Sheridan. Wonderful passer of the ball – but he'd lost his pace, too,' says Pleat. 'Never had much pace, in fact. And John wasn't an easy player to control. He was difficult.'

As Pleat now acknowledges, though, he might have used Waddle and Sheridan more in that first season. They might have helped out more, especially considering how, post-Christmas, the season had drifted and Wednesday's ability to unpick opponents had diminished.

'Hindsight's a fine thing though, isn't it?' says Pleat. 'Maybe in particular I could have built the team around Sheridan, got closer to him and tried to integrate him more in the team. Maybe I should have done. But it was difficult.'

Pleat also had problems with David Hirst, despite him being his top scorer in 1995/96. 'I found Hirst tremendous on his day but treading water another,' says Pleat. 'He'd had problems with injuries and probably had a little bit too much weight on him.

'But still, even while I was there, we had Joe Royle wanting to sign him for Everton. That one got close. But I got a phone call from Joe saying he couldn't sign him. "We've just had his medical papers through," he said, "I'm afraid we're not going through with the deal." Hirst was absolutely distraught and any chance of an ongoing relationship between us was now destroyed.'

Still, regardless of what Pleat's assessment was of the golden trio of Waddle, Sheridan and Hirst, whatever part he did or did not envisage for them at the club going forward and whatever plans he had for the team in general, one thing was certain: season number two for Pleat needed to be better.

6

Development

T HE summer of 1996 brought the European Championship
to England, with Sheffield and Hillsborough happily sharing
the fixtures of one of the groups with Nottingham and the
City Ground. National flags hung from the posts leading up to
Hillsborough along Penistone Road; as they had for the World
Cup back in 1966, the last time England and Sheffield had hosted
a major international football tournament. The sun mostly shone
and a buzz spread across the city and the country for what was to
be a fantastic three weeks of football.

Kicking things off in Sheffield, the day after England and
Switzerland had played out a draw at Wembley in the opening
game, were holders Denmark against Portugal. Thousands of
friendly Danes descended on the city for the tournament – they
were everywhere, having a brilliant time, drinking the pubs dry
and enjoying knockabouts in Hillsborough Park. In the ground,
they filled Wednesday's Kop and led the crowd in a rendition of
'Stand up if you hate the Germans'.

Great players were in town for the Denmark–Portugal game:
Peter Schmeichel; the Laudrup brothers, Michael and Brian; Luis
Figo; Rui Costa. The best goal though would come in Denmark
against Croatia – the latter competing in their first international
tournament since breaking from Yugoslavia in 1991 – when the

majestic Davor Suker beautifully chipped Schmeichel to score one of the finest goals seen at the old ground for some time

Before the tournament and over the previous few years Wednesday had been busy developing Hillsborough, with the club modernising to varying extents, yet at great expense, each of the ground's four sides. The lower tier of the Leppings Lane end was converted to all-seated at a cost of £800,000 (though many believed that the stand – where in 1989 so many had lost their lives – should have been demolished and replaced entirely). The Kop, which back in 1986 had been given a new roof to give Wednesday fans shelter from the elements, was in 1993 converted, at a cost of £750,000, from all-standing to an 11,210-seated bank. Further changes came in 1997, when the wooden seats of the 1960s North Stand masterpiece were replaced with plastic ones – 'SWFC' plastered in white against blue. But definitely the most comprehensive work undertaken in the mid-90s took place on the South Stand.

The South, designed originally by the celebrated Scottish engineer Archibald Leitch, then responsible for an increasingly impressive collection of football stadiums' stands across the country (recognisable for their criss-cross steel balconies and brick façades), had been built in 1914. 'The Wednesday Football Club Ltd', it read in white across its gabled top. Its 1990s upgrade saw a number of improvements.

First, the bottom tier was re-seated and a whole new roof constructed; complete with a crisp, triangular gable reminiscent of Leitch's original design and topped by a golden ball finial, courtesy of chairman Dave Richards' company, Three Star Engineering. The cost for this first phase of upgrades was £1.8m.

A further £5m was spent on phase two, as a new 3,000-seated top tier grandstand was added, providing towering views over the pitch and – from its back concourse – lovely views over Hillsborough Park; along with 30 executive boxes for the local business community, further executive seating, new club offices and a bridge over the River Don, rushing below. The expanded new South Stand, visible through the trees on the approach through Hillsborough Park, along Penistone Road or down Wadsley Lane, became an impressive, imposing and dominant sight.

The stand, Dave Richards would gush in the club's 1995/96 accounts, was 'one of the finest facilities in the Premier League'.

Richards also said how the development was 'vital for Sheffield Wednesday, because with today's spiralling wages for the better class of footballer, you have to generate the revenue... it has to come from somewhere'. Big things, in particular, were hoped of the new corporate facilities, which were much more swish that the catering and toilet services offered elsewhere in the ground (as anyone who ever had to have a piss against the brick wall 'toilet' at the bottom of the Kop might recall).

Richards's board wasn't stopping at Hillsborough with the upgrades though. Half a mile up the road from Wednesday's home, the club's training ground at Middlewood also received a facelift. The main day-to-day base of the players and the coaching staff, the training ground was where the preparation for the main event – the match – took place. And just like the South Stand at Hillsborough, it had to be up to Premier League standards. A further £2m–£3m would, then, be spent on improving Middlewood's facilities: a two-level clubhouse with changing rooms and manager's office was constructed, along with a canteen and medical centre. Later, improvements to playing surfaces for the senior teams and youth teams would also be made.

All of these upgrades and developments to the stadium and to Middlewood had, for a variety of reasons, been necessary. At Hillsborough, not only did the ground have to meet the demands of the post-Hillsborough disaster Taylor Report (that is, to be safe and all spectators seated) – Wednesday, more than *any* other club, had to do that properly – but it also had to be set up as a modern, more comfortable and inviting venue. Something suitable for the Premier League era that was now upon the club.

The problem was, all of the development had also helped to stretch the club's finances to the limit; the £8.3m lump of debt that would be reported in the 1995/96 accounts (compared with £2.6m the year before), upon much of which the club by now was paying out over £500,000 a year in interest to the club's main lender, the Co-operative Bank.

However, the necessary investment in the club's infrastructure wasn't the sole reason for this financial situation. Between 1994/95 and 1995/96, the club's wage bill had grown from £5.7m to £6.4m. Net spend on players had been just under £1m. And in 1995/96, the club posted a £2.3m loss (albeit following a modest profit of

£983,000 the season before). But when a football club makes a loss by investing in its team, even if only modestly, while at the same time investing heavily in its infrastructure, helping to drive up the debt even more significantly (even if that investment has the long-term aim of spurring greater financial returns), there may be trouble ahead.

Back in the 1960s, Wednesday's secretary Eric Taylor had battled with manager Harry Catterick as he invested in the stadium – the infrastructure – ahead of the first team. Thirty years later, guided by chairman Dave Richards, Wednesday were adopting a quite different approach: the club was happy to do both. Happy to spend. Happy to open the chequebook and borrow more from the bank. Whatever, it seemed, the cost.

'You can't have penny and bun, son,' Dave Richards is said to have once remarked to some of his colleagues in the game. Which is to say: two things cannot be had together, at the same time. You can't have one thing and another as well. But for Wednesday, under Richards, it was a different story.

A new expensive stand? Penny.

An expensive new player or two, too? Bun.

'You can't have penny and bun, son.'

Yes you could, it seemed.

7

Flying High, Charterhouse and Shooting Yourself in the Foot

FOLLOWING the fairly narrow escape from relegation at the end of David Pleat's first season in charge of Wednesday, few people, if any, would have expected his team to be topping the Premier League at the start of his second. But somehow they were. Four games into 1996/97, the Owls sat top of the tree. Four wins from four: Aston Villa, Leeds United, Newcastle United and Leicester City all beaten. Twelve points from 12. Number one. It was a remarkable turnaround.

Pleat had spent the summer revamping his squad, fully putting his stamp on the team in the hope of finding improvements moving forward. Incoming was Andy Booth, a strong leader of the forward line from First Division Huddersfield Town who cost Wednesday £2.7m. Booth had netted 21 times for Town the previous season, attracting considerable interest from the scouts of Premier League clubs. Liverpool, Aston Villa and Manchester United had all been there, taking a view of the powerful Yorkshire lad. And though they were put off by his price tag and, perhaps, his lack of pace, the Owls were not. Pleat had watched Booth himself several times and had liked what he'd seen – a brave, unselfish player who ran the channels well with a commanding aerial ability – and signed him up.

For the young Booth, it was a great move. 'Obviously I jumped at the chance to play Premiership football,' he says. 'There were some fantastic players at the club and I thought it was a great opportunity. It didn't take me long to decide to sign.'

Pleat's other purchases that summer included the midfielder Scott Oakes, £450,000 from Luton Town (he'd played for Pleat before); Wayne Collins, £600,000 from Crewe; and, to provide back-up for Kevin Pressman, Rotherham's young keeper Matt Clarke (£325,000).

In all the summer's spending was over £4m; covered by the sales of Darko Kovacevic and Marc Degryse. While Kovacevic's sale had not been much of a surprise, Marc Degryse's certainly was, especially considering how well his first season in Sheffield had gone. Degryse had created and scored goals; but there were some issues with the training and the way the team had been playing.

'The manager's biggest thinking was to play more continental,' explains Degryse. 'But if you want to try and play continental football you have to think and change your thinking of how you prepare your team. That was not done and for sure was part of the disappointment for me.'

So he was sold on to PSV Eindhoven for £1.8m; £300,000 more than Wednesday had paid for him the year before. PSV and European football proved a significant draw for him, 'I was attracted to be playing for them,' he says. 'To play for the title and to play in Europe. To play for a better team – that was the reason.'

Never mind. Those first four games of the season showed Wednesday could do okay without the promising Yugoslav and the creative Belgian. The Owls had been playing well; they looked confident and hungry, solid and strong, and most importantly were *winning* – four from four. Top of the Premier League.

* * * *

In that excellent opening run, it had been Des Walker and Dejan Stefanovic at the back providing a strong shield for Kevin Pressman. The unglamorous trio of Wayne Collins, Mark Pembridge and Guy Whittingham were compact across the midfield, protecting the defence. Dutch winger Regi Blinker was allowed to roam and create from out wide, while the new strike force of Andy Booth and the youngster Ritchie Humphreys were taking care of the goals.

Humphreys was an 18-year-old prospect brought in from the reserves by Pleat, in place of the injured David Hirst and Mark Bright. In those opening games, he scored a series of excellent goals. Against Villa: a first-time top-corner volley. Against Leeds: striking low across the keeper inside the box. And best of all against Leicester: picking up the ball in the centre circle, he dribbled on before chipping over the keeper from outside the area. What a talent, many believed. Andy Booth meanwhile added to Humphreys's notches with a couple of goals himself.

Life wasn't great for everyone at the club at that time, however. Wednesday legend Chris Waddle, aged 36 and being used less and less by his manager, found his days at the club to be over. 'Waddle was gone,' says Pleat. 'He'd been fading. He couldn't do it anymore. He could still do his tricks but he wasn't progressive. Not the future.' So Waddle was off to find a game: first with the Scottish club Falkirk, then Bradford City. Goodbye Chrissy Waddle. Hero of the Wembley 1993 season. Exciting. Exhilarating. Brilliant. Gone.

John Sheridan would also be on his way out of the club. He came off the bench a couple of times early on in the 1996/97 season, but was eventually sold to First Division Bolton Wanderers for £225,000. Though he had been the goalscoring hero of the 1991 League Cup Final, his vision and passing ability was now surplus to requirements for Pleat.

'I just walked out of the door as if I was going home, like on any other day in the previous seven seasons,' Sheridan would recall of his final day as a Wednesday man. 'Nobody said thank you.'

Despite their terrific start to the season, Wednesday couldn't stay at the top of the Premier League forever. Never mind any feelings from the fans of things being about to turn for the club; of the Owls being on their way back to somewhere near the upper reaches of the league. The drop-off would come.

No wins from the next eight games – four draws and four defeats. That was more like it.

Goals would be leaked (four against Arsenal and four against Wimbledon). And with Waddle, Sheridan and Degryse all now departed, the only real inventor left in the squad was Blinker. The rest of the players worked hard; played a tight, stifling system well. But at the same time, this provided only limited spark.

The light of the young Humphreys had shone bright at the start of the season, but by October 1996 he was already fading (how could he better or even maintain such an explosive start?). Hirst was somewhat a shadow of his former, devastating self, his injuries continuing to take their toll; nine games in, he was yet to find the net. Mark Bright was out of favour and also on his way out of the club. This left Andy Booth, who was now being relied upon to bring the goals: a big burden for someone who the season before had been playing First Division football.

Assessing his team, Pleat knew what was required. 'After Waddle, we still needed a personality,' he says. 'Someone who the crowd would get excited by.' So Pleat phoned up an old friend in Italy: a man who at the time was in charge of Serie A giants, Inter Milan.

At Inter, the future England boss Roy Hodgson had at his disposal a talented and expensively assembled squad – but he didn't have room for everyone. And with the likes of Ivan Zamorano, Maurizio Ganz and Marco Branca among his choice of forwards, Hodgson was unable to give everyone a game. One such player was the young Italian Benito Carbone. Perhaps Pleat could take him to Wednesday?

Carbone was an extremely skilful forward who could, Pleat thought, provide the inspiration that he was after for his Owls. 'I rang Roy,' remembers Pleat. 'He was on the Inter Milan bus coming back from a game. He said to me, "He's got all the quality in the world, a clever player, terrific touch, powerful shot, unbelievable skill. But he's a sulker. He's sitting at the back of the bus now sulking because he didn't get on today. But that's Benny."'

But this was Inter Milan. What if he came to Wednesday? Pleat *would* pick him. *Would* play him. So no problem. 'It didn't put me off,' says Pleat. 'I knew what I was getting.' Pleat wanted him. Carbone wanted to come to England. And the deal was done.

The only problem was, Wednesday's pockets at that time weren't that full. Carbone would cost £3m; the club had around half that. But Pleat needed him, needed his spark, so the rest would be found from the extra £2m of borrowing that was provided to the club that season by the friendly Co-operative Bank (by that point, the Co-op had been the club's bankers and supporters for over two years, the relationship between lender and borrower getting closer and closer and more special by the year – the extra £2m lent to Wednesday coming on top of the £8.2m already provided to the club).

Despite Carbone speaking only basic English, he settled in quickly. Starting out wide, and given Waddle's vacated number-eight shirt, 'Benny' brought great energy, skills and inventiveness to the side. His short, defence-unlocking passes kept the pace and flow of the matches going and created chances for others. His goals – including a spectacular effort at home to Nottingham Forest – indicated that he was, perhaps, something quite special.

And over the next few months Carbone's influence doubtless helped the Owls recover their form after their sad slide from the top of the tree; the team losing only twice between mid-October 1996 and mid-April 1997, rising as high as sixth and even reaching the quarter-final of the FA Cup (and disappointingly losing at home to Wimbledon). With such momentum, there were hopes of claiming a European spot – hopes that grew and spread until a sudden end-of-season collapse, which culminated in a 1-1 home draw against Liverpool at Hillsborough, during which Andy Booth ended up in goal after first Kevin Pressman was stretchered off and then his replacement, Matt Clarke, was red-carded, meaning the Owls would finish 1996/97 in seventh place. Despite the end-of-season dip, it was in all a season of progress for Pleat and the team.

For the club, however, having borrowed more and more money from the Co-op Bank to upgrade both Hillsborough and the training ground, it was a different story. Combined net spending on player transfers for 1995/96 and 1996/97 reached £5.4m, with the wage bill ramped up over the same period from £5.7m to £7.6m. The club realised that they needed cash – lots of cash – from someone other than the Co-op Bank (which of course was charging interest on the millions it was owed), and soon.

To bring in the kind of figure that was needed, rather than pass the collection plate around the local business community, as once a club like Wednesday might have done, the club through 1996/97 had begun looking at a different source of funding: namely, the financial markets and associated institutions of the City. It was here, the Wednesday board believed, that the type of large funding they were looking for could be found.

Thanks to the remarkable early growth of the Premier League and the rising revenues of its member clubs, investors smelt money. Football, these investors observed, was a fast-growing industry (in terms of revenues), benefitting from a uniquely captive customer base of supporters that by and large would continue to follow their club regardless of its fortunes (certainly, for as long as said club remained in the top division). Broadcasting deals alone were handsome: the initial £304m 1992 deal for the Premier League was soon to be surpassed by a £670m four-year one from 1997/98; the investors also noted rising attendances and rising ticket prices too.

Manchester United, listed on the Stock Exchange since 1991, had been the real success story of City investment, initially raising £7m to help redevelop its Stretford End stand. By 1997, the time Wednesday started looking at raising their own funds, United's market value was over £400m. Newcastle United, Sunderland and Aston Villa would each be floated on the London Stock Exchange through 1996/97; Villa was initially valued at £126m. Even Sheffield United, at that stage a First Division club, would be floated, bringing in £12m to the club. At Wednesday, these financial developments did not escape the board's notice.

So, back in March 1997, the club had released a prospectus that outlined its plan to raise finance via institutions of the City. It was decided, the document explained, that 40 per cent of the club would be made available for purchase via the issue of new shares. This process would dilute the shares of the club's existing few thousand shareholders, while raising cash that could be used to reduce some of the £8.3m of debt the club had held at the end of May 1996, and which had been creeping up since. In effect, this process would help pay off some of the costs relating to the previous years' stadium development and over-activity in the transfer market, while going towards further improving the club's facilities and providing cash for David Pleat to buy more players.

The thinking was that investment would ultimately lead to on-field success and thereby boost the status of the club. At this point

Wednesday, with its 'manageable' and reduced debt and 'captive market' customer base (its fans), would be able to present itself as a sound proposition for even more investment, perhaps even going for a full Stock Exchange flotation, either on the main London Stock Exchange or the Alternative Investment Market. And the draw for the early-to-the-trough, pre-listing investors would be that if they did buy into the proposed new share issue, they would, after the value of those shares had risen substantially (following the club's hoped-for progress and success), be able to sell them on and cash-in big time. Whoopee!

Before even that point, however, there was money to be made. Quite a bit of it, potentially. On paper, at least.

* * * *

Towards the end of the 128-page prospectus was detail of the recent share-buying activity of the club's directors. Essentially, the document showed, in the lead-up to investment between October 1996 and February 1997 – during which time it is said that plans to issue the new shares had at least been informally developed; the official negotiations beginning in January and to be concluded by April – some of the board had been buying up shares.

Apparently, it was usual for shares that were coming up for sale to be put in front of the board and bought by them if they wanted them. The document showed that through that October 1996–February 1997 period, director Keith Addy had purchased seven 'A' shares (the most valuable); finance director Bob Grierson had bought one; and chairman Dave Richards had bought five. And with the release of the prospectus in March 1997, a number of eyebrows were raised at the directors' activity, including those of another board member, the MP Joe Ashton. Suspicious of what had been going on, Ashton would proclaim, 'I knew they [his fellow directors] were buying them up. But there was no way I was getting involved in it.'

By the time the investment came, in April 1997, the value of those original shares would have risen, on paper at least, from around £6,250 each to over £18,000. Chairman Dave Richards, the lead custodian of Sheffield Wednesday, would make a paper gain of over £130,000 (a gain only to be realised, though, if and when the shares were ever sold on).

Because the directors purchased their shares while Wednesday were still just a limited company, such activity – 'making money by dealing in shares with inside knowledge that their value is going to increase' – could not be considered insider dealing. And despite the subsequent misfortunes of the Owls and the consequent fall in value of the shares and the club meaning that those paper profits would not materialise, as David Conn comments in *The Beautiful Game?*, the whole episode, while not illegal, did give 'an appearance of gold-rush profiteering'.

In the end, the share issue would be undersubscribed by existing shareholders, many opting not to take up the opportunity of purchasing new shares in a football club/business that was losing millions of pounds a year (over £2m was lost in 1995/96; over £3m would be lost by the end of 1996/97). So, it would be Charterhouse Development Capital Funds (investment portfolio over £1bn) that emerged as the main buyers. Charterhouse would take 36.7 per cent of the club's total share capital for £15.6m. A further £1.4m would come from existing shareholders. The exercise effectively valued the club at £42.5m.

Curiously 18 million of the new shares created through the issue, most of which were purchased by Charterhouse, were non-voting shares, meaning their owners were not entitled to vote on club matters at the Annual General Meetings (£15.6m to have no voting rights). Meanwhile the previous ordinary voting shares were converted to around 32 million new ones.

According to Charterhouse, the club represented 'good value' thanks to it being 'securely placed in the Premier League'. To keep an eye on things, Charterhouse put their own man, Geoff Arbuthnott, on the plc board, joining Dave Richards, Bob Grierson and Howard Culley; the likes of Geoff Hulley and Keith Addy would remain on the football club board.

For the club's then secretary Graham Mackrell, the moment the Charterhouse money came in was when 'the club changed'. He explains, 'All companies like that are interested in is growth. And all they [Charterhouse] were interested in was money. But football is not the best model in which to achieve growth. By definition, you are not going to progress up the league every season. So that's when it became quite difficult. From then on, we weren't sure if we were a football club or a business.'

FLYING HIGH, CHARTERHOUSE AND SHOOTING

* * * *

With the new £17m pot of cash from the shares sale and a mission to 'grow' Sheffield Wednesday, the ~~football club~~ business got spending. By the end of the upcoming season, 1997/98, the debt held just with the Co-op Bank would be reduced by £3.8m to £6.4m. Further cosmetic development work would be carried out to the stadium and at the training ground at Middlewood, with a few more million pounds spent there. Meanwhile, ahead of his third season in charge at the club, Pleat was able to bring in new players for good transfer fees and see the wage bill increase.

Those new joiners included Patrick Blondeau, a highly regarded right-back in France who had been an important part of a league-winning Monaco side that featured Emmanuel Petit, Gilles Grimandi and an emerging Thierry Henry. He arrived in Sheffield for £1.8m, with Wednesday supposedly beating Inter Milan to his signature. David Billington and Mark McKeever were youngsters signed from Peterborough just after the Charterhouse cash had landed: £500,000, potentially rising to £1m, for the teenagers who between them would go on to play five times for the club. In September 1997 the tidy midfielder Jim Magilton would come in from Southampton for £1.6m; 'the next John Sheridan' some said optimistically. But best of all was the capture of the fancy Italian forward Paolo Di Canio, who for the past year had been dazzling in Scotland for Glasgow Celtic.

Back in Italy, earlier in his career, Di Canio had starred for his hometown club Lazio; then Juventus, Napoli and AC Milan. After falling out with Giovanni Trapattoni, his manager at Juventus, and Fabio Capello, his manager at Milan, Di Canio had moved to Celtic to rediscover his playing verve. After one season he was voted Scottish Player of the Year but following another falling-out, this time with the club's chairman Fergus McCann, he would be moving on again. Interested in the Italian maestro, Pleat had travelled north to take a look.

Pleat remembers his trip to Glasgow well. 'When I arrived at the airport I got in a taxi to the hotel. The driver recognised me and said that there was only one player I had come to see, Di Canio. I had a coffee at the hotel and got another taxi to the ground. And that driver spent the journey telling me about how good Paolo was as well. Unfortunately, when I got to the ground I found out he wasn't playing, so I left early for the airport. And on the way the third taxi driver spent the journey eulogising about Paolo, too. "Three taxi drivers can't be wrong!" I thought to myself. I went back up to watch him again and we eventually signed him.'

Pleat recalls one part of the subsequent negotiation process. 'It was during pre-season training in Holland. We were in the taxi on the way to the airport to meet Di Canio. I get a phone call from his agent: "Look," he says, "we've got a problem. Paolo won't be there today. He's stuck somewhere and he's not feeling too well. But don't worry about it."

'The chairman [Dave Richards] was sitting next to me. He says, "Dave, if Di Canio 'asn't got decency to come t'airport to meet us, I'm telling you now laddy, we're not going to fuckin' sign him." That's what Dave Richards said to me in the car.'

Richards, it seemed, had a change of heart though.

'Three hours later,' explains Pleat, 'and everything had been agreed.' For £4.5m – £3m cash plus Reggie Blinker, rated at £1.5m (a £1.2m increase in his value in 18 months) – Di Canio was a Wednesday player.

* * * *

In the Owls' opening game of 1997/98 at Newcastle, Di Canio would come off the bench for the last 20 minutes. He received a warm reception from the travelling Wednesday fans, but that day the Owls would lose; as they would to Leeds in their next outing and Blackburn a couple of matches after that (the latter a 7-2 humiliation).

Losing games. Defensively poor. Not good for business.

The season plodded on. Wednesday lost 5-2 at home to Derby in an awful performance and by the end of September had won only once. Not even the creativity of Di Canio could arrest the slide.

At least the new man seemed capable of getting something going, though: gliding across the pitch with the ball, making incisive creative passes and linking the play.

* * * *

At this time, autumn 1997, Pleat moved to finally complete the break-up of the 1993 cup finals side, four years after the process had been begun by his predecessor, Trevor Francis. And the Owls' legendary striker David Hirst – much-adored by the supporters – was sold for £2m to Southampton.

Hirst's departure ended an almost 12-year association with the club, during which time he had given 128 goals. And though his blisteringly powerful runs and jackhammer-shot goals had provided great memories for the fans, his terrible fortune with injuries – torn thighs, broken ankles, bad knees – had blotted his final years with the club. Hirst had been top scorer in Pleat's first year in charge, but more recently he could not be relied on to provide a less interrupted season of games. So the cash on offer from Southampton was taken. 'Great business,' reckons Pleat.

The other move was to bring in the lanky Norwegian midfielder Petter Rudi from Molde for £800,000. He would inspire the excellent chant from the Wednesday fans, 'Tutti frutti, Petter Rudi.'

The team shake-up had given some new impetus, but thanks to Wednesday's difficult form through the opening of 1997/98, pressure on Pleat was growing. The rumours that his time in charge might be running out were becoming louder and stronger.

Pleat himself sensed something was awry. He observed how his chairman, Dave Richards, was becoming colder towards him. 'He was beginning to get milky,' was how Pleat put it, 'wasn't supportive any longer.' The 6-1 defeat in November in the unforgiving arena of Old Trafford against Manchester United didn't help matters.

It was a grave day in Manchester: a game in which, as Pleat recalls, his talented all-Italian strike partnership of Di Canio and Benito Carbone 'hadn't tried a leg' (both were taken off at half-time with the score at 4-0).

After Old Trafford, there was no doubt that Pleat's days as Wednesday manager were numbered.

'Things had gone poorly since the previous Christmas,' he says. 'We were on a downward spiral and the board thought they had to arrest it. The United game would be the last game of my tenure.'

That evening, having returned to Sheffield, the phone rang at Pleat's home. 'It was Dave Richards,' he recalls.

'"What you doing tomorra?" he said.

'"I'm coming into the club as normal," I said.

"'Unfortunately, we've got bad news for you. We're going to have to say cheerio.'

"'I understand,' I said. 'That's football.'

"'Unfortunately,' he said, 'I won't be at the club tomorrow because I've got a meeting in London. I'm catching the Master Cutler in the morning.'

"'Chairman,' I said. 'You'd better be there. You hired me, you should have the decency to get rid of me, face to face.'

"'All right, laddy, okay. I'll go on a later train.'"

Down at the club Pleat was told, face to face, by his chairman that his time as manager of Sheffield Wednesday was over.

'He told me that even though it was still early in the season, results had not been good. I think I should have fought my corner more, but I didn't. That was it and I drove off.'

The Owls' next game, at home to Bolton, saw them stroll to a 5-0 win. Andy Booth, one of the previously injured, but now fit players (though he had been out of action for ten weeks), bagged an 11-minute hat-trick. Pleat could have done with that. As the ex-Wednesday manager says today, 'That's football.'

* * * *

The rumours went round of who would replace Pleat. Bobby Robson, at that stage general manager of Barcelona, was again linked with the club; Howard Wilkinson, now technical director of the Football Association following his departure from Leeds United, was too. Also in the running were the former Arsenal boss Bruce Rioch, Barnsley's Danny Wilson (who was attempting to keep the Tykes in the Premier League after getting them there from the First Division), Derby's Jim Smith (a Wednesdayite) and West Bromwich Albion's Ray Harford. Through that whirr of speculation, however, emerged one main contender. The man who'd brought Wednesday the glory of 1991's promotion and the League Cup Final win. And the man who'd then controversially abandoned the club for Aston Villa. 'Judas' Ron Atkinson.

Since leaving Wednesday, Atkinson had won another League Cup, with Villa. Eight months later he had moved on, ending up at Coventry City, where he lasted a couple more years before being pushed out of the door. Atkinson, of course, knew the Owls. He'd saved them before, in 1988/89, and though he took them down a year later, he did bring them back up. Aged 58, he was at the time one of the country's more experienced managers.

As told in his autobiography, *Big Ron*, Atkinson had just returned from the cinema when he learned of Wednesday's interest via a message left on his car phone to call chairman Dave Richards. Funnily enough, Atkinson had been to watch the film *The Full Monty*, the tale of unemployed Sheffield steelworkers turned strippers, which had been released a couple of months earlier.

The message requested that the two men meet. When they did, the chairman offered him the Wednesday job. As Atkinson tells it in his book, '"Ron," he [Richards] begged, "you just have to come back... we have to stay up."'

On offer to Atkinson was a lucrative three-year deal to once again turn the club around. After mulling it over, Atkinson wasn't sure if the Wednesday fans would accept him back after what had happened in 1991. The walkout to Villa: the betrayal. 'If there had been a mass reaction against me,' Atkinson would later say, 'and a general no-no, I'd have said, "Forget it."'

But there wasn't a general no-no (Richards certainly wanted him back), and so his return was agreed. Atkinson signed up until the end of the season (for now, he would reject Richards' original offer of three years, preferring instead to see how things went: his mission was to keep Wednesday up and then see what was what).

His welcome back to Sheffield was warm. The *Sheffield Star* gave away car stickers to mark the occasion – 'Big Ron's Barmy Army' – and they seemed to be everywhere in the city. All was not forgotten, but the general view was that Atkinson was the right man for the job.

From the start, he ordered double training sessions for the players, working them hard and whipping them into shape. He and his coaches made sure they were organised; his head could be seen peering out of his office window at the training ground at Middlewood, overseeing it all. And so work began on that simple objective: achieving Premier League survival.

The results were instant. Wins came over Arsenal, Southampton and Barnsley. 'Atkinson's Barmy Army!' chanted the crowd. The Owls were alive again: out of the relegation places and up to the relative comfort of mid-table.

* * * *

Before he departed the club, David Pleat's net spending on player transfers during 1997/98 had reached over £4m. Atkinson didn't have a great deal of cash available for making changes. But following the New Year sales of the French full-back Patrick Blondeau (off to Bordeaux for £1.2m; a £600,000 loss on his original transfer to Wednesday) and Wayne Collins (£400,000 to Fulham), there was some in the pot.

Atkinson moved to bring in Niclas Alexandersson, a winger from Gothenburg who provided quality, energy and an urgent thrust down the right-hand side of the pitch. After being made aware of a buy-out clause in his contract, the Wednesday manager was able to get the Swede for £750,000. Experienced defender Earl Barrett was brought in on a free transfer from Everton, and from the same club came the England left-back Andy Hinchcliffe, signed for £2.75m in January 1998.

Hinchcliffe was a top defender; he had won the FA Cup with the Merseysiders in 1995 and earned four England caps along the way (as he would three times while a Wednesday man). He defended tough and his left boot could swing over deep accurate crosses or strike a fierce free kick. But he had problems with injuries.

A few weeks before joining Wednesday, Hinchcliffe had failed a medical at Tottenham Hotspur after they had had concerns over his ankle. Earlier a much more serious cruciate knee ligament injury had sidelined him for nine months. Hinchcliffe, though, was able to pass Wednesday's medical no problem and sign up for wages reputed to be at least £16,500 per week.

Also bought by manager Atkinson at this time was the Macedonian defender Goce Sedloski, signed from Croatian club Hajduk Split. Originally, Sedloski had been set to join Wednesday for £1.75m.

But, unlike Hinchcliffe, he initially failed his medical. When he recovered, the club came back and managed to get him for a cheaper £750,000 (the extra £1m payable as and when he had made a sufficient number of appearances for the club). The transfer proved disastrous, however; once the inevitable injury problems came, he would play only *four* times for the club before being let go for *nothing* a year later.

Another, slightly more astute, bit of business carried out by Atkinson was the signing of the towering Brazilian-born Portuguese centre-half Emerson Thome, picked up from Benfica in March 1998 – for free.

After receiving a tip-off about him, Atkinson gave Thome a trial in Sheffield, playing him in a reserve game. Impressed with what he saw, the manager invited him to join the club. And after he bought himself out of the remainder of his Benfica contract, Thome joined Wednesday on a three-month deal.

Speaking down the phone from Portugal, Thome remembers the circumstances surrounding the move and his initial time in Sheffield. 'Ron was a very experienced man. He had great knowledge about the game and was very passionate. We shared the same passion and he bet on me straight away. When I came to Sheffield nobody knew about me. I was something out of the blue. I couldn't speak the language; nothing at all. But all I needed to do was express myself on the pitch. I needed to prove how good I was. And I did. My relationship with the supporters gelled straight away and I heard them singing my name, making music, and that proves a lot.'

Indeed, such was the new man's popularity with the supporters that he soon had his own song. To the tune of 'The Little Drummer Boy' and referencing a previous, 'similar'-looking Wednesday player, it went, 'He looks like Paul Warhurst, He's Emerson Thome.'

Thome exuded presence and quality at the back; he was strong and commanding and would eventually form a great partnership with Des Walker. 'To be fair to us,' remembers Thome, 'it was quite hard at the beginning because communication between us wasn't the best. But we gelled together on the pitch and that was the most important thing. The partnership worked well and I was proud to play next to such a great centre-back.'

Though Thome was a free transfer, the other players did not come cheap. Since the Charterhouse investment, the club had by now spent over £7m net on new players; its annual wage bill increased by £4.2m in a year to £11.3m by the end of 1997/98. Of course, while the normal inflows of a medium-sized Premier League club (gate receipts, television money, merchandise, corporate sales and so on) could to some extent support this expenditure, the club's recent spending had reached such a level that the £15.6m of

Charterhouse cash that had flowed into the club (along with the £1.4m from other shareholders) at the time of the share issue was now, pretty much, gone.

Fortunately, the Co-operative Bank was still there to support the club and its post-Charterhouse-cash spending. The relationship between bank and club, more loss-making than it was profitable, was set to gradually deepen and become even more 'special' as the months and years passed.

* * * *

Undoubtedly one of Atkinson's key strengths was his ability to man-manage the different characters that made up his team, getting the best out of them for the benefit of the collective, to achieve the common goal.

His preferred forward pairing for his Owls side was the Italian duo Paolo Di Canio and Benito Carbone. And under Atkinson the pair, both subbed at half-time in David Pleat's last game in charge, thrived. They would go on to make an invaluable contribution over the remainder of the season.

Di Canio's goal at Everton, where in the club's orange and white away strip he danced over the Goodison Park pitch to confirm the 3-1 win, plus his marvellous overhead kick in a vital win against Manchester United in front of a full house at Hillsborough, helped bring vital points. Meanwhile his accomplice Carbone helped set up the bullets for his compatriot to fire. At times, the pair would link up fabulously on the field: poetry in motion. 'We spoke the same language,' Carbone would later say of himself and Di Canio. 'Not just Italian, but in football terms.'

They were massive characters for the team but both, while able to dazzle, could be known to sulk and strop and disrupt. Complaints and gesticulations would come from each of them, be it on matchday or at the training ground at Middlewood. Di Canio, for instance, would be known to criticise others in training if he believed their efforts were not matching his. Yet he was an excellent worker. 'A great professional,' says one former Wednesday teammate, 'first on the training pitch, last off it.'

And he cared. Wisely, Atkinson worked to nurture the temperamental pair, accepting the difficulties that would come with such an approach, while at the same time ensuring that their talents and efforts were channelled in an effective way. 'I love flair,' Atkinson would say, 'but I like it to be productive flair. Both have got immense talent... what we've got to do is harness their talent to our team play.'

As Atkinson's influence on the team grew, having blended the quality new recruits with those he'd inherited and nurtured, he was able to reap the success that followed. Eventually, enough wins were taken to complete the job – to turn the club around and retain the club's Premier League status. Job done, Big Ron.

Wednesday, it seemed, had turned the corner and were about to make some progress.

Then they shot themselves in the foot.

'Ron has a contract until the end of the season,' chairman Dave Richards had remarked the previous November, not long after Atkinson had returned to the club. He had added ominously, 'Wednesday will then take a look at the long-term effects and see whether he is the man to take us forward.'

When Atkinson had re-joined Wednesday, he'd said, 'I'll stay on board until the end of the season... at the moment there's no need to look beyond that.' Now, though, having assured the club of its Premier League status, he definitely fancied another year or two at the helm. He envisaged working with a young assistant, to whom he could eventually hand over the reins; and he had Nigel Pearson, a well-respected figure and captain of the 1991 League Cup-winning side, who had just retired from playing with Middlesbrough, in mind for that role. Stay a year or two, then pass it on, was Atkinson's plan. But Richards had other ideas and was not, it seemed, in favour.

Richards wanted more stability in the role; more certainty for the future than Atkinson's hand-over-the-reins-to-a-younger-man plan provided. So, at the end of the 1997/98 season, having just saved the club's skin, Atkinson was sacked by Sheffield Wednesday.

'[W]e've taken a decision which we feel is necessary for the long-term future of the club,' Richards announced. 'We're looking at the long-term picture.'

Atkinson was shocked, angry and 'numb with betrayal' at the decision. It was certainly a strange one, considering how the previous season had just played out.

Some suspected an act of revenge from the club: getting Atkinson back for his abandonment in 1991. Atkinson, in 1998, had kept the club up; now, he could bugger off – Wednesday could finish with *him* as he had done with them. '[M]aybe we should call it a draw,' Atkinson had said to his chairman as his second spell at the club neared its end. Richards's response to that comment, 'put me [Atkinson] in the dole queue,' as Atkinson would tell it in his book; 1-1.

But surely it wasn't that petty?

Another influencing factor may have been the £487,500 of league prize money the club had lost following the last-day defeat at Crystal Palace. Kevin Pressman and Des Walker's collision had led to a gift winner for Palace, which meant that Wednesday finished 16th instead of 13th – thereby foregoing that wad of prize money.

Hardly Atkinson's fault, though? Yet as he would recall, 'After the Selhurst Park result, I felt a considerable change in the boardroom mood and attitude towards me. The vibes were extremely negative. The chairman, maybe feeling the boardroom pressure, bleated on about the lost half-million pounds. Finances were tight, he said.'

Of course, the Charterhouse money had been spent and the club was on course to post a £10m loss that season. Now, they had just lost an extra £487,500. But surely it wasn't just about half a million pounds?

Whatever the reasons, Big Ron was out. In what seemed like a flash, a relatively stable situation had now been destabilised.

It appeared as if the thinking from within the club was that 'big club' Sheffield Wednesday was too good for relegation. That Wednesday looked up and not down. And that others would always be worse off. The club had now been in the top flight for seven years – so would always be in that division. Right?

But life in the top tier, with its three-team trap door, fierce on-field competition and escalating wages and transfer fees, was precarious. Despatching with a manager like Ron Atkinson, whatever the concerns surrounding short-termism or lost prize money, and even forgetting any potential desire for revenge, would in the eyes of many – both at the time and in hindsight – prove a huge act of folly by the club.

8

Anatomy of a Fall

I

IN the frame to replace Ron Atkinson as Wednesday boss, to become the club's fourth manager in seven years, were two Frenchmen and one Scot.

Frenchman number one was Philippe Troussier, then the manager of South Africa. It was the summer of 1998 and his team were in France for the World Cup. According to Troussier, Wednesday chairman Dave Richards travelled to meet him at the South Africa base in Vichy, four hours away from Paris. 'We had a ten-minute chat,' Troussier would say, adding assuredly, 'and I'm very happy that I'm going to Hillsborough.' Troussier appeared to be suffering from a spot of premature triumphalism, however, because as Richards would point out, pouring cold water on Troussier's hopes, 'Nobody has been offered the job. Several candidates have been spoken to... [but] we will keep interviewing until we decide on the one we want.' In the end, that wouldn't be Troussier.

Frenchman number two was Gérard Houllier, at that stage technical director of the French Football Association and previous manager of the French national side. Wednesday did make an approach for Houllier and were close to appointing him.

Houllier cannot now remember if Richards came to visit him at the French camp during the World Cup, as he had with Troussier in Vichy. But, as he recalls today, speaking down the line of his mobile, meetings between him and the club would take place both over the phone and in London.

'I knew Sheffield,' says Houllier. 'I knew the club and I knew some of the players. And I had a good relationship with Dave Richards. He was very keen to sign me. I explained a few ideas of how I wanted the team to play and things like that and I had a good feeling about what we could do at Sheffield Wednesday. I practically gave my agreement to join.'

But there was one condition. Houllier explains, 'I would be given a divorce clause. This was where if the club for one reason or another had to sack me, they would pay me a certain amount of money. I'd never been sacked in my life, but things don't always go your way and sometimes a club has to take a decision. So I just wanted protection for myself. Dave Richards was very good about this part of the negotiations and told me that their lawyer would get in touch to agree the sum of the clause. The lawyer came to me, it took him some time to do so, and I said I wanted this amount of money. It wasn't even a year's contract. But he said, "It's too much. Can you lower it?" "No," I said.'

With other clubs on the scene and interested in Houllier, among them Celtic and a few in France, the talks with Wednesday dragged on. Then, with no agreement ever reached, Houllier eventually moved to Liverpool to become their joint-manager with Roy Evans. Within three years he would win an FA Cup, League Cup and UEFA Cup treble.

'It's not Dave Richards's fault,' reflects Houllier today of the Owls' failure to bring him to Hillsborough. 'Unless he gave instructions to the lawyer to make things linger. I don't know. I don't think so. It's more to do with the fact they were slow in finalising the divorce clause and the contract. If they had agreed on the terms of the divorce clause, I would have been Sheffield Wednesday manager.'

After Houllier had got away, and Troussier discarded, there then emerged the Scot: Glasgow Rangers' successful manager, Walter Smith.

After winning a wheelbarrowful of titles and cups in Scotland, Smith was now ready for a move south to England, and it seemed Wednesday was to be his destination. A three-year deal was lined up: the club reportedly claimed that the deal was agreed and a press conference was planned to unveil him. However, late on, Everton came in with a better offer; one apparently providing a bigger pay packet and the promise of a transfer kitty larger than Wednesday's. So Smith went to Goodison Park instead, leaving Dave Richards and the club 'extremely disappointed by Mr Smith's late change of mind'.

Troussier. Houllier. Smith. None out of three for Wednesday.

Richards now had a headache. Time was ticking – the opening weekend of the 1998/99 season was only six or so weeks away – and the pool of suitable, available candidates was diminishing.

What, though, about a young up-and-coming English manager? Someone who had played for the club; had even lifted a trophy in a Wednesday shirt; an honest bloke who understood and cared about the club? An intelligent man who in his brief managerial career had already achieved some success, and who might be able to build upon what Ron Atkinson had started? That'd work, wouldn't it?

Twelve miles up the road from Sheffield, in Barnsley, the rumours had been going round for a while: one day, their manager would leave them for Wednesday.

Danny Wilson, starter in the 1991 League Cup Final in the centre of the Owls midfield, had been a willing early casualty of Trevor Francis's post-1993 clear-out, following Viv Anderson to Barnsley to become his assistant player-manager. Though initially unpopular with the fans thanks to his Wednesday background (the Owls considered by Barnsley to be more of a rival to them than, say, Sheffield United), Wilson, having now taken over from Anderson as boss, had managed to win over the Oakwell crowd.

Back in 1994/95 Wilson's Barnsley had been knocking on the door of the First Division play-offs. Two years later, his hardworking, committed and (apparently according to the Barnsley fans) Brazil-esque-in-style side had taken the club to the top flight for the first time in their 110-year history.

'When Danny Wilson took us to the Premiership, he was seen as a god in Barnsley,' says the Tykes supporter and poet Ian McMillan, sitting one afternoon in a Salford Quays coffee shop. 'He really was someone who could do no wrong.'

And even though the Premier League adventure had ended with the inevitable relegation, many people associated with the club still believed that Wilson would not be leaving them anytime soon – even if 'big' Wednesday down the road did come sniffing. But they'd be wrong. Wilson had first been linked to the Wednesday job the previous October (1997) when David Pleat was sacked by the club. But with Barnsley early into their Premier League adventure, Wilson, when questioned about his link to the Owls job, made it clear where his loyalties lay, 'I don't think you should be asking me questions like that at a time like this,' he would say (Barnsley had just beaten Liverpool at Anfield). 'I've got a job to do here.'

Later that same season, when Wednesday had visited Oakwell, the travelling Owls fans had mischievously chanted 'Danny's coming home' to the 'Three Lions' Euro 96 England tune. 'No way!' shouted back McMillan and the Barnsley fans.

'But,' recalls McMillan, 'I remember thinking then, "I wonder if he will go?" Would Wednesday come and take our manager?'

Wilson's comments on the Oakwell pitch after the last game of the previous season indicated that he would stay; he made his position quite clear, in fact. 'This is Danny Wilson,' he said over the speakers. 'I just wanted to say I'm going to stay in Barnsley and try to bring the club back into the Premier League.' That was 10 May 1998.

Yet as the summer moved on and Wednesday flirted with Philippe Troussier, Gérard Houllier and Walter Smith, only to land none of them, the Owls were now more desperate. By 30 June, when the England national team were walking out to their World Cup second-round tie against Argentina in St Etienne, Wednesday's chairman Dave Richards was under increasing pressure to make an appointment.

At half-time of that game, with the score 2-2, Richards, according to the then Barnsley chairman John Dennis, picked up the phone. 'I'm so sorry, John,' Richards is said to have told Dennis, 'this is the call that I never wanted to make, but can we please have permission to speak to your manager, Danny Wilson?'

Dennis decided that if Wednesday did want their Danny, they wouldn't be getting him cheap. It would cost them. Barnsley demanded £2m in compensation (even though Wilson's contract apparently would actually have enabled a move for £250,000). Richards didn't like that. £2m? For the manager of Barnsley? Don't think so.

Dennis recalled what happened next. 'In the subsequent conversation, he [Richards] explained that, in view of our hugely optimistic demands, there was little point in wasting time trying to negotiate... they [Wednesday] were intending to proceed to talk to Danny with or without permission... [and] were perfectly happy for the dispute to be settled by arbitration.' Naughty, naughty 'big' Wednesday.

In the end, and despite having assured the Barnsley fans on the Oakwell pitch that he would not be leaving the club, the 'emotional pull' to move 12 miles back down the road to Hillsborough was too great for Wilson to resist. In the end the Owls had got their man for £500,000 (still double the price they apparently could have got him for).

Meanwhile back in Barnsley, Wilson overnight went from hero to villain.

'I was upset when it happened,' recalls McMillan. 'You thought, "God, this is terrible, this really is bad. Why has he gone to Wednesday?" It was like some favourite person that you know very well, suddenly saying they don't like you. And we all felt a sense of betrayal and disappointment because he'd done such a great job here. But Wednesday was his club, so your head said, "Well, he had to go."

'In a way, the whole thing felt very poetic to me, almost in a Shakespearean sense. Here comes the young prince to take on this thing. Then he betrays you and is off to the big rival across the water. It had that kind of narrative element to it. That's what I thought anyway.'

* * * *

Ahead of 1998/99, there wasn't too much for the new Wednesday manager to spend on his team, what with the Charterhouse cash spent up and the club still £6.4m in debt with the bank. He had, however, inherited a group of players that had been revived and improved under his predecessor, Ron Atkinson. And probably, initially at least, the group would require only a few tweaks of his own.

Those tweaks...

First was the signing of the PSV Eindhoven and Dutch international midfielder Wim Jonk, a cultured ball player once of Inter Milan who'd played six times for his country in that summer's World Cup. Jonk, it was thought, would bring quality and a cutting pass to the Wednesday team. He cost £2.5m and was reputedly handed the astonishing clause in his three-year contract that provided him with a £5,000 bonus for every game Wednesday played... whether he was in the team or not. That, on top of a basic salary believed to be £12,000 per week (perhaps even as high as £18,000).

Second was the signing of the right-back Juan Cobian who, following a trial on the training pitches at Middlewood, arrived from Argentine side Boca Juniors for £250,000.

Initial impressions of Wilson's tweaked Wednesday were mixed. While early on, comprehensive wins came away at Tottenham and at home to Blackburn (both 3-0), these triumphs would come alongside three tame 1-0 defeats. And with Wilson set to face an early challenge from a couple of individuals in his squad, he soon found his man-management capabilities tested to the limit.

A League Cup second-round tie against Third Division Cambridge United brought the first controversy: a poor performance at Hillsborough that resulted in a miserable 1-0 defeat and some scathing post-match criticism from Wilson. '[I]t was a performance bordering on complacency and was disrespectful to Cambridge,' he vented. 'We had no work-rate and team spirit... We did not have enough people willing to roll their sleeves up and have a go.'

Wilson then appeared to single out his two tricky Italian forwards, Paolo Di Canio and Benito Carbone, both of whom had had a poor game. 'I won't stand for that kind of commitment,' said Wilson. 'Two players [believed by everyone to be the Italians] think they can turn performances on and off like a tap, but it doesn't work like that.' Adding, with reference to the pair's general play that night, 'All that fancy dan stuff is just c***. They are so self-indulgent and it's detrimental to the team.' Di Canio was unimpressed by the comments. '[P]erhaps he thinks attacking his own players in public is a way to show strength,' Di Canio would say dismissively.

Naturally, the episode did not do much for Di Canio and Wilson's relationship. 'He [Wilson] was considered a rising star among managers,' Di Canio would recall in his autobiography, 'but

I could tell right away he lacked something. He didn't carry himself with any kind of confidence.' A rift had emerged.

Four days after the second leg of the Cambridge tie (a draw which dumped Wednesday out of the competition 2-1 on aggregate), things came to a head when Arsenal visited Hillsborough.

* * * *

Saturday 26 September 1998 was a significant day in the recent history of Sheffield Wednesday. A day that not only would mark the beginning of the end of Di Canio's Owls career, but also more fatefully the beginning of the end for Sheffield Wednesday as a Premier League football club.

That Saturday afternoon saw a good first half of football between Wilson's Wednesday and Arsène Wenger's title-holders Arsenal. Dennis Bergkamp, Marc Overmars and Patrick Vieira were on show, and a decent Premier League game unfolded down on the Hillsborough pitch. Then Wednesday's Wim Jonk tugged on the shirt of Vieira – and everything changed.

Retaliating to the tug, Vieira shoved Jonk, who took a theatrical tumble. Then Di Canio, other blue and whites, and red shirts came together, all pushing and shoving. Arsenal's fearsome centre-half Martin Keown moved Di Canio out of the way, using his elbow to do so, and caught Di Canio on his nose in the process. Di Canio kicked Keown in response and both were sent off.

The Owls' Italian didn't like that: he was only protecting a colleague. So he pushed the referee, Paul Alcock. For what seemed like an age, Alcock stumbled backwards, before falling to the floor in a heap. 'The severity of the incident is unquestionable,' a shocked Danny Wilson would say of the episode. 'I just don't know what went through his mind.'

Tipping point.

Di Canio walked off towards the dressing room, gesticulating a bit with his arms, and on the way had a moment with the Arsenal defender, Nigel Winterburn. 'You're done! You f**king Italian bastard! You're finished!' Winterburn is said to have told Di Canio, who in response raised his hand as if to punch him (Winterburn hilariously then reeled back in shock).

Wednesday would go on to win the match, Kevin Pressman's saves and Lee Briscoe's 89th-minute edge-of-the-area wonder chip bagging them the three points. But, naturally, afterwards all of the attention focused on Di Canio and his actions. The media, of course, set to condemn him.

After the incident, Di Canio had driven to Heathrow and caught a flight home to Italy. Finding his way to Terni, a village north-east of Rome, he would for weeks train isolated, far away from Sheffield, his teammates and his manager.

Wednesday apparently had gone quiet on him. 'Nobody from the club called me,' Di Canio would later say. 'Not Wilson, not Richards... several weeks passed before I heard from the club. I felt totally abandoned.' And whether this was absolutely accurate or not – the club did claim they had been in touch, at least via his agent – certainly they were not defending him in public.

A few weeks after the push, Di Canio was back in Sheffield, England to attend his disciplinary tribunal (held across town from Hillsborough at Sheffield United's Bramall Lane). Dressed smartly in shirt and tie, Di Canio would be accompanied by his lawyer and three club representatives. His manager Danny Wilson and his chairman Dave Richards would not attend.

* * * *

An aside. Why was Richards absent? Why had there been a general lack of support from the club towards Di Canio following the incident? It may be as simple as: what exactly were they meant to say? After all, the player had manhandled a referee. But could there have been more to it than that?

As Wednesday's chairman, Richards had sat on the Premier League's one-club-one-seat board since its inception, sharing the room with characters like Chelsea's Ken Bates and Manchester United's Martin Edwards. Having observed the ways of those wealthy and strong-minded men, and building on what he had learned from his time on the Wednesday board and as head of his own Sheffield business, Three Star Engineering, Richards, it is said, had become a most adept boardroom player.

Since 1994 he had also sat on the FA Council, the board that determined the overall policies of the FA. And, it is understood, he had shaken enough hands, spent enough time on the phone to colleagues and peers, and made enough friends to position himself as a somewhat influential figure in the game. Someone perhaps destined for a top role, someday? It was certainly possible. Back in 1996, he had gone for the job of FA chairman, losing out, along with Geoff Thompson, to the then Southampton vice-chairman Keith Wiseman. But that didn't mean he would not try again in the future.

And as Di Canio would speculate, 'Dave Richards couldn't care less whether I got banned forever or not. You see, the last thing he wanted to do was make waves. If he stood up to the judges at the disciplinary hearing, he risked upsetting the powers-that-be. From his point of view it made much more sense to roll over and play dead, entrusting my future, my career, to the judges. That way he wouldn't run the risk of upsetting anybody at the FA.' Not, perhaps, something that ambitious Dave Richards wanted to be doing, either directly or via the football club of which he was chair.

In the end, Di Canio would be handed an 11-game ban for his push on the referee – three games for the red card itself and eight for the push – plus a £10,000 fine. Di Canio accepted the punishment. 'I am very, very sorry for what happened,' he said. 'I had a fair hearing, for which I am grateful.' 'We are satisfied with the outcome,' a club representative said. 'There will be no appeal.'

After the hearing, Wednesday told Di Canio to go back to Italy and train while he saw out most of his ban. As it turned out, though, he would not play for the club again.

Beyond the difficulties of a club defending a referee-pushing player and even ignoring the theory of Richards being more interested in politicking for a future top vacancy in the game than protecting one of the club's players, Wednesday had seemingly done little to support Di Canio. If only from a commercial viewpoint, more might gave been done to protect the value of an individual who was at the time the club's most valuable playing asset. Yet by not doing so – in public at least – Wednesday had signalled that they were willing to drop their talented-yet-difficult-to-handle player and depressing his transfer value in the process.

Just over a year before, Di Canio had been brought into the club on a £4.5m deal; his performances since then would at least have kept that value static, but now it was in sharp decline. As Di Canio himself would explain, 'Instead of protecting me, instead of maximising my value, they did everything they could to destroy me… Sheffield Wednesday created a situation for themselves where they had no choice but to sell me.'

By January 1999, after his ban had been served, a get-out for both Di Canio and Wednesday appeared when the West Ham United manager, Harry Redknapp, spotted a bargain. Seeing a rough diamond to be polished, Redknapp offered a lifeline to the Italian maestro and a drop-down £2m fee to the Owls. Like that, Di Canio would be gone. Under his new manager, he settled fast and shone bright, becoming an integral part of the Hammers' side.

'Could we have handled it better?' the club's former secretary, Graham Mackrell, now asks of the whole affair. 'Possibly. We took the moral high ground. Did we support him enough? I'm not sure.'

Though the Owls had done okay during Di Canio's ban, picking up three wins and four draws, the challenge now was how Danny Wilson's Wednesday would cope with the loss of such a creative talent.

Andy Booth and Benito Carbone now became Wilson's favoured pairing up front: big and small; Yorkshire brute and continental flair. They were backed up by a generally solid midfield of Petter Rudi, Danny Sonner (a £75,000 capture from Ipswich Town a few months into the season), Wim Jonk and the adventurous winger Niclas Alexandersson. Then an even more solid defence, featuring at its heart the duo of Des Walker and Emerson Thome, themselves supported by Kevin Pressman or Pavel Srnicek (the former Newcastle United man who had been brought in by Wilson on a free transfer from Czech club Banik Ostrava) in goal.

This solidness would be reflected in the end-of-season statistic that had Wednesday with the fifth best defensive record in the league. Worryingly, though, they had failed to do much in front of goal – 1-0s, 0-0s and 0-1s were the more familiar score lines of 1998/99, with the reality that the squad had now become an unimaginative and wearisome team to watch. It was grey ordinariness from Wilson's Owls as they drearily saw out the season, finishing 12th.

It was decent, but really not decent enough. It felt like the club was in a slow decline that had rumbled on for years now. Perhaps it had begun back when Andy Linighan had broken hearts at Wembley, in the last minute of extra time in 1993. And now, post-

Di Canio, post-tipping point, it felt very much like the iceberg might be coming.

II

For Danny Wilson, joining up with Wednesday the previous summer, only six weeks before the 1998/99 season had begun, had not been ideal preparation. Prior to his second season in charge, though, he now had time to prepare fully for the campaign ahead and to tweak his squad as he thought necessary. This was the summer Wednesday would truly become his team.

He knew, once again, that he didn't have much money to spend. The club would post a £9.4m loss for 1998/99 which helped increase its debt to £11.7m – with more lending provided by the ethical Co-op Bank in Manchester. For 1999/00, therefore, Wilson had his work cut out to identify some pretty canny signings.

He had earlier outlined exactly what he would be needing come the summer: strength in depth for the squad and a cutting edge up front to complement his already strong defence, and also had sought a more elegant, technical, continental style of play for his team.

He found two players he liked. One, Simon Donnelly, was once compared to Kenny Dalglish (perhaps because he was slight, had good vision and passing ability, was a forward, was Scottish and played for Celtic); he had been tied to a pre-contract agreement by Wilson earlier in the year, and would arrive at the club that summer. Donnelly would be joined by his compatriot Phil O'Donnell, a midfielder. Both Scots had played for their country, were fairly highly regarded, and in choosing not to renew their contracts with Celtic were able to move to Wednesday on Bosman free transfers. The pair had signed their pre-contract agreements in Sheffield in March 1999, completing their medicals at the same time, it is understood.

Curiously, at this pre-contract signing stage, neither player was actually playing for Celtic: both were injured. Donnelly had not featured since the month before due to a knee problem, and would not play again until early April; before that, he'd had a pretty flawless injury record. O'Donnell, meanwhile, had not appeared since mid-February due to a back injury, and would not play again until early May. He had played only 22 and 20 games for Celtic over the past two seasons. For Wednesday, though, none of this appeared to be considered much of a problem.

Both Scots were signed on four-year deals with reputed weekly wages of up to £14,500; figures which supposedly included signing-on fees at the start of the deal, possibly inflated beyond normal terms due to there being no transfer fee in the first place. But though the players passed the Wednesday medicals, it wasn't long before injuries hit for both of them, during their very first season at the club. They would go on to make only a handful more appearances between them.

Also brought down to the club from Scotland had been the central midfielder Philip Scott, joining back in March 1999 on a three-year deal for £75,000. York City's young forward Richard Cresswell had the same day also joined the club for £950,000.

Next into Hillsborough during the following summer were the forwards Gilles De Bilde and Gerald Sibon.

De Bilde was a reasonably well-known name at the time. A Belgian international playing for PSV Eindhoven, he was efficient in the box and able to finish a chance and bring others into the play. At £2.8m he seemed a reasonable deal; the cutting edge, perhaps, that Wilson had been after.

The new man had a reputation as a laid-back individual, but also somewhat contrarily, one who came with some baggage – namely, a history of violent confrontation on and off the pitch. Incidents involving violent De Bilde include him once breaking the nose and shattering the eye socket of an opposition player, with one punch; head-butting two boy-scout leaders; and doing the same to a male nurse, after being refused entry to a hospital room where his ill father was being treated. Following the punching-another-player incident, De Bilde's coach at the time suggested that he might see a psychiatrist. The Belgian's wages at Hillsborough would reportedly be in the region of £15,000 per week. His contract, like Donnelly's, O'Donnell's and Scott's, was four years long.

The Owls' other capture, Gerald Sibon, meanwhile, was an 11-foot-tall (or 6ft 3in according to official stats) forward with apparently excellent football skills. He cost £2m from Ajax, where he had been lurking mainly out of the first team, and he too would be handed a four-year contract. His reported wages: £14,400 per week.

Wednesday's total commitment for those five new players over their four-year contracts would be well over £12m (maybe even £14m, depending on which reports are most reliable). They would help grow the club's wage bill to £14.4m for 1999/00 (the fourth *lowest* in the Premier League that season).

* * * *

After the new signings, however, early indications of Wilson's 'improved' set-up for 1999/00 were not that encouraging. Aside from the results – five defeats from the opening six games – the team's play appeared as stagnant as it had towards the end of the previous season. And even once the new signings had adjusted to a new league, the Owls did not ignite.

As De Bilde and Sibon scored no goals in those opening games, it was left to Benito Carbone to contribute the most, bagging each of Wednesday's two goals so far that season; despite now only being used by Wilson as a substitute.

Carbone the sub was not, however, happy with the situation. Down at Southampton, having learned that he again would be made to sit on the bench, he naughtily walked out of the Wednesday changing room, took a taxi to Gatwick airport and got on a plane home to Italy.

Wilson, whose team lost that day, was 'absolutely disgusted' with Carbone; he fined him two weeks' wages and, when the Italian returned to Sheffield, made him train with the youngsters. Some of his senior teammates stopped talking to him and adopted some sophisticated dressing-room banter, such as putting up various signs that read things like 'RIP Benny'.

Carbone would find himself back on the bench for the Everton game (another defeat for the Owls, following the Southampton reverse) but his days as a Wednesday player were numbered. Eventually, he would be sold to Aston Villa for a miserly £250,000 (three years earlier Wednesday had paid Inter Milan £3m for him).

'We don't miss Benny,' said one of his teammates at the time, adding, fantastically, 'but we miss someone who can score goals.' Carbone had been Wednesday's joint-second top scorer when he left.

'RIP Benny'? For the Owls, sitting bottom of the table after seven games, it was increasingly looking like RIP Sheffield Wednesday of the Premier League.

* * * *

With goals now even harder to find, Wednesday relied more than ever on their defence being as tight as it had been the year before. Alas, it was not.

The same pairing of Des Walker and Emerson Thome still prowled the middle of the back four, working alongside a combination of full-backs: Andy Hinchcliffe, Lee Briscoe, Jon Newsome, Ian Nolan or Peter Atherton. But so far that season they, and their keepers – Kevin Pressman or Pavel Srnicek – had been shipping a worrying number of goals: 15 in the first seven games, compared to the five conceded by the same stage the season before.

Then, on a dreadful day up at Newcastle, on the great Bobby Robson's first game in charge as their new manager, the floodgates would really be opened; 8-0 to the Magpies. Eight fucking nil.

At 0-0, Andy Booth had had the ball in the net for the Owls – offside – before having his lob cleared from the line. But that was as good as it got for Wednesday as the goals came, all eight of them; five from Alan Shearer. Danny Wilson would describe it as 'the most humiliating and embarrassing day of my career'.

If Paolo Di Canio's push on the referee Paul Alcock the previous September had been the tipping point that had triggered or accelerated Wednesday's fall, this performance – a hapless team collectively throwing in the tea towel – was the moment that confirmed exactly where the club was heading.

Down. Down. Down.

How long could Danny Wilson last now? 'If you're asking me will I keep my job,' said the Wednesday boss following the Newcastle deluge, 'it's not a question I can answer. As far as I'm concerned, I'm sticking in there. But I'm a realist. I can't keep getting results like that.'

* * * *

With his team sat at the foot of the Premier League, Wilson wasn't helped by stories of apparent splits between various dressing-room factions. Apparently core to this was the divide between some of the foreign and British players, a divide symbolised by and manifested in the two separate changing rooms at the club's training ground, Middlewood. As Andy Booth recalls, 'We probably had all the English lads in one dressing room and all the foreign lads in the other. That wasn't ideal. You want everyone together, to have the banter in the dressing room, to be a team.' It would be several years before someone had the idea of knocking down those walls.

Some believed that a few of the imported players, who had the most talent and were definitely among the club's highest earners, were 'divisive' mercenaries, disinterested in the club and just there to collect their big pay cheques each week, perhaps not giving everything they could for the cause. Attitudes like this from the £2.8m Belgian Gilles De Bilde, revealed years later, wouldn't help, 'The only way foreign players amused themselves,' he would write in his autobiography (not published in English), 'was talking about money. It was the only reason we were still playing in England.

'In that period the Dutch players [Wim Jonk and Gerald Sibon were on the club's books at the time] and I made a calendar. Each of us made a drawing of how he saw his future. I drew a nice villa in Spain with a waiter serving me while a plane dropped pounds over me.'

Of course, it would be unfair, not to mention unjustly xenophobic, to blame Wednesday's on-field demise on one particular contingent. As the miserable defeats continued to come, most of the players, wherever they came from, had their share of below-par performances that season. Really, it had been pretty terrible from most of them for *all* of the season.

Yet worse was still to come for Wilson. Halfway through the season, he had to sell Thome to Chelsea for a pitiful £2.5m. Having excelled since his arrival from Benfica during the 'Ron Atkinson Returns' days, Thome had wanted another, improved contract from the club. When he wasn't given one, Chelsea swooped in with a bid way below the towering defender's true value, but Wednesday – still rock bottom of the table and with a debt on course to reach over £15m by the end of the season – were hardly in a position to turn down the London club.

'I'm sure they didn't want to sell me,' recalls Thome today of the move, 'and in a way I was disappointed to leave. But things had gone wrong from the beginning of the season and the club needed some money.' Within a year of him joining Chelsea, his new club would sell Thome on to Sunderland for a £2m profit.

As 1999/00 wore on, doubts about whether Wilson was a good enough or strong enough manager to cope with the challenge of keeping the Owls in the Premier League became ever-louder. Despite being generally liked in the game, he now had some particularly staunch critics.

The departed, and admittedly controversial Paolo Di Canio was, for one, never impressed with his former manager, '[W]ith Wilson, there was nothing,' he would later comment. 'No personality, no guidance, no real strength… he was simply way in over his head at Hillsborough.' Meanwhile Di Canio's compatriot Benito Carbone, who had initially got on well with Wilson (before his subs'-bench sulking also earned him a move away from the club), would explain how his former boss 'didn't have any sort of character… didn't know how to impose himself and get what he wanted'. Their comments could simply be the complaints of disgruntled former employees; or perhaps astute observations from two passionate individuals.

Poor Danny Wilson. At least he wasn't the only one at Hillsborough feeling the pressure around that time.

III

At the club's Annual General Meeting back in October 1999, Wednesday's directors were challenged by a group of shareholders to allow one additional board member to join the plc board. Specifically, someone from the fan base who would provide more of a voice for the ordinary supporter – a figure who, it was increasingly thought, was becoming more and more detached from their club and the existing board, its custodians.

The candidate put forward by the shareholders was David Coupe, a fanatical supporter who a year earlier had helped set up the Shareholders' Association, a group whose aim was to constructively challenge the club on behalf of its members. According to Coupe, he initially was told that it would cost him £500,000 to join the board, should he be successful in his bid. 'No,' he replied, or words to that effect, 'I need enough votes.'

Unfortunately for Coupe, when it came to the vote, as he had not come to the table in a more 'usual' way (that is, he hadn't been invited to join the board by any of the existing directors), his skills and expertise were dismissed; and the shareholders were advised by their board to vote against him and his bid.

At this point, past and present board members of Wednesday controlled only around ten per cent of the club's voting shares, either via their own individual shareholdings, or ones owned by companies that they ultimately controlled (such as Dave Richards's Globalfare Limited, which owned 237,600 shares). David Coupe's Shareholders' Association represented around 14 per cent of the voting shares (per the original terms of their investment deal, Charterhouse, owners of 36.7 per cent of the club's capital, were not at that stage entitled to vote, however).

And while in the end, Coupe lost in his bid to join the board – 9.9 million votes were cast against him, 4.1 million for; over 16 million possible votes not cast at all – apparently the Wednesday board had been 'rattled' by the fact that Coupe and the Shareholders' Association had achieved almost 30 per cent of votes that had been made.

* * * *

One further tangible, and less political, reflection of the rising apathy and discontent now being felt by the club's supporter base was the fall in attendances in recent seasons at Hillsborough, as the decline really set in.

In 1997/98, the average attendance had been 28,706. By 1998/99, it had dropped to 26,745. By the end of 1999/00 it would be down to 24,855.

One explanation for this drop would, of course, be the deteriorating fortunes of the team, but perhaps even more influential was the cost to the average fan of watching this deteriorating team – the fans were now required to hand over significant, increasing amounts of money as they passed through the turnstiles. After all, the players they were watching were taking home more and more in wages (in 1999/00 the wage bill would be £14.4m, 80 per cent of the club's turnover, up from £6.4m, 64 per cent of turnover, five years earlier in 1995/96). For the Manchester United game in 1999/00, for instance, it cost an adult Owls fan £18 to sit on the Kop. For the same fixture in the same stand back in 1991, the year Wednesday finished third in the table, £7 (though, admittedly, you would at that point have been stood rather than seated).

A survey conducted in 1998 had gathered the views of supporters across the country on such matters as ticket pricing. Over 100 Wednesday fans were spoken to and in general the view from the blue half of Sheffield was that the 'main' reason for them going to fewer matches at Hillsborough than they had before was ticket prices.

The comments of one interviewed Owls fan seemed to sum it up well, 'I've just been to see Wednesday,' he said, 'it cost 43 quid for me and our two young 'uns… and it was absolute crap.'

Danny Wilson. The board. The quality of football. The ticket prices.

'[A]bsolute crap.'

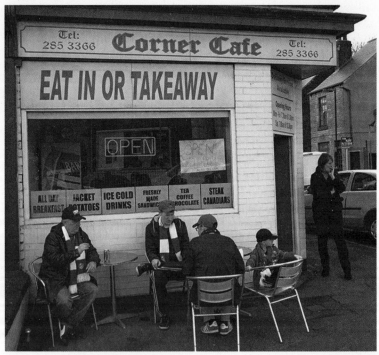

[Louis Clay]

IV

Despite some positive results at Hillsborough through the post-Christmas period (seven points from 12 since Boxing Day), Wednesday still were struggling hard. For manager Danny Wilson, the last thing he needed, as he battled to turn around the increasingly hopeless situation, was to become the subject of some exceptionally undermining public criticism from, of all people, four Wednesday-supporting Members of Parliament. Yet in January 2000, that is what happened.

During a one-hour meeting with the Charterhouse investors, who since 1997 had held 36.7 per cent of the club's shareholding, the MPs David Blunkett, Bill Michie, Clive Betts and Joe Ashton took it upon themselves to voice their concerns at not only how the club was being run at the time – where the debt had come from and how Charterhouse saw its role in the future of the club – but also questioning the performances of the first team and asking whether Wilson should still be the man to manage Sheffield Wednesday.

Afterwards, news of the meeting 'somehow' found its way to the press, which prompted the MPs to come out and clarify their individual stances. 'In my opinion, it would be best for the club if Danny Wilson was to leave,' said David Blunkett. 'Any other Premiership club would have sacked the manager by now,' commented Clive Betts.

It was remarkable. Concerns which would usually have been reserved for the stands, on the radio phone-ins, in the letters pages of the papers or in the pubs were now being raised by four Wednesday-supporting MPs who, controversially, were using their positions of apparent influence (provided to them by the constituents who had given it them) to air their own concerns, first in private with the club's main shareholder, then in public, about their football team and its severely under-pressure manager.

The four MPs:

David Blunkett, MP for Brightside (Sheffield). Former leader of the once 'radical' Sheffield City Council and now Secretary of State for Education and Employment (and about 18 months away from being appointed Tony Blair's Home Secretary).

Bill Michie, a former engineer and shop steward. MP for Heeley (Sheffield) since 1983.

Clive Betts, MP for Attercliffe (Sheffield), who back in the '80s had followed in the footsteps of David Blunkett in becoming leader of Sheffield City Council. Betts was its figurehead at the time of the Hillsborough disaster in 1989, when the ground's safety certificate had been out of date; the leader of the body that, according to Lord Taylor's report into the events of the disaster, had shown 'a serious breach of duty' in not revising or amending the certificate.

Finally, Joe Ashton, MP for Bassetlaw (an area covering Worksop and Retford, about 20 miles from Sheffield) since 1968. Ashton had grown up a Wednesdayite and until recently had, for almost a decade, served on the club's board; his position giving him the opportunity to influence things from the inside.

Wilson's response to them was great; one of his better moments that season, in fact. 'I just think it is pathetic timing,' he said. 'If they want to keep blasting their mouths off, I can't do anything about that. [But] I have got better things to do than get involved in a slanging match with MPs. I would have thought people of their stature would have known better. I am really disappointed by the whole thing.'

One of the four MPs, David Blunkett, would express his regret at the whole affair, embarrassed perhaps by his actions (or by the fact that news of the Charterhouse meeting had got out). 'I offer apologies for causing offence,' he would say. But the damage had been done. Negative publicity had been created surrounding the club when positive publicity had been needed.

V

Fortunately for the struggling Wilson, he at least had the backing of his chairman, Dave Richards. After all, he hadn't sacked him yet and, when it came to the MPs' attack, he did come to his manager's defence. 'My initial reaction is to tell them to get on with the business of politics while we get on with the business of football,' said Mr Chairman. 'Everyone at Sheffield Wednesday has to concentrate on working to stay in the Premiership,' he continued, adding, 'I truly believe at this moment the best way to do that is by offering every support to both manager and players.'

Richards's own definition of staying in the Premier League, however, appeared to take on a different meaning when, a month after the MPs' episode in February 2000, he announced that he would be leaving the club: to take on the role of permanent chairman of the Premier League.

Already Richards had held the role on a temporary basis for a year, during which time he had been able to remain as Wednesday chairman as well. Really, though, the league's chairman had to be independent from its member clubs; so when he was handed the job on a permanent basis, the writing was on the wall.

It is believed that Ken Bates, the Chelsea chairman, had championed Richards for the £176,667-a-year role (in a decade, that salary would rise to over £300,000 a year). Quite how Richards had managed to rise to one of the most important and powerful positions in the game, both domestically and globally, and exactly what qualified him for that role was, though, to many observers at least, something of a mystery; especially considering the plight of the club he had just left behind, both on and off the field.

But in the football industry his stock had been rising. As Wednesday chairman, he'd sat on the Premier League board since its inception, watching and learning from those around him (Bates and company). And apparently now he was emerging as an ever increasingly supportive figure in the game, particularly at Premier League HQ: a figure who could mediate between clubs; nip problems in the bud before they escalated; generally being the man to whom you could turn if a matter needed resolving, all in a 'leave it to me, I'll sort it out, I'll help you, chuck' kind of way.

On the other hand, as MP and former Wednesday director Joe Ashton would comment of Richards's appointment to the top Premier League job, 'It's like the captain of the *Titanic* being appointed First Lord of the Admiralty.'

Along with having been Wednesday's chairman, Richards was witnessing the demise of his Sheffield business, Three Star Engineering.

Having been made a director of Three Star back in the early 1970s, Richards would by the early 1990s come to own the business via another company, Globalfare. Under his guide, Three Star had posted modest profits as its turnover rose steadily – up to over £9m by 1998 – and the company moved to new premises out at Attercliffe, in Sheffield's once-thriving industrial east end.

Between 1996 and 2000, the Globalfare group was profitable and Richards, as 88-per-cent shareholder, did okay for himself, sharing over £1.1m in wages and dividends with one fellow director. Through that same period, however, the group had run up a debt with the Co-operative Bank – the same bankers Sheffield Wednesday had – which by June 2000 would stand at over £1.2m.

Then things downturned for the business and the company went under, with 131 Sheffield employees losing their jobs. The Co-op Bank would be owed over £1.5m.

Certainly, for the journalist Dan King, who in 2006 would write those articles on the controversial 1992 Inland Revenue club-employee payments story, Richards's appointment to the Premier League's top job is baffling. 'Richards,' says King today, 'is one of those characters whom you cannot fathom how they got to where they are. What anyone thought qualified him for that role, I have no idea. Failed business? Failing football club? "Come and run what's turning out to be the biggest league in the world." It doesn't make any sense.'

Nevertheless, as 1999/00 neared its end, that was where he was. Indeed, on the same day that Wednesday would lose woefully 4-1 to Coventry City, Richards would not be there with them. Rather, he would be at Manchester United, standing on the champions' platform in the middle of the Old Trafford pitch, smiling on as United captain Roy Keane was handed the Premier League trophy. For many Wednesday fans, it was a pretty bitter pill to take (in 2006 Richards would be knighted for 'services to sport').

* * * *

Meanwhile, for Wednesday, as they limped on through 1999/00, the poor performances and the poor results continued.

Back in January 2000, Danny Wilson's men had been turned over 3-1 by Second Division Gillingham in the FA Cup, a last half-hour collapse knocking a cowering Wednesday out of the cup. Then in March came another calamity, this time at Pride Park, Derby.

Leading 3-1 with 89 minutes gone, the game was almost done and dusted for Wednesday. Three much-needed points were almost in the bag. But then they gave it away, conceding two sloppy goals in injury time and dropping two vital points.

Afterwards, in the dressing room, one Wednesday player is said to have echoed the widely held view of the time that the team really would be relegated. To this, Danny Wilson apparently 'went berserk', according to one former player.

At least someone in the camp had some passion left. For that day at Derby, whatever fight or spirit might still have remained in the group seemed, at that point, pretty much gone. Wednesday now stood little chance of avoiding the drop; they were heading out of the Premier League. 'There's always light at the end of the tunnel,' Wilson had said after Derby. But there wasn't.

* * * *

By now the departed Dave Richards had been replaced as Wednesday chairman by Howard Culley, a managing partner in the law firm Irwin Mitchell, who had served as a director of the club since 1995.

In mid-March, following a 1-0 defeat at lowly Watford – which left Wednesday seven points from safety with nine games of the season remaining – Culley and the board did what Richards had not. They did what the four MPs had wanted; what most Owls fans accepted had to be done. They sacked Wilson.

'The thought process is that we can still avoid relegation,' said Culley optimistically, 'and we thought a change of the coaching side might improve our chances.'

* * * *

With only those nine games remaining, however, had the move come too late to prevent the club from dropping into the First Division?

Taking charge of the team for the run-in would be Peter Shreeves, a respected coach who had previously worked for the club under David Pleat, Ron Atkinson and, briefly, Wilson himself. He would be assisted by the Wednesday legend Chris Waddle, previously player-manager with Burnley and more recently, since December 1998, back with the Owls as a coach.

The new pair Shreeves and Waddle certainly gave it their best shot. Although initial defeats came against Middlesbrough and Aston Villa, the Owls, all of a sudden, started playing more confidently, less carelessly, and were seemingly stronger and harder to beat. Two wins, at Wimbledon and then at Hillsborough over Chelsea, put them back in reach. Five points behind now, with five games left to play.

Hopes, though, were still slim. And after losing to Sunderland, Leeds and Coventry, the fateful, inevitable moment was to come one early May evening at Arsenal.

Your team, about to be relegated from the Premier League. How the fuck did this happen?

* * * *

It was seven years on from the heartbreaking Wembley finals of 1993 when Wednesday and Arsenal had seemed on a par. But seven years on, the London club, led now by super Arsène Wenger, were by far, and in every respect, the bigger and better club. Their crowds, finances, quality of team... As Wednesday were poised to drop out of the division, Arsenal would finish the season second only to Manchester United.

That night in north London, the Owls fought hard. Shreeves, Waddle and the travelling Wednesdayites looked on as Gerald Sibon, Gilles De Bilde and the youngster Alan Quinn remarkably gave the Owls a 3-1 lead at half-time. But, alas, it wasn't to be. In the final 12 minutes of the game, Arsenal would peg themselves back, 3-1 to 3-3.

Three months earlier, at Derby, such a comeback had been a devastating blow. But that night at Highbury, however, it was not an upset, nor even that much of a blow. Rather, it seemed the inevitable, damning full stop to a miserable campaign.

The dejected Owls players walked off the north London pitch. Sheffield Wednesday, relegated from the Premier League.

The slow drift to that painful position – a decline which for many had begun in the mid-1990s with the dismantlement of the defeated Wembley team, progressed during David Pleat's 18-month period of upheaval and then been made certain with Ron Atkinson being pushed out of the door to make way for Wilson's lacklustre reign, all before Paolo Di Canio's tipping-point push – concluded at last.

Shreeves and Waddle had had a hopeless task – five points from safety with little or no spirit left in the camp – but they'd given it a good go. They had won games; even delivered a points ratio that would have kept them in the division had it been achieved and extrapolated over a full season (comfortably so, in fact). But it hadn't quite been enough.

Five days after Highbury, Wednesday would wave goodbye to the top division with a 4-0 win over Leicester City at Hillsborough; the team that day doing what they might have, should have, done more often that season: perform.

With their burdensome bank debt of £16.2m, owed to the Co-operative Bank, a wage bill of £14.4m and a split squad not good enough for the Premier League, Wednesday were going down.

Down, down, bloody down.

Act II
Wilderness

[Louis Clay]

9

Adjusting

AS of the summer of 2000, Sheffield the city was over a decade into its post-industrial revitalisation journey.

In the traditional industries, the focus now was on the production of less steel – but more specialist and of higher value – by a much smaller workforce than in the past; similar drops in workforce numbers had been seen across engineering and other manufacturing sectors too. And while in a few years' time the Advanced Manufacturing Park would be built at the edge of the city on the old Orgreave site, where coal miners and police had violently clashed during the 1984–85 strike, providing at least some continuation of the city's innovative engineering, steel and manufacturing heritage, there was no doubt that the composition of the city's economy had transformed drastically over the previous couple of decades.

Indeed, in 2000 the majority of Sheffield's working population would be placed in the broadly defined 'service' industries (which ranged from those toiling in call centres and Meadowhall shops, to those supporting the city's young and dynamic 50,000-plus population of students at the two universities and serving massive public-sector organisations like the NHS).

Recent years had seen significant investment in the city's infrastructure with many cranes now dotting the skyline. In town, notable new constructions would include the sleek Millennium Gallery and revamped Peace Gardens beside the Town Hall (with the beautiful curved wooden framed and glass Winter Garden to follow), along with the surrounding office blocks and hotels that sought to encourage people and businesses into the city.

Grander schemes for the regeneration of the city centre's retail areas would be harder to realise, however, and even less successful would be the ill-conceived National Centre for Popular Music museum, a £15m flop opened in March 1999 that had closed only 15 months later (they built it and nobody came, leaving a distinctive four-drum steel building that eventually would find a use as a students' union). The airport, built out at Catcliffe in 1997 – only to close five years later – was a similar dud.

Strides were being made to place Sheffield as a top leisure destination, its green spaces and adjacent Peak District 'golden frame' a focus of its tourism promotions. In addition, the notion of Sheffield as a city of sport (two football clubs, excellent post-World Student Games swimming facilities, a rich boxing heritage and so on) and a city of culture were also pushed.

At the beginning of the 2000s Sheffield: Steel City was a changed and still-changing place. However, for all its efforts, Sheffield remained, as the academic Larry Bennett had noted back in 1997 in his study, *Neighbourhood Politics*, 'an industrial city whose economy has not managed the "turn" necessary to generate large numbers of jobs in corporate management, business services, communications, or travel/tourism.' Steel City was still finding its way.

* * * *

Ahead of the 2000/01 season, following the misery of relegation from the Premier League, Wednesday too, like Sheffield, had to find their way and prepare for life as top flight exiles. The club had a large debt, an unsustainable wage bill, covering large long-term contracts for players who had taken the club down, and its income was about to reduce drastically (for commercial income, including broadcasting monies, would drop by £3.9m, while average attendances would also be set to reduce by over 5,000, contributing to an £845,000 dip in income in that area alone). Not only that, but chairman Dave Richards had left for the Premier League earlier in the year, leaving the lawyer Howard Culley in charge in his place. And, following the decision not to keep the Peter Shreeves–Chris Waddle partnership together, despite the pair having had a good go at keeping the club in the Premier League during the final games of the previous season, the team was now leaderless.

Whoever the new Sheffield Wednesday manager would be, then, they would need to be ready to cope with the challenging situation in which the club now found itself. They would have to accept that they would have very little money to spend on new players, cope with the loss of a number of experienced players (albeit ones who had been part of a group that had taken the club down) and then, somehow, achieve success in what was a very difficult second tier.

Who would take on such a challenge? Former Wimbledon manager Joe Kinnear was close to signing up. But when it became clear just how little cash there would be for him to spend on new players – an ocean away from the £10m he had eyed – coupled with the fact that he would be required to move on some of the big-earning players so as to lower the wage bill, he pulled out of the running.

Bruce Rioch, who had once taken Bolton Wanderers to the top flight and briefly been in charge of Arsenal, was linked too, as was the former Sheffield United manager Steve Bruce, then at Huddersfield. But neither joined. Nor did future Everton and Manchester United chief David Moyes, who was high on Wednesday's target list but supposedly (justifiably) saw more chance of success with his rising Preston North End side. After that, Wednesday turned their attention to Bradford City's up-and-coming boss Paul Jewell.

Jewell had guided City to the Premier League and kept them there at the same time as the Owls were dropping out of the division. Citing a difference of opinion with his chairman at Bradford, Jewell, however, would announce he was to leave the club in the summer of 2000. Not long after that, Wednesday signed up the 35-year-old as their new manager.

At his Hillsborough unveiling, Jewell outlined how he saw the situation. He said simply, 'I have to put belief and passion back into the players.'

* * * *

Job one for Jewell was to reduce the club's substantial wage bill. To do that, he had to move out some of the club's big earners, before trying to blend and galvanise what remained of his squad with bargain-price additions and emerging youngsters.

Amongst the departing high earners would be the Swede Niclas Alexandersson, who brought a decent £2.75m from Everton, and Richard Cresswell, who was sold to Leicester for £750,000. Danny Sonner, Pavel Srnicek, Lee Briscoe, Peter Atherton and Ian Nolan all moved on to other clubs for no fee (although the latter two were offered new contracts). Jon Newsome retired and early into the season Petter Rudi would be loaned back to Molde, his old club in Norway. Jewell would also receive the following proposition from the agent of one of his players: said player would leave Wednesday if they were to buy out the remaining three years of his contract – at a discounted £1.6m. This offer would not be taken up.

Of course those departures helped with the wage-bill savings. Yet at £13.4m, the club's total outlay on player contracts in 2000/01 would still come in only about £1m lower than the previous year in the Premier League.

Remaining, then, of the high-earners were Kevin Pressman, Des Walker, Andy Hinchcliffe, Phil O'Donnell, Simon Donnelly, Andy Booth, Gerald Sibon, Wim Jonk and, after Derby County pulled out of a potential £3m move for him, Gilles De Bilde. None of them had drop clauses in their contracts, which would have helped further curb the wage bill; for a club previously confident of their Premier League place, such arrangements had been considered unambitious and impractical. In addition, as their then chief executive, Alan Sykes, would explain, 'Most players at the top level won't move on that basis... they just won't accept it. You're trying to sell players the attractions of coming to Sheffield Wednesday. You're not presenting much ambition, talking about relegation.'

As Bradford boss, much had been made of Jewell's ability to work wonders on a shoestring budget; for example, the £3m shoestring he had been provided with through his first full season as City manager. At Wednesday, by comparison, the shoestring he was handed seemed a thin thread, his options for new players for his Owls team extremely limited.

Ashley Westwood, a centre-back, was brought into the club from Bradford for £150,000. He'd played five games in the Premier League but few were convinced he was even First Division standard. As the season got under way, Westwood would be followed in by Ian Hendon, a £40,000 right-back from Northampton; the young utility man Aaron Lescott, £100,000 from Aston Villa; and Steve Harkness, an average left-sided defender-midfielder once of Liverpool but picked up now from Blackburn Rovers for £200,000.

Completing the mix of experienced and well-paid pros and new lower-league, lower-calibre signings making up Jewell's Wednesday side were a handful of the club's youngsters. Alan Quinn and Steve Haslam had seen a number of games the year before in the Premier League and had done okay at times. Their progress and first-team exposure would continue through 2000/01 in the First Division. Joining them through the season, to various extents (at first filling the substitutes' bench before creeping into the first team, more out of necessity than anything else), would be the winger Matthew Hamshaw, Owen Morrison (a forward whose light, which first shone bright after a few spectacular goals, would ultimately fade fast), the defender Tony Crane and Derek Geary, an energetic and committed Irish full-back.

Despite all of this upheaval and change in the team, expectations in Sheffield were high for the upcoming season, with much of the fan base believing 'big' Wednesday, a Premier League-sized club with some Premier League players, would make their return straight away. Striker Andy Booth thought so too. 'I think we went down thinking we were going straight back up,' he says. Yet, as he now acknowledges, 'We might have been a bit over-confident.'

The reality of the struggle to come hit home on the opening weekend of 2000/01 at Wolves. In front of the Sky TV cameras, Wednesday keeper Kevin Pressman got things off to a tricky start when, 13 seconds into the game, he was red-carded for handling the ball outside the area. His replacement, another youngster, Chris Stringer, deputised admirably and Wednesday managed to take a draw, but the calamity of Pressman's sending-off seemed immediately to set the tone for the whole season. Indeed, after the 3-2 home defeat to Huddersfield the following Saturday, it already seemed apparent that this season the Owls, rather than looking up to the promotion places, were more likely to be looking down at relegation.

'Well,' says Jewell today, remembering those difficult early days of his time in charge of the team, 'I think that when a team gets relegated, no matter which team it is, they lose confidence. Obviously Wednesday hadn't been a great team because they had got relegated from the Premiership. And some of the players hadn't been good enough for the Premier League; the results had proved that.

'There were some impressive names on the team sheet, but I realised very, very quickly that the lack of belief and spirit around the place was bad.

'I think our first game of pre-season was Chesterfield away. After the first 15 minutes, some of the supporters were booing the players and I thought, "This is going to be difficult." There was a bad feeling there and I think that the supporters felt let down by the players for getting relegated.

'In the Huddersfield game, we played really, really well for the opening few minutes, but we still found ourselves 3-0 down after about forty minutes. There were shouts of "you're not fit to wear the shirt". I mean, when you hear that in the first home game you know that it's going to be a long and arduous season.'

After Huddersfield (game two), Wednesday went on to post a club-record eight consecutive league defeats; a run which included the embarrassment of a 5-0 home turnover by Wimbledon. Dire stuff.

* * * *

Off the field, meanwhile, things were becoming stickier too. Chairman Howard Culley had to face up to an increasingly despondent fan base; a fan base concerned about the unfolding situation at the club, including its significant financial problems. As Wednesday had slid out of the Premier League, the independent Shareholders' Association had made rumblings of discontent about the leadership of the club, and back in the summer of 2000 the Association, having gathered the required level of shareholder support to do so (ten per cent), called for a vote of no confidence in the club's chairman Howard Culley and finance director Bob

Hillsborough, Sheffield. [Colin McPherson]

Captain Don Megson and the Wednesday lads take a losers' lap of the Wembley pitch following their 1966 FA Cup Final defeat.

After the horror.
Leppings Lane
terrace, April
1989. [Getty]

Le Magicien.
Chris Waddle
celebrates
his wonder
strike against
Sheffield United,
Wembley 1993.
[Colorsport]

Pete McKee depicts 'Big Ron' Atkinson's return to the club in the pages of the Sheffield Telegraph, *1997.*

Chairman Dave Richards (left, beside stairs) watching on as Wednesday slide. [PA]

Tipping point: Paolo Di Canio pushes referee Paul Alcock. [Getty]

Cardiff 2005. Paul Sturrock (right) and his team celebrate their League 1 play-off final victory. [PA]

Dave Allen, Wednesday chairman 2003 through 2007. [PA]

Mark Lewis, the lawyer who defended the Wednesday fans being sued by their own football club. [Getty]

Happier days. One of those fans, Nigel Short (centre) enjoying life with his family on Wembley Way, 2016.

This is Sheffield.
[Louis Clay]

*Paving the way.
Lee Strafford's
work as
chairman led
to much needed
change at the
club.*

2010. Relegation from the Championship. [Colorsport]

2012. Milan Mandarić and a beach ball, and promotion back to the Championship. [Colorsport]

Revival. Head coach Carlos Carvalhal and owner Dejphon Chansiri. [Getty]

From Rosario, Argentina, Fernando Forestieri, the light and drive of Carvalhal's side. [PA]

Grierson; a move that could have led to the pair's removal from the Wednesday board.

At the Extraordinary General Meeting, held in front of almost 500 shareholders at the Ponds Forge leisure centre in town, tensions ran high. However, a move made before the meeting in fact meant the die was cast against the Association even before the vote was held. For before the meeting, investors in the club, Charterhouse had given up its *non-voting* shares in exchange for ordinary voting shares – and in so doing, remarkably, gave up the majority of its original £15.6m investment – just so it could vote on club matters; in this case, it seemed, to vote to protect two board members.

So Culley and Grierson managed to survive the vote of no confidence.

The normal tally of votes would have been around 8 million in support of the two directors, against around 7 million not in support (with 16 million votes not cast): a close-run tie. However, it was only thanks to the votes cast by Charterhouse, the additional 18 million, that made the vote wider than it would otherwise have been (in effect around 24 million votes in support of the two board members to 7 million against).

Later, at the club's AGM in October 2000, the board would face further challenges from the Shareholders' Association. Again though, supported by the votes of Charterhouse, the existing directors would be able to ride the waves of discontent and would not be moved on. 'My position is quite clear and that is that I intend to see this job through,' Culley would say after that meeting.

Away from the politics and back on the pitch, for Jewell's Wednesday, despite having earlier slightly recovered (and beating their hated city rivals Sheffield United in the League Cup; the Blades, managed by the pantomime villain figure Neil Warnock, overcome 2-1 on an electric and hostile night at Hillsborough), were by December amid another run of poor results; one which had begun with a miserable 4-2 home defeat to Stockport County. County's third goal that day had come following an embarrassing mix-up and collision between stalwarts Kevin Pressman and Des Walker. Another new low for the Owls that season.

At Bradford, Jewell had managed to engender a battling, work-to-the-end attitude from his team, getting the most out of what was a fairly limited group of players. That was what had helped to take them up to the top level and then kept them there. At Wednesday, though, as the months of the season passed, the cracks in the squad that had already been there would grow and grow. Some players in particular seemed distinctly uninterested in the cause.

Jewell recalls, 'The club was riddled with players who didn't want to be there; riddled with players who were earning lots of money and, to be brutally honest, weren't bothered about playing. They'd got relegated and shrugged their shoulders. There was a lack of energy and a lack of desire there. No heart. I found that very difficult to cope with.

'Don't get me wrong, the problems weren't with every player. And it's easy to say that foreign players were the cause. But that wasn't the case. They didn't all speak in foreign tongues.

'At Bradford, I'd been used to the lads running through brick walls for each other, scrapping for each other. But at Wednesday I think I was banging my head against a brick wall. When you looked around the dressing room at Hillsborough, you wondered how many of them were going to fight for each other, let alone fight for the shirt. And frankly, quite a lot of the players didn't care who they were playing for, as long as they got paid.'

At this point the quote from striker Gilles De Bilde's autobiography again comes to mind, 'The only way foreign players amused themselves was talking about money. It was the only reason we were still playing in England.'

De Bilde: Jewell recalls a couple of telling exchanges with him. 'One day Gilles said to me, "Why did you come to Sheffield Wednesday? Why have you come here?" And I couldn't understand that. "What do you mean," I said, "Why have I come here?" When he asked the question, he wasn't being nasty, he was just wondering why I would want to come to Sheffield Wednesday. He had absolutely no feeling for the club whatsoever. I found that difficult to comprehend.

'One low point I remember,' Jewell goes on, 'was when Wimbledon beat us 5-0 at Hillsborough. In the changing room after the game, Gilles asked me to help him with his tie because he was going to a party that night. Without wanting to put everything on Gilles De Bilde, this was the type of situation we were dealing with. And we couldn't replace these players with anyone else because we didn't have the money.'

De Bilde would eventually be loaned to Aston Villa, off the payroll momentarily, before returning to Sheffield after a few months to pick up his wages and chip in with a few goals. At the end of the season, he would join Anderlecht on a free transfer, a 100 per cent loss on the £2.8m Wednesday had paid for him two years before.

* * * *

Author – Dear Mr De Bilde, …Would you be willing to spare some time to discuss your time with Sheffield Wednesday?

Gilles De Bilde – No, thank you.

* * * *

Along with having to deal with the players who didn't want to play for the club, Jewell also had to contend with the issue of those who couldn't play because they were injured; with some experienced and highly-paid players frustratingly unavailable to him and his struggling side deprived of some much-needed extra experience.

Andy Hinchcliffe, the highly-paid left-back signed by Ron Atkinson not long after he'd failed a medical at Tottenham Hotspur, had a torrid 2000/01 in the First Division with knee problems (a cruciate ligament injury had put him out of action for a long spell back when he was an Everton player) causing him to miss months of the season. He would play less than ten games of the campaign for Wednesday.

In addition, Wim Jonk missed all but two games of the season through injury, leaving him to run down the last year of his contract (and all the while supposedly still picking up that £5,000-per-game, get-paid-whether-you-play-or-not bonus). Phil O'Donnell and Philip Scott would suffer similar problems with injuries, with both of them absent from the team for months.

Simon Donnelly, meanwhile, would miss all but three games of 2000/01. Donnelly's problem, as he explains today, 'was a pelvic imbalance that was leading to my hamstrings continuously going'. He says, 'I picked up the injury in the first season, and it was ongoing into the second.'

For Donnelly, it was a long and exasperating ordeal. 'You want to be fit,' he says. 'It doesn't matter if you're on £100 or £100,000 a week, you want to play football. I'd picked up an injury and that had lasted around a season and a half. I was sick of the sight of the gym. I was in there all the time, trying to get back. Eventually, I went down to see a guy at British Athletics. I worked with him for eight weeks on an intensive strengthening programme, working every day from seven in the morning. I paid for it out of my own pocket, the hotels and everything, and was away from my family. But I wanted to get back. Eventually, it worked out. He turned it around for me.'

But for Jewell, mid-season, that turnaround was nowhere in sight. With half his team on the treatment table, and with little resources to sign new players, Jewell was forced to turn to the loan market to help plug the holes in his sinking-ship side. Middlesbrough keeper (and former Wednesday youngster) Marlon Beresford would briefly keep Kevin Pressman out of the team; Blackburn's Simon Grayson and Middlesbrough's Robbie Stockdale were used at right-back. Terry Cooke, a former Manchester United trainee then at Manchester City, did a bit of a job on the wing while Efan Ekoku helped out up front, before being signed permanently.

Another loanee, Con Blatsis, seemed to best encapsulate the desperate post-Premier League reality the club now faced, having to rely on players borrowed from other clubs just so they can get a half-decent team out on to the pitch. A tall Australian centre-back who had played only twice for Derby County's first team, Blatsis first appeared alongside Des Walker one cold afternoon in Huddersfield just after Christmas.

* * * *

Author – That season you had a player on loan called Con Blatsis?

Paul Jewell – Who?

Author – Con Blatsis, from Derby.

Jewell – He wasn't there when I was there.

Author – He was Australian. His first game was at Huddersfield.

Jewell – You know what, I do remember him now. There you go. That's how good he was, wasn't he? I'm ashamed to say that I can't remember a lot about him, to be honest.

* * * *

Over the years, the list of borrowed players that the club would rely on for the team would grow and grow.

Further transition in the squad that season would also see striker Andy Booth leave the club. Four and a half years after he had joined from Huddersfield Town, his wages would be removed from the payroll as part of the continuing drive to save cash. His last game would come at Southampton in the FA Cup in January 2001, after which he was sent on loan to Tottenham Hotspur. Booth wouldn't play for Wednesday again and ultimately would be sold back to Huddersfield for £175,000.

By February 2001, Wednesday were amid what seemed like a helpless drift. With one win in nine in the league since early December, the club was bottom of the First Division. A hopeless team. A sinking ship. Following one more defeat, to Wimbledon, Jewell was sacked as Sheffield Wednesday manager.

'We'd lost 4-1,' remembers Jewell. 'I came into work on Monday morning and Howard Culley came into my office. "Sorry," he said, "it's not good news. We're sacking you." They felt they had no option and I understand that.'

Although his time as Wednesday boss had not gone quite to plan, Jewell today is philosophical about his time at the club, acknowledging just how difficult his job had been.

'Don't get me wrong,' he reflects, 'it's not the only club where I've been sacked, so maybe it's me. I do take responsibility. I'm not here to put all the blame on the players; I hold my hands up. I was a naïve young manager and I made mistakes. But I think when you see the results from before I went there and after I left, there were a lot of managers who tried to put things right there but who couldn't.

'Wednesday appealed to me because it was such a big name. But without being rude, and if you want me to be frank with you, that was about the only good thing it had going for it at the time. When I look back at the size of the club against the quality of the team and the quality of the people at the club – and that isn't everybody, I should say – I probably wouldn't have gone there if I'd known better. Sheffield Wednesday will always be a team that will play some part in my life because it's a great club, but it probably wasn't the right club for me at the time. Right club, wrong time, you could say.'

After packing up his things from his office and saying a few goodbyes, Jewell would be gone. Over to the next man.

After sacking Jewell, Culley decided that it was time for him, too, to step down from his position, with Geoff Hulley, a board member since 1980, stepping into the void to replace him.

Hulley's first move was to put Peter Shreeves back in charge of the team. Following his and Chris Waddle's attempts to keep the club in the Premier League towards the end of the previous season, Shreeves had stayed on as part of Jewell's coaching staff and again was ready to step up.

With Wednesday at the foot of the table, he had 15 games to save the Owls from relegation. '[I]t would,' said Shreeves, 'be a sad, sad day if we went out of this division.'

Prior to his dismissal, Jewell had handily set up the loan signings of two experienced midfielders; a pair whose impact would prove transformative for the team and Wednesday's season, without question making Shreeves's task easier than it would otherwise have been. The pair: Southampton's experienced Trond Egil Soltvedt and Coventry's Carlton Palmer, the former Owl returning to the club more than six years after leaving for Howard Wilkinson's Leeds United.

In Shreeves's first game, an evening kick-off against Tranmere Rovers at Hillsborough, Soltvedt and Palmer helped give the new manager win number one: 1-0. All of a sudden, with those experienced heads in the team, Wednesday seemed a stronger, more confident and more able proposition. Immediately, things were looking up.

Another win came at Nottingham Forest; Wednesday again giving a robust and commanding display in another 1-0 win. The Dutch forward Gerald Sibon, a figure of such frustration at times since his arrival at the club during the Danny Wilson days – his lethargic manner often exasperating, but his ability sometimes mesmerising – was the hero that night with a fantastic long-range, low drive. In the Forest away end, for the thousands of Wednesday fans who'd travelled down the M1 from Sheffield, it was all jumping and shouting, pushing and hugging. A corner had been turned.

Soltvedt recalls, 'When me and Carlton arrived, we were bottom of the league and had nothing to lose. And we came in with a lot of experience, which took a bit of the pressure off the younger players. Tranmere was the perfect start, and Forest gave the whole squad a lift and the belief that we could stay up.'

In the end, Wednesday would be safe with a game to spare. Eight wins from 15 for Peter Shreeves. Job done – well done. The awful year of post-Premier League adjustment over. On now to the next season.

* * * *

For 2001/02 Shreeves, rightly, was given the manager's job on a permanent basis. Coaxing results from his ever-changing roster of players – the experienced big earners, cheapo signings and youngsters carrying too much of the burden; those injured and those who didn't want to be there – would continue to be a massive challenge, however.

Costs still had to be cut down. Who knew how the growing debt (standing that summer at £16.3m) was going to be coped with?

A few of the higher earners would be on their way: Des Walker's contract had ended, concluding his mostly excellent eight years with the club; so had Wim Jonk's, his mostly disappointing three years with the club now over. In their place came Danny Maddix, Queens Park Rangers' experienced centre-half; Luton Town midfielder Paul McClaren; and Pablo Bonvin, the young Argentinian joining on what would be an unimpressive year-long loan from Boca Juniors. The changes would see the club's wage bill reduce a further £2m. Now, it was down to *only* £11.4m.

As the season got under way – and in spite of the best efforts of Shreeves – decent results from what was a dwindlingly talented group would be very hard to come by. Sadly, after 13, mostly winless games, an exasperated Shreeves quit. 'In the best interests of both Sheffield Wednesday and myself,' he said, 'I felt the honourable thing to do was to offer my resignation.' Terry Yorath, Paul Jewell's assistant since their Bradford days, and later sidekick to Shreeves, would take over the reins.

Manager number three since Danny Wilson.

Yorath knew the Wednesday players well and would manage to coax from them an upturn in results. And not just in the league, as Wednesday reached the semi-final of the League Cup, though they eventually succumbed over two legs to Blackburn Rovers at that penultimate hurdle.

Fortunately a good gate for the home leg of the semi-final enabled Yorath to purchase a new striker, the fast and strong, barging Finnish-Kosovan Shefki Kuqi. Bought from Stockport County for £700,000, his goals in the league helped push the team over the line – by the end of the season, the Owls would just about have done enough to stay up, missing relegation by a single point. The threat of the drop had never having quite left the camp all season, though.

* * * *

Ahead of 2002/03, Wednesday were operating against a backdrop of reduced gate receipts and broadcasting income. The latter was an area set to get worse thanks to the ending of the £4.5m Premier League parachute payment and the demise of the broadcaster ITV Digital, which would leave the club around £2m short that season. Wednesday still had to support several of the contracts which remained from the Premier League days, however; namely, those of Kevin Pressman, Simon Donnelly, Phil O'Donnell and Gerald Sibon (who would move back to Holland part-way through the season). At least Andy Hinchcliffe, another big earner, had just retired.

For Yorath, the options available to him ahead of the new season for new players was still restricted to loan signings and free transfers. The young forward Leon Knight was borrowed for a year from Chelsea, while the Beatles-haircut-flop defender John Beswetherick arrived for nothing from Plymouth Argyle. The 'top' signing, striker Lloyd Owusu, came in from Brentford, also for a free.

As the new season got under way, the depressingly settled pattern for post-Premier League Wednesday resumed, as they dreadfully shipped goals and lost games. It would be another year of looking downward, battling again just to stay in the second tier.

One of the challenges faced by Yorath and the team that season was that some of the new, inexperienced players were seemingly incapable of handling the pressures of playing for Wednesday in front of 20,000-plus Hillsborough crowds. This was something the Wednesday manager recognised in particular with his three new recruits, Owusu, Knight and Beswetherick.

As Yorath would recall, 'In his first few games, he [Owusu] kept collapsing. He would fall to the ground and throw up. I'd seen players be sick in the dressing room before a game, but never on the pitch… I think it was nerves. Lloyd couldn't cope with being at such a high-profile club like Sheffield Wednesday.

'[N]either could Leon Knight… he couldn't hack it either. Maybe it was the big crowds or the aura of the place, the ground itself.

'The worst case was John Beswetherick. He was a left-back who I'd had great reports about… he had a good left foot on him, but just couldn't play at Hillsborough… the club was miles too big for John. It was all down to nerves – he just couldn't handle it.'

Recently, Wednesday's various managers had faced issues of disinterest, inexperience or injury among their squad. The problem now seemed to be an inability to cope with the pressure of playing in a big stadium for an apparently big club. In the years to come, Yorath would not be the last Wednesday manager to encounter this problem.

As the struggles continued through the opening stages of 2002/03 (excepting a bright light-against-the-darkness home victory against city rivals Sheffield United), Yorath was, following defeat to Burnley in October, given a month – four games – to turn the situation round.

He won one of those matches but, giving in to the hopelessness of the situation, decided to quit before he was sacked. 'Results haven't gone for us and it can't keep going this way,' he said on his way out.

Manager number three since relegation from the Premier League was gone as Wednesday sat hopeless amid the relegation places.

Mooted for the job were some familiar names; Peter Reid, sacked that month by Sunderland, was the club's number-one choice. Yet he declined. George Burley, recently out of the Ipswich Town job, was the favoured option of one director, but the consensus of the board was not with Burley. Rather, Hartlepool's Chris Turner, a former Wednesday player and goalkeeper in the 1991 League Cup Final, was the preferred choice.

And it was Turner who became manager number four in less than three years for the club.

Arriving at Hillsborough, the new man spoke of targets like getting Wednesday into Europe within five years (he actually said it 'could' happen).

However, what Turner brought instead was eight wins in 29 games and, bloody hell, relegation to the third tier. The last time the club had stooped so low had been over 20 years before in 1979/80.

10

Dave Allen

THE 2003/04 season would represent a new stage for post-Premier League Sheffield Wednesday. While from the outside looking in, things appeared pretty bad – just relegated from the First Division, no money – happenings both on and off the pitch would get the club on a firmer footing, and set them off on a supposedly more forward-looking path.

First, more of the high-earning players were now leaving the club – Simon Donnelly and Phil O'Donnell were out of contract and off the wage bill; Gerald Sibon had moved home to Holland earlier in the year. That left Kevin Pressman, Alan Quinn and Steve Haslam of the remaining relatively 'high' earners.

Second, Owls manager Chris Turner was able to bring in a number of new faces to freshen up the squad. Faces that would help form the basis of what would be a more balanced and eventually settled side.

Third, the club had a brand-new chairman.

* * * *

In his 70-plus years, Dave Allen has achieved a lot in the world of business. A son of Sheffield, he began his working life in the 1950s at the cutlery firm Viners. Music, though, seemed more of an interest for him and by the 60s, aged 22, he became the leader of a touring Mecca band. After that, he headed his own outfit, The Dave Allen Sound.

Later, he took over the lease of a nightclub in Rotherham, The Charade, borrowing money from family and friends and putting up his house as collateral to do so. Over the next few years, he would open scores more across the country. One of them, Josephine's, opened in 1976, was in Sheffield, in the Fountain Precinct building just over from the City Hall.

Over the years, many Wednesday players would be spotted there, even manager Jackie Charlton. And though things were beginning to get tough for Sheffield at that time – the high unemployment that came from the erosion of its steel and manufacturing industries, along with the collapse of mining – Josephine's was packing them in and Allen's business, The A&S Leisure Group, survived and thrived.

Along with the nightclubs were the casinos, including, in Sheffield, Napoleon's on Ecclesall Road and his flagship outpost in Leicester Square, London. In 1991, A&S took over the greyhound and speedway stadium at Owlerton, half a mile down the road from Wednesday's Hillsborough home.

Overall, Allen had built a strong, customer-focused business with an ethos of providing good facilities and good value for money – all underpinned by stringent cost control. A later *Sunday Times* Rich List would have him worth £70m.

It was back in 2000 that Allen joined the Wednesday board. He would serve on it for seven years, four of those as chairman following his move up to the top role ahead of the 2003/04 season.

* * * *

Sitting one early summer afternoon in his grand office inside the headquarters of A&S Leisure, Allen recalls how his relationship with Sheffield Wednesday began.

'I was first approached to become involved with the club by Howard Culley,' he says. 'He came to see me here.

'"What can I do for you, Howard?" I said.

'"Do you fancy the job of chairman of Sheffield Wednesday?" he said.

'"I bloody don't," I said.

'Then he said they were looking for another member of the board. Would I be interested in that?

'"I'll have a think about it," I said.'

Allen had a think and, feeling the twinge of temptation to get involved with the football club just up the road, went to Hillsborough for another meeting. Wednesday at that time had just been relegated from the Premier League and it was thought his experience of running a successful business in the leisure industry would be helpful. Ultimately, he agreed to join the board.

Most serious for Wednesday at this time was the massive amount of debt that the club was carting about (£16.3m in 2000/01, the club's first season outside of the Premier League), along with the losses that were being made. And new board member Allen was concerned.

'My impression was that the finances seemed a little out of control. The operating costs were high. It was very much overstaffed, particularly in the office region, and I was shocked at the amount of money the players were earning. Some of the contracts… Andy Hinchcliffe was on just short of £1m a year. The two lads from Scotland, Donnelly and O'Donnell, were on £750,000 a year apiece. De Bilde was on about the same. Frankly, I couldn't believe what the club had let themselves in for.'

The wage bill stood around £14m; Allen believed it needed to be nearer £5m.

'I can remember the first board meeting I had. I said, "Chairman, these costs are completely out of hand. You've got to get them under control."'

His concerns, though, appeared not to resonate with his fellow board members.

'At the second board meeting, I said, "Chairman, if you don't get these costs under control then there'll be real problems."

'And I said that at the third meeting I went to, and the fourth, but nothing ever happened.'

Another early focus of Allen's was the Charterhouse shares. It was in March 2001, four years since the investment house had purchased 36.7 per cent of the club for £15.6m, that Allen set up a deal to buy them out.

'I said to Howard Culley, "Why don't we try and buy these shares? We can't run this business unless we properly own it."'

At the time, the current-serving directors controlled only around five per cent of the club, though would likely be able to count on about another five per cent from supportive 'associates', such as past board members. But that wasn't *control*. As demonstrated at the EGM in the summer of 2000, when Culley and finance director Bob Grierson had faced a vote of no confidence, the Charterhouse votes were a big help in keeping them securely in place.

'Howard said, "God, we won't be able to afford them, Dave."

'"Let me go and talk to them," I said.

'I met him [Charterhouse's Geoff Arbuthnott] on the motorway at Watford Gap services.

'I said, "Look, I've got some money in the bank, I was going to invest it in my share portfolio, will you take £1.5m for these shares?" He said yes without thinking about it.

'On the way back I thought, "Christ, what have I done?"

'I came back and said to the board, "Look, we can buy the shares for £1.5m. But I don't want 37 per cent of the club. Does anyone else fancy 'em as well?" Geoff Hulley said he'd have some. Keith Addy said he'd have some too.'

Allen, then, joined forces with two of his fellow board members and split the cost and the shares: £1.5m for 36.7 per cent of Sheffield Wednesday Football Club (Sheffield Wednesday plc). Charterhouse's disastrous relationship with the club was over as the shares were sold at a massive loss from their original £15.6m investment.

Not all of the newly acquired shares could be kept by Allen, Hulley and Addy, however. Per stock-market rules, where over 29.9 per cent of a publicly listed company is owned by one party, that party, upon reaching that milestone, must make an offer to buy the rest of the shares. And the trio, while not individually owning that percentage, would've been seen to have been acting as one when the Charterhouse shares were bought, and thereby triggered the 29.9 per cent rule. 'And I wasn't going to be making a full takeover bid,' says Allen, matter-of-factly.

So some of the shares were given away, with the newly formed Owls Trust supporters' group (one separate to the Shareholders' Association) the happy recipients of 9.46 per cent of the football club for free. 'I wasn't fully familiar with the fans' trust,' admits Allen, 'but they seemed okay to me.' While early on the relationship between club and trust was positive, things would turn sour between the two parties, prompting Allen now to describe the handing over of those shares as 'definitely the worst decision that was ever made'.

* * * *

All of this off-pitch activity had first occurred against the backdrop of Wednesday's post-Premier League 2000/01 adjusting season, followed by their slide down the second tier. In April 2003, as the Owls headed toward the third tier, Dave Allen took over from Geoff Hulley (who a few years earlier had taken over from Howard Culley) as chairman of the club. At last, thought Allen, he would now be able to grasp the club by its neck and start running it more like he believed it should be run.

'My intention,' he now says, 'was to put my stamp on it. Get the club back into the Premiership. Hand it back to them and say, "Right, don't let it get into that mess again."

'To do that, you've just got to run it like a business. You can't pay out more than you get in. It's the only way you can do it.'

Staff costs were streamlined, particularly on the administrative side. 'It was just totally out of control,' says Allen. 'They had secretaries for secretaries. I soon chopped it all down. I parted company with Alan Sykes [the club's then chief executive] and merged two jobs, commercial director and chief executive. That was Kaven Walker. After that, the business side of the club revolved around Kaven and myself on a day-to-day basis, with the help of Bob Grierson as financial director and Paul Johnson as company secretary and chief accountant. That's how it worked: the four of us.'

A more common-sense approach to player recruitment was also implemented. 'When players came to the club, I insisted that they went through a proper in-depth medical so that we weren't signing crocks, which had been happening for years before,' explains Allen.

Meanwhile, any notion of the club going into administration, clearing the debts and starting again, as many had speculated would one day happen at Wednesday, was dismissed completely by the new chairman. 'I do not believe in going into liquidation, bankruptcy or anything else. That wouldn't have happened while I was there. You would have left too many little people hurt. We made sure the local creditors always got paid.'

'In all,' Allen accepts, 'I made some very unpopular decisions. But in business, if you're going to get anywhere, you have to make unpopular decisions. You always have to think: the business comes first and you do what's in the best interests of the business. That's what we did. And we turned it around.'

That turnaround: in his first season as chairman, 2003/04, losses were reduced to £4.1m, down from £8.3m the previous year. '[W]e have certainly steadied the ship,' Allen happily reported in the accounts that year.

Through his time at Wednesday, Allen would also dip into his own pocket to help out with things like bringing in new players. £119,834 would be gifted to the club and almost £3m loaned at times when it was needed; when the Co-op Bank, lenders to the club since 1994/95, but at May 2003 owed over £20m, were less willing. Those loans and the interest accrued on them would not ever be fully paid back to Allen.

On the pitch meanwhile, following relegation to the Second Division at the end of the 2002/03 season, many had been thinking of a quick return for Wednesday in 2003/04. Certainly Owls manager Chris Turner knew what was expected of him and his team, and his sights were set appropriately high, 'We need to be out of the Second in two years,' he said, 'but hopefully we'll be out this year.'

However, despite fairly positive beginnings to the season, a dreadful, dreary and hopeless mid-season drift would see the club drop into the bottom half of the table, struggling to overcome the likes of Wrexham, Rushden & Diamonds and Wycombe Wanderers who each came to Hillsborough, raised their game and took away points. In the end, despite changes made by Turner to both tactics and personnel, Wednesday would finish 16th in the table, the club's worst final position for nearly 30 years.

* * * *

Back to the boardroom and the finances, one plan of Dave Allen's to raise significant funds for the club was to sell Wednesday's second biggest asset: the training ground at Middlewood. Losing the site would be a pity (the fairly recent upgrades, funded in part by the Charterhouse investment at the end of the 90s, had made the facility a decent base for both the first team and the academy), but it was thought around £10m might be raised through its sale, so a plan to sell and relocate was put in motion.

First up was Asda. They hoped to build a supermarket on the site, though this plan would be blocked; the town planners concerned about traffic congestion and the effect on local shops.

Disappointed, though not discouraged, the club turned next to housing and the developers Bloor Homes. Bloor wanted to build 250 new homes on the Middlewood site and, late in the summer of 2004, agreed a £10m deal with the club (it is unclear how that figure would have been split between Wednesday, who held only the leasehold of the land, and the council, holders of the freehold).

Early indications were positive this time around. Allen too was feeling hopeful, having attended a 'cordial' meeting with the council about the new plan. In the background, the club worked to identify a suitable site for their new training base; the frontrunner was a 28-acre plot at Mosborough, out at the edge of the city. A planning application for the new homes was duly put forward.

Alas, as with the supermarket application, this plan would also run into problems. And in advance of the application being heard, the club was informed that it was likely to fail, so it was withdrawn completely. Allen was not happy.

'We found out at the 99th hour that they were going to refuse it,' he remembers. 'I was extremely annoyed and disappointed with the council. We'd done a lot of work and put a lot of effort into it.'

Back, then, to the drawing board for ways of raising substantial funds for the club. How about seeking out and bringing in considerable external investment?

* * * *

But how do you get someone to invest in a football club like Sheffield Wednesday?

'Well,' explains Allen, 'who's going to invest in a football club anyway? Nobody with any sense. People invest money so they can get a return on it, don't they? So what good is investing in a football club?'

Despite this viewpoint, Allen had his ears open to people who were seriously interested in the club. People who could show they had the money to make a deal happen, and the best interests of Sheffield Wednesday at heart.

One early (and controversial) runner in the long takeover/ investment saga, which was ultimately to engulf the club over the next few years, was the notorious former Chelsea owner Ken Bates, fresh from having sold off his share of the London club to the Russian billionaire Roman Abramovich for a reputed £17m (part of a £60m takeover).

'He loves a battle, and usually finds one... never hesitating to stir up a hornets' nest or challenge the status quo,' one author once wrote of Bates. 'I'm difficult to deal with because I'm not logical,' Bates said of himself. He now came on to Wednesday's radar; put on to the club by its former chairman, Dave Richards, now chairman of the Premier League; his and Bates's friendship forged at those top flight league meetings; Richards had apparently asked Bates if there was anything he could do to help the club.

The events that followed were not an entirely pleasant affair.

Through the early months of 2004, it was reported that Bates had had three face-to-face meetings with the Wednesday board regarding his possible involvement with the club. Initially, it was explained that Bates was just looking to offer advice to the club surrounding its general financial situation. To Allen's mind, though, rather than requiring such an advisory service, what the club needed was a serious offer of investment. As he recalls of the initial interactions with Bates, 'Geoff Hulley brought him to the table, brought him to my boardroom and I said to him, "Before you come and sit down with me, you prove that you've got £10m in the bank." And he brought me proof of that.'

Following that stage, Allen wanted a written proposal outlining Bates's actual intentions. Bates, though, would deny that such a request was made, so a proposal did not arrive.

Controversially, the story then took on another party: the Owls Trust (later renamed Wednesdayite), the supporters' group that had been gifted some of the Charterhouse shares that Allen, Hulley and Keith Addy had purchased back in 2001. It appeared to some, not least Allen, that the Trust had come out in support of Bates – and therefore against him, after its chairman, Jim Harrison, had sat next to Bates at a press conference in which the latter pressed the club's board to release figures he was after which would allow him to make a fuller assessment of the club's finances; the indication now being that Bates was ready to make a takeover bid for the Owls.

The Trust though would later insist that rather than supporting Bates specifically, they were simply supporting the *notion* of the club releasing documents to potential suitors, so as to help with future potential investment.

Things would then come to more of a head between the Trust and Allen around the time of Wednesday's last game of the 2003/04 season, at home to Queens Park Rangers. First, Bates was hosted in the executive box of Trust chairman Jim Harrison, before later being feted as the special guest at a Trust meeting at the Dial House working men's club in Wisewood, just up the road from Hillsborough. At the meeting Bates, centre stage, confirmed that he did now wish to take over the club. 'I want one more challenge,' he announced to the crowd of Trust members, outlining how once a deal was in place he supposedly intended to invest at least £10m into the club, with a focus being made on team investment.

Allen, though, was not pleased. Not with the Trust – to whom the majority of its Wednesday shareholding had been handed by him and his two fellow directors – for providing Bates with this very public platform. Nor, it seemed, with Bates, whose proposal was ultimately rejected, '[T]he indicative proposal [received from Bates] is unacceptable to the board,' a club statement read. 'When the offer did come,' Allen adds today, 'after all the meetings and everything else, it wasn't anywhere near to what was required.'

Relations between the Trust and club would go further south after that. As Allen reflects today, 'Giving those [Charterhouse] shares to the Trust was the worst decision ever. Because all they did was cause a bloody nuisance. Just shows how dangerous a little bit of power can be, doesn't it?'

As for Bates, he would turn his attention to Leeds United, sealing a £10m takeover of their club in early 2005, with the ensuing years providing a glimpse of what life under him might have been like for the Owls, 'eye-watering' ticket prices, relegation to the third tier and administration with debts of £38m.

He had also tried to sue Allen.

Back in May 2004, Allen, as Wednesday chairman, had sent a letter to shareholders and season-ticket holders in which he was scathing of Bates, questioning his motives for wanting to become involved in the club and attacking his attempts to carry out a takeover. In reaction to the letter, Bates took a libel action against Allen.

'He said I'd libelled him so he was going to sort me out in court,' recalls Allen. 'He asked for £50,000 and he'd withdraw. I told him to get lost. "I'm not giving you a tenner," I said.

'It was a very long case; 18 months approximately. Every morning my fax machine had mountains of paperwork coming out of it. It's a wonder it didn't pack up.

'But he hadn't got a case, and before he was going into the witness box he had to withdraw. His barrister had phoned my barrister and said, "I'm just going to have to beat your client up in the witness box because we haven't got a lot."

'Then my barrister said, "You won't beat him up in the witness box; he's an experienced witness."

'I've done a lot of court applications for casino, nightclub, greyhound licences, and I'm quite *au fait* with what goes on in the witness box.'

And so, in the end, Bates would abandon the action.

'He picked the wrong 'un when he picked me,' says Allen. 'When you're a bully, you've got to be careful who you try and bully.'

* * * *

For the 2004/05 season Chris Turner and his Wednesday side had to deliver a much better return than the season before. His chairman had been supportive of him, but another let-down, 16th-place finish like the one just gone would not be acceptable.

In common with each of the recent close seasons for non-Premier League Sheffield Wednesday (their fourth since the drop from the top flight), the summer months therefore meant further upheaval of the squad, as the wage bill was further, and necessarily, reduced.

Keeper Kevin Pressman ended his 17-year association with the club and moved on to Leicester City; Alan Quinn, Leigh Bromby and Derek Geary (via Stockport County) would each cross the city to join Sheffield United. Meanwhile John Beswetherick, the full-back who had never impressed for the club, and Steve Haslam were also out of the door.

Shrewdly (there was of course no other option), Turner would spend only £230,000 on their replacements. These included full-back Paul Heckingbottom, Livingston's energetic winger Jon-Paul McGovern, strikers Steve MacLean (from Glasgow Rangers) and Lee Peacock (Bristol City), Glenn Whelan (a promising passing midfielder out of the Manchester City reserves), the experienced Chris Marsden, the versatile journeyman Lee Bullen and the goalkeeper David Lucas. Chris Brunt, the gifted young Northern Irish winger who had come in on loan from Middlesbrough towards the end of the previous season, also signed up permanently.

Turner then worked to blend and forge the new players into a strong, promotion-chasing side. Beginnings were bright (LWWW), yet as the team then began to underperform (LDDDL), the boss found himself under massive pressure. By only mid-September, following a 1-0 home defeat to Bournemouth, and with Wednesday now sitting 14th in the table, Turner was let go by the club. 'They [the supporters] were shouting and bawling at him,' remembers Dave Allen. 'The pressure was unbelievable. So we parted company.'

Another Sheffield Wednesday manager, gone.

The departing Turner was philosophical. 'When I took the job,' he said, 'I knew from Wednesday's track record there was a fair chance of not being successful. But I took it because I'm confident in my own ability and I believe if we had had more time we would have achieved what we set out to achieve. We brought a whole new team in this summer, we've changed the culture and have left them with a lot of good young players. We just needed more time.'

But time was not what he had.

Allen's next move was crucial if Wednesday were going to achieve what was required: getting out of the division.

'I sat down with my chief executive Kaven Walker and said, "Look, the one guy that can manage football in the Second Division is Paul Sturrock. Set up a meeting."'

As a player, Sturrock had spent his career playing in Scotland for Dundee United, winning the league in the 80s and appearing in a UEFA Cup Final. He'd later managed the club, before, in 2003, guiding Plymouth Argyle to the Third Division title (then doing three-quarters of the job of winning another promotion to the First Division). His next move, to Southampton, interrupted that success – though things didn't quite work out for him there and he lasted only six months as a Premier League boss. Nonetheless, he was considered to be a manager who could get a team going in the lower leagues: motivate a team and get the most out of them. *Get them promoted.* He was just what the Owls needed.

* * * *

'I came up and had a chat with the chairman,' says Sturrock today, recalling, one warm Cornwall evening, his initial contact with the club. 'He seemed impressed with what I'd done for Plymouth. The season before I'd taken the team to Sheffield on a Wednesday night and it had gone well [Argyle won 3-1]. And he was very impressed with that.'

At the meeting, Sturrock became convinced of Allen and what the chairman wanted the club to achieve. Allen, in turn, was convinced of Sturrock. He was offered the job there and then.

Some of the new manager's opening remarks were music to the ears of Wednesday fans. 'You play football to win and the aim for this season is promotion,' said the new man in town, making it clear to his players exactly who was in charge.

'Basically,' remembers one of them, Steve MacLean, 'he laid the law down straight away and got stuck into us. It was very much that it was going to be his way or the highway. If you weren't going to do what he said and tune in to his way of thinking then you were no longer going to be required. It was a bit of a shock to the system for a lot of us, but probably it was what we needed at the time. A little bit of a kick up the backside.'

The turnaround wasn't quick; Sturrock's early win ratio was not much better than Turner's, in fact. 'I'm not going to turn this around overnight,' he explained. But better days would eventually come and with the team now more organised, and the play moved to a more brute-over-finesse style, the good results came.

In the midfield, the youngsters Glenn Whelan and Chris Brunt were each becoming ever more classy and influential presences; to Wednesday's benefit, their smooth passing and play-starting ability developing well with each week; their influence on games ever increasing – two popular young men; two Premier League players in the making.

Lee Bullen, now captain of the team, was helping hold together a strong defence, at the same time earning big respect from the supporters for his passionate and committed, pull-you-up-by-the-scruff-of-your-neck style performances – few forwards in the division would have had a quiet day when going up against this tough defender.

While up front Steve MacLean and Kenwyne Jones (the latter borrowed from Sturrock's old club Southampton) were bringing the goals. MacLean would reach 19 goals in the league that season, naturally becoming a fans' favourite. Jones's seven in seven before Christmas helped massively as the team climbed up the table.

The smiles were back at last at Hillsborough and by mid-March, with eight games of the season left, Wednesday sat seemingly comfortably in the play-off positions.

Then the slip.

Nervousness, perhaps, set in. The goals dried up (it hadn't helped that key man and top scorer MacLean had gone down with an injury earlier in March; it wasn't known if he'd be seen on the pitch again that season) and in a seven-game spell, it was only draws and losses for the Owls, no wins. After the 3-0 turnover at a wet Hartlepool, Wednesday dropped out of the top six.

'We had a couple of sticky results,' remembers Sturrock, 'and Hartlepool, the night the rain came down, was a really disappointing performance. A lot of people thought we'd blown it at that point.'

A week later, they had clawed back their play-off place. But still, travelling to East Riding and grimmest Hull at the end of April, with only two games of the season remaining, Wednesday were in desperate need of the three points.

In Hull, the Owls fantastically went ahead and led for much for the first half. Yet on the hour they were pegged. Going into injury time, Wednesday's play-off hopes again seemed in real jeopardy.

At 1-1, as injury time was about to begin, Sturrock, getting ready to castigate his players, exited down the tunnel towards the dressing room. 'I didn't used to watch injury time,' he explains. 'It was 1-1 and we'd basically blown our chances. We might have lost our place in the play-offs. I was a wee bit angry and frustrated because we'd played okay in bits in the game but we could have done better. Then they all came in jumping up and down and being all happy.'

Sturrock wasn't aware that James Quinn had put away a last-minute winner to secure Wednesday's place in the play-offs. 'I was ranting and raving at a few of them,' he remembers, 'then one of them piped up and told me that they'd scored in the last minute. That kind of put my gas at a peep. I was dumbfounded and a bit embarrassed. I hadn't heard the crowd. But I was delighted of course.'

So, with that late drama in Hull, it was onwards to the play-offs for the Owls.

11

Talking Football: Cardiff 2005

Featuring Sheffield Wednesday manager, Paul Sturrock, the belting left-footed winger Chris Brunt, and the super Scottish goal-getting machine Steve MacLean.

FOLLOWING the win at Hull, Wednesday had secured their place in the League 1 play-offs. Brentford, who had finished in fourth position to Wednesday's fifth in the league table (but had beaten the Owls 2-1 and drawn with them 3-3 during the season), would be their opponents in the two-legged semi-final – the winner destined for the showdown final at the Millennium Stadium, Cardiff.

Some 28,625 were there at Hillsborough for the first leg and that night, with the big crowd spurring on the team, Paul Sturrock's Owls side battled through a difficult game to take the win: Jon-Paul McGovern's grounded shot from the right side of the box early into the game beating the Brentford keeper and sending the crowd bananas. 'It wasn't the best game in the world,' recalls winger Chris

Brunt, a very late substitute that night, 'but we got the early goal and just played it out to the end.' Advantage Wednesday.

Down to west London and Griffin Park for the second leg, with the final in Wednesday's sights, Sturrock, noting a nervousness in some of his players, and knowing how there was still a big job to be done, his players needing to be focused and their heads in the right place, gave a speech to ease the tension.

'Before the game,' he recalls, 'the players all were tetchy and bickering with each other. You could tell they were worried, so I sat down and gave them a wee speech, just to break the ice. I talked about everything apart from the game. Talked about myself, actually. How I was nearly 50 years old. How when I ate bread I got heartburn. How sex wasn't as good as it used to be. They were all looking at me like I was an alien. Then at the end I said, "This is a day to be enjoyed.

'"You've got all of those things coming to you, so just live for the day and enjoy it while you're young." We had a good laugh about it and it definitely took the pressure off them before they went out.'

Wednesday, now ready, took to the field and took care of business: Lee Peacock striking first – 1-0 on the night (2-0 on aggregate) – before Chris Brunt made it 2-0 (3-0 aggregate).

'Towards the end we showed a bit of resilience,' says Sturrock, 'because you know, they threw everything at us in the last 15 minutes.' Brentford would get a goal back. 'But we had a lot of good characters in the side and it really showed.' It finished 2-1 on the night (3-1 on aggregate).

Wednesday were on their way to Cardiff, to the final, where they would face Hartlepool United, whom Wednesday had beaten 2-0 earlier in the season before more recently losing to them 3-0.

For the final, the club's biggest game in recent history, Wednesday's first allocation of 33,500 tickets would go quickly, as would most of the second allocation of over 7,000, people having queued up at Hillsborough in the cold and wet night to get their hands on their tickets. Wednesday had averaged just under 25,000 for the season. Everyone, it seemed, was going to Cardiff.

* * * *

29 May 2005. Millennium Stadium, Cardiff. The big stage. 40,000-plus travelling from Sheffield for the League 1 Play-Off Final

For the club's most important game in years, Sturrock had his plan and as with the Brentford semi-final second leg, he wanted his players calm and relaxed for this massive game.

Sturrock – We decided that we'd do it like a normal game, like if we were playing Cardiff City away. So we trained the day before then drove down. Everyone picked a song they liked and we put together a tape to play for the journey. When we got there, we did all the interviews and everything, had a nice meal in the hotel, then got up the next morning and went to the game.

Sturrock, his players and his coaching staff got on the team bus and made their way through Cardiff to the stadium. As they got nearer, they were met with a brilliant scene.

Sturrock – When we were driving along to the stadium, as we turned the corner it was incredible, all blue and white down both sides of the street. Thousands and thousands of fans. We couldn't believe it. It looked like ten to one Sheffield. The noise was unbelievable.

Steve MacLean [a substitute that day following a lengthy spell out due to injury] – When we were driving in and saw all of the supporters, we were absolutely buzzing. We just couldn't wait to get there and wanted to do so well. We wanted to please all of those fans, wanted to send them home happy.

As the team bus moved through the crowds and to the ground, Sturrock's focus was still to keep his players as calm as possible.

Sturrock – When we got inside the stadium we still kept it low-key. The players came out in their tracksuits, they didn't have suits or anything like that, and they were ready to play. It was hot and when we got to look at the pitch we saw that it wasn't in good nick. But basically, I still thought, if you couldn't play in that atmosphere there was something wrong with you.

Kick-off approached at the Millennium Stadium. 'Hi-Ho Sheffield Wednesday' rang out from the 40,000-plus Wednesdayites in the stands and the flags waved as Sturrock proudly led out his players on to the pitch. One photograph captured the look of wonder on the Wednesday manager's face as he surveyed the brilliant and deafening blue and white landscape before him. The players looked confident.

Chris Brunt – The atmosphere was brilliant. We knew there was going to be a lot of Wednesday fans there but I didn't really appreciate it until we walked out on to the pitch. It was my first kind of experience of a stadium and an occasion like that, and it's one that will always live with me.

Kick-off

The Wednesday Boys lining up that day had taken the club this far – on the verge of a return to the second tier – and were ready now to take them there: Lucas, Bullen, Heckingbottom, Wood, Bruce, Whelan, McGovern, Brunt, Rocastle, Peacock and Quinn.

Relaxed and confident, they played their game, backed all the way by the incredible travelling support from Sheffield, and gave it their best. A couple of chances came the Owls' way – Chris Brunt then Lee Peacock going close – but they couldn't get through. Then, another opportunity: Craig Rocastle, somewhat uncharacteristically majestic that day, crossing low to reach Jon-Paul McGovern who managed to put it away at the back post. In the stands the 40-000-plus from Sheffield went bonkers and, at 1-0, the Owls had the upper hand.

Sturrock – We played very well in the first half, very well, and I thought we were unlucky with some of the chances.

At half-time the players left the pitch, and walked with their manager and his staff down the tunnel and into the changing rooms leading the play-off final 1-0.

Sturrock – After the goal I thought I'd be able to give them a fantastic half-time team talk. But they all came in looking a bit worse for wear because of the heat that day. I had a chair in the middle of the changing room and sat there. 'Right boys,' I said. 'I know what you're feeling like. It's hot and you're knackered. But you're winning. Can you imagine how the other lot are feeling?' It was just to try and rally them a bit. The team talk didn't work that time, though. About two minutes after half-time, it was 1-1 [Eifion Williams the scorer for Hartlepool], and about 25 after that, we were down 2-1 [Jon Daly].

Trailing 2-1 with 15 minutes to go and everything was going wrong for Wednesday. The game and the minutes and the promotion hopes were slipping away. Something had to be done.

Sturrock made three changes – a last-ditch attempt to salvage the game – and went all out with a triple substitution. On came defender Patrick Collins and the strikers Drew Talbot and Steve MacLean to freshen up the team and, in the latter pair's case, add extra attacking impetus to the side (though MacLean had been out injured for over two months, he'd still managed to score 19 times for the Owls that season).

Sturrock – Steve [MacLean] was injured but had a knack for scoring goals. He had trained on the Thursday, trained on the Friday and it was one of those scenarios: do you put him on or not? In the end I did.

MacLean – I found out an hour and five minutes before the game that I was going to be involved. The gaffer used to like keeping things close to his chest and wouldn't tell us until quite late on who was playing. He'd read my name out last and I was absolutely buzzing. I desperately wanted to get out on to that pitch as soon as possible.

Sturrock's bold and necessary move paid off, and with ten minutes of the play-off final remaining, Wednesday, still trailing, won a penalty: a hand on the back of the energetic substitute Talbot causing him to fall in the box and the kick was given. Hartlepool's Chris Westwood was shown the red card.

The Wednesdayites in the stands celebrated for a bit, then bit their nails. A golden chance to get back into the game.

Penalty

To some the penalty decision looked a little soft. But...

Sturrock – It was definitely a penalty, yes. It doesn't matter how many times you look at it, it was.

MacLean – Yes, I thought it was. I've never actually thought it wasn't.

MacLean, the substitute, would take the responsibility and take the kick.

MacLean – I definitely fancied it. I remember Chris [Brunt] saying to me, 'Do you want it?' Obviously I'd not been on the pitch long, but I grabbed the ball. There was no way anybody was taking it off me. Normally I'm quite a laid-back person and I did feel a lot of pressure, but I was quite confident I'd score.

MacLean, the pressure of a whole football club on him, stepped up, struck hard and scored. 2-2. Wednesdayites everywhere went mad with joy and relief, the noise in the Millennium Stadium deafening.

MacLean – It wasn't the greatest of penalties ever, the keeper got a hand to it, but it crossed the line. The feeling when it went in was exceptional, one of my best feelings in football.

To the end

The play-off final was now level and Wednesday, back in it and with a man advantage following Westwood's sending off, had the impetus and were soon to have the ascendency.

Sturrock – After we scored, you could see the Hartlepool players' heads dip a wee bit. The game had definitely shifted to us.

Brunt – I was sort of thinking it was our day then... we never looked back really.

Wednesday's third goal came three minutes into extra time. Glenn Whelan, the youngster excellent in midfield that day, capped a strong season with the club when he won the ball outside the area, took it on with three touches, then stuck it wonderfully into the left corner of the net. A tremendous goal. Wednesday now led 3-2.

In 1991, the League Cup had been won for the Owls after John Sheridan's strike from distance at Wembley. Now, in 2005, in the League 1 Play-Off Final, it looked as if Whelan's own spectacular big stage effort would win the day for Wednesday too.

MacLean – I remember him [Whelan] running through. I think I can remember actually asking for him to pass me the ball! But of course he didn't need too. It was such a great finish into the corner.

Wednesday's fourth came in the last moments of the game: the young substitute striker Drew Talbot winning the ball and racing free towards goal. Floating on, he rounded the Hartlepool keeper and finished for 4-2.

They'd won it now. Victory in the play-off final for Wednesday. Promotion back up to the Championship. The supporters partying in the stands.

After the whistle

The celebrations could now begin. Captain Lee Bullen, a big presence that day at the back and a brilliant influence on the team that season, lifting the trophy with his teammates jumping about all around him.

More hugs and more cheers in the stands – the flags still waving. And Paul Sturrock and his chairman Dave Allen walking along the pitch, arms round each other's shoulders, taking it in, savouring the moment.

When he got into the dressing room, penalty-scoring hero Steve MacLean took a moment to reflect on the game, what had just happened in Cardiff and his own difficult journey to this moment.

MacLean – Well, I'm a big softy and get a bit emotional with things like that. Back in the dressing room, I put a towel over my head so none of the boys could see me and just sat and took it in for a few minutes. Thinking that I wasn't even going to make the game, then to get on there and then score, it was amazing.

Party

After the Wednesday Boys had picked up the trophy, celebrated then changed, they joined the 40,000-plus Wednesdayites on the exodus back up the M50 to Sheffield, the party following them all of the way home.

On the way, as the team bus got caught in the subsequent gridlock, some of the players took the opportunity to celebrate on the motorway.

Escaping through the back of the bus, they piled out on to the road and proceeded to celebrate, trophy in tow, between the cars of the jubilant Owls fans and confused members of the public, also sharing the road with them that day.

Sturrock – 'They're out in the road with the trophy,' the driver said to me. They were walking over cars and dancing around in the middle of the road. People had scarves and everything dangling out of the cars. Then they saw the cup and got out of the cars. Everyone was dancing together. Incredible.

Further on up the motorway, when the team bus stopped at the services for a comfort break, the celebrations continued.

Sturrock – There were hundreds of fans all there, all around. Of course the toilets were up the stairs so the boys did the conga into the place and up the stairs. All the fans joined on to the back. Then they were stood up at the top of the stairs singing with the Wednesday fans. It was fantastic.

Happy days at last for the club. Five years after dropping from the Premier League, something proper now to smile about for the club and all of its supporters.

Sturrock – Nothing will ever beat Cardiff.

12

Cretins and Scum

'WE'D had a terrific day in Cardiff,' recalls Dave Allen of Wednesday's play-off win. 'Then we came back to Sheffield to celebrate at Napoleon's into the early hours of the morning.

'One thing I remember about that night was something Paul Sturrock's coach, John Blackley, said to me: "Savour this occasion, Dave," he said, "because there's a lot of bad times in football." He was right, of course.'

Following the joy of Cardiff, the sole aim for the Owls in 2005/06 was to consolidate the Championship place they had just regained. Their budgeted wage bill of around £5m would be the fourth lowest (in a division where, as in the Premier League, there existed about a 90 per cent correlation between expenditure on wages and final league position; so the more you spent on wages and not transfers, the higher you were likely to finish in the table), representing the club's prudent spend-what-you-earn approach to finances. And with that manager Paul Sturrock got to work planning for the challenge of the season ahead.

First, he had some difficult decisions to make.

'Nobody knows this,' explains Sturrock, holding court in a Cornwall bar, 'but because of the lateness of the play-offs, I had to release some of the players the *day* after the final.

'It was the worst thing. The night before I was drinking and celebrating with them in the casino, then I was calling them in in the morning to release them. Hammy [Matthew Hamshaw] was the first one. He had to get off because he was going on holiday. I freed him. "Sorry mate," I said, "we're not giving you a contract for next year." That's the two sides of football.'

Out of the door along with Hamshaw would be James Quinn and the more peripheral Lewis McMahon.

Replacing them were players that hopefully would be of better quality and better suited to the second tier. In came Burton O'Brien, a tidy enough midfielder from Livingston; Graham Coughlan, a strong, rugged defender and leader from Plymouth; John Hills, a left-back from Gillingham; Drissa Diallo, a centre-half from Ipswich Town; and Frankie Simek, an excellent young American right-back out of the Arsenal academy. They all arrived on free transfers, while Wigan's Scottish striker David Graham joined for £250,000, a decent fee for Wednesday at the time.

While decent enough, the new boys weren't all necessarily Sturrock's first choice, however. 'We couldn't afford the players I would have liked to have taken in,' he says. 'That's no detriment to those I did bring in. They did well for us. But one of them, as an example, was probably fourth or fifth in line of what I was looking for. But I had to fit a budget.'

Still, his team for the new campaign would be a robust and well-organised outfit that would give everything for the simple cause of keeping Wednesday in the division. The football wasn't all that pretty to watch, but the team were capable of gradually, week by week, game by game, building up enough points to keep the team's head bobbing above the water and out of the relegation places.

The memory that season of Lee Bullen appearing in every position of the 4-4-2 at one stage or another, and even in goal at Millwall, seems to sum it all up and define a season of endeavour and all-togetherness.

In the New Year Sturrock had been able to bolster his squad, bringing in the forwards Deon Burton (£110,000 from Rotherham United) and Marcus Tudgay (a reputed £200,000 from Derby County). They added firepower to his side and helped the survival job tick on.

By the end, Wednesday would have won about a point a game on average; enough to get them safely over the line. The aimed-for Championship survival achieved. A successful season (and so what if across the city at Bramall Lane Neil Warnock's Sheffield United were on their way back to the Premier League after over 20 years away?).

* * * *

Ahead of 2006/07 chairman Dave Allen made it clear to his manager how he wanted the early part of the new season to pan out. While satisfied with the previous survival campaign, Allen now wanted to see improvements not only in terms of results and league placing, but also style of play (which in the season just gone had been efficient and effective; the team having ground out enough points to survive). 'Paul,' Allen surmised to his manager on this point, 'we've got to get this right.'

This was a concern for Sturrock. 'I knew it would be a problem,' he says. 'The style of football we played was one that will get you promoted out of football leagues.' And in 2004/05 it had; though admittedly it was not the most attractive and stylish to watch.

'I've had a number of promotions in my career,' he adds, 'so I know exactly how it needs to be done. But I realised then that there were going to be a few slight problems with that that season.'

The club's finances were still tight. A £457,000 loss had been posted for the season just gone and earlier that summer, in May, the club's overdraft had reached £8.5m.

During that year the Co-op Bank had generously helped out, 'parking' £6m of the loans they held in the club, effectively re-calibrating part of the bank debt so that *no* interest would be charged upon it. The £6m – very possibly by now written down in the bank's books – would be reduced whenever possible, in the event of a player sale for example. Additional to the 'parked' debt arrangement was the £7.75m loan relating to the Middlewood training ground, with only notional interest to be accrued on that debt, and due to be paid over only upon the site's seemingly unlikely sale.

The ship-steadying approach to spending was set to continue and Sturrock again provided with only limited resources for new players.

Into the club that summer came Crewe Alexandra's petite midfielder Kenny Lunt (no fee), Southampton's combative midfielder Yoann Folly (fee undisclosed), Milton Keynes's pacy winger Wade Small (undisclosed), and Madjid Bougherra, an Algerian defender brought in from the French club Gueugnon for around £250,000. Bougherra had impressed while on loan with Crewe the previous season and would prove a fine capture. Lunt, by contrast, would not.

Unfortunately for Sturrock, early performances and results in 2006/07 were not good: one win in the first four games; no wins in the next six. Just before he had left for his late-summer holiday, Allen had told Sturrock that by the time he returned a good number of points needed to have been won. But when he got back, those points had not been won. Despite what Sturrock had done for the club – Cardiff and promotion, then second-tier consolidation – his chairman felt something had to give.

'Paul had gotten us out of League 1 and into the Championship,' Allen says, 'but I had reservations about whether he could manage in the Championship.'

At the end of Wednesday's next game, at home to Barnsley, with the Owls heading for a draw Allen had risen from his seat in the directors' box and walked down to the boardroom, in anticipation of making the decision there and then... 'Then,' he says, 'in injury time Brunty scored a goal and we won 2-1.' The goal brought Sturrock a reprieve, but only a brief one. 'We then went down to Colchester,' Allen continues, 'played Bullen on the left wing [usually a defender, but in the past he had played further up the pitch] or something and lost 4-0. I said to Kaven Walker, "I think we'll have to part company." So we did.' Paul Sturrock was sacked as manager of Sheffield Wednesday.

Naturally, Sturrock was massively disappointed with the decision. 'I was gutted to be leaving,' he says, 'because I really enjoyed it in Sheffield. I did feel the pressure going down to Colchester though. We needed to get a couple of results and I'd been disappointed with the performances so far. I knew it was on the cards. There were also a few other things that had happened. We had a couple of meetings, two really heated board meetings where I mooted my opinion on all of the board members, and those meetings were contributing factors to me getting the sack.'

Later, reports would also emerge of Sturrock rowing with the club's chief executive, Kaven Walker.

Striker Steve MacLean remembers the 'horrible day' his boss was dismissed. 'Paul was a great manager and ended up being a great friend as well. I was really sad to see him go.' Captain Lee Bullen would recall how Sturrock 'looked like a broken man' as he said his goodbyes to his players following his dismissal.

The fans were upset too, and angry; the belief of many was that Sturrock was still the right man for the job – that eventually he would have got the team going again, would have kept them up and kept them safe.

In response to that, Allen today is pragmatic in his view. 'All the fans were carrying on because they thought he was a lovely bloke. But we were near the bottom of the league. "How dare you sack him" and all that. What is the matter with these people? I thought.'

As Sturrock himself reflects today, 'He [Allen] made the decision to move me on and that's how it went.'

As a temporary fix, academy director Sean McAuley was put in charge of the first team. 'I sat down with Kaven Walker,' remembers Allen, 'and said, "Look, I think we've got the right players here to play attractive attacking football. Bring Sean in. Let's have a talk to him." I say to Sean, "There's no pressure on you, just play 4-4-2 while I look round for a manager." Sean had four games. He won three and drew one and they played well. Smashing.'

Allen was so impressed with the upturn in the team's form that he suggested keeping McAuley on permanently. 'I said to Kaven, "I don't think we should appoint a manager. Let's give it to Sean until the end of the season." But Kaven said, "If you don't appoint a manager, this lot [the fans] will slaughter you."' So the hunt continued.

Former Everton and Manchester City manager Joe Royle was linked, but he ruled himself out. The former Wednesday players Nigel Worthington and the tough midfielder and former captain in the 1980s, Gary Megson (who was also a big Wednesday fan; his father, Don, was also a former club captain in the 1960s) were interviewed, as was Bryan Robson, but it was Scunthorpe's Brian Laws who, according to Allen, came across best.

Laws was something of a rising name having twice guided Scunthorpe out of the fourth tier, setting them on course to another promotion from League 1. Before Scunthorpe, at Grimsby Town, he had punched out one of his players, Ivano Bonetti, after the Italian had thrown some sandwiches at him from the post-game buffet. Before that, he had worked under Brian Clough as a ball-playing full-back for Nottingham Forest.

Laws and Allen met three times. Laws was pleased to discover that Allen 'told things as they were, no messing about', while Allen, impressed by the Scunthorpe boss, made an offer.

Laws had his reservations. He was doing well at Scunthorpe and, as he would later note in his autobiography, 'Wednesday had been chewing up and spitting out managers at the rate of nearly one a year.' Would the same happen to him?

In the end, of course, the pull of a club like Wednesday proved too great and so Brian Laws became the Owls' latest manager.

'Don't change much, Brian,' were Allen's instructions. He didn't – and the excellent run, begun under Sean McAuley, continued wonderfully. Fantastic wins came at Leicester (four long-range belting goals that day), Norwich, Barnsley and Leeds (3-2 at Elland Road, Chris Brunt notching a splendid lob from out near the touchline).

January 2007 saw the sale to Premier League Charlton Athletic of the excellent, if at times erratic, Algerian defender Madjid Bougherra for £2.5m. Such quality would be a loss to the team, but if an opportunity arose where a player could be sold on for a good price, it still had to be taken. A portion of the fee appears to have been used to pay back an interest-free loan of £429,000 that Dave Allen had made to the club, with a further £78,000 being repaid to the Co-op Bank.

Happily, Brian Laws managed to plug the gap in his defence and the good times continued.

The win at Leeds came early on in an eventual 11-game unbeaten run; one which had many believing Wednesday might even sneak themselves into the play-off positions by the end of the season. Winger Chris Brunt recalls, 'After the battle of the season before, there was a lot of people in the team getting used to the Championship now.

When Brian Laws took over, we started to play a bit more football and obviously it was a lot better to watch. We had a good team and went places with no fear and great confidence. Everybody was enjoying themselves and everywhere we went we expected to come away with a result.'

Sadly, a loss at Birmingham would ultimately count Wednesday out of the play-off race, their surge of form proving fractionally too late. Nevertheless, it had been a fine first six months as manager for Laws.

The immediate future was starting to look bright.

[Louis Clay]

Away from the field, in the Hillsborough boardroom, Allen still had his ears open to offers of investment in the club – although, as had been the case with the Ken Bates saga a few years before, he was not about to entertain any approaches that he did not consider to be in the best interests of the club.

One apparently interested party was a consortium that included the Sheffield boxing promoter Dennis Hobson and which, according to the *Sheffield Star*, had between them more money than Allen. No deal. 'Just hot air,' says Allen.

Another was the Hong Kong businessman Carson Yeung, who would hold talks with Wednesday and visit Allen and the club twice. But a deal would not happen (this all came before Yeung took over at Birmingham City, got convicted by a Hong Kong court of laundering over £55m and got sentenced to six years in prison).

In early 2007, someone seemingly more suitable came forward.

'Originally I think Paul [Gregg] rang up and spoke to Bob Grierson [the club's finance director],' recalls Allen. 'Bob said to me, "We've got a guy who I think is genuinely interested, Dave. He's just come out of Everton."'

Paul Gregg's background was in the entertainment industry: Allen's industry. Considered by some to be something of a hard-nosed businessman, Gregg and his wife, Anita, had built up the Apollo Leisure Group, owners of theatres up and down the country. In 1999 Gregg and his family sold Apollo, netting a reported £129m, after which he was persuaded by fellow theatre impresario Bill Kenwright to join him and others in taking over Everton. Gregg's share was a reputed £7m.

Following an acrimonious split in Liverpool, Gregg would sell his shares and walk away, reportedly netting up to £9m. Seemingly Gregg was ready to invest in another club.

'We did a bit of research on him,' remembers Allen, 'then he came to talk to us. We got on very well, Paul, Bob and myself. We sat down and worked it all out. He spent a lot of time examining the business and preparing for what he was going to do there. We provided him with all the figures he wanted and he did his due diligence. He spent about £20,000 on that, I think.'

Time moved on, but things appeared to be going in the right direction. 'He'd got his bank sorted out. He was going to buy Geoff Hulley's, Keith Addy's and my shares. And pay off all the directors' loans [which by the summer of 2007 would stand at over £5m, including accrued interest, much of which was owed to Allen]. We'd taken him across to see the Co-op Bank too and they were happy with him; he was going to reduce the debt.'

Allen was sure of the whole thing. '"God," I thought, "we've got a genuine guy here." Paul had been meaningfully going about it and definitely wanted to be there. He was happy. It was all going to be sweet. The guy was going to take over the club, invest and everything.'

Then the deal died: Paul Gregg pulled out and walked away. Allen was shocked and what followed would be the beginning of the end of his involvement with Sheffield Wednesday.

* * * *

The reasons given for Gregg's about-turn were outlined in a letter sent from his solicitors to Allen, a letter which would feature heavily in a press conference that the Wednesday chairman was about to call to make an announcement about the collapse of the deal. It was the summer of 2007.

For over a week few people, if any, outside the club came to know of Gregg's withdrawal. Then came the press conference.

Fielding some of the enquiries about the nature of the upcoming conference was the club's chief executive Kaven Walker. 'Turn up on Friday to find out,' he is said to have explained, bluntly. 'No further comment.'

Turning up that Friday, then, were numerous members of the local and regional television, newspaper and radio press, many of whom were still expecting to hear the announcement of a successful Gregg takeover.

John Gath, then vice-chairman of the Wednesdayite group (formerly the Owls Trust, which owned over ten per cent of the club's shares), had also made his way to the ground to hear the announcement. Though, unfortunately for him, he wouldn't be allowed in to do so. 'When we arrived we asked the stadium guys if we could come in,' remembers Gath. 'But they refused. They'd been told not to let us [Wednesdayite] in and had closed the gate across the bridge. So we stood outside, just on the entrance to the bridge.'

Inside Hillsborough, when Allen walked into the press conference and sat down beside Walker, ready to begin, he was stern-faced.

First from Allen came the mini bombshell that Paul Gregg would not in fact be investing in the club. And that it appeared to have something to do with the Wednesdayite group.

With Gregg's solicitors' letter in front of him, Allen, glasses on, read aloud. '[O]ne of the crucial reasons why our client decided to withdraw,' Allen read, 'was [his] recognition that the acquisition of only 30 per cent of the club could be delivered with any definitive certainty [that is, the shares that were controlled by the board, namely, by Allen, Keith Addy and Geoff Hulley].

'However,' Allen read on, 'it was felt that control was necessary for our client.' Adding, 'the potential blocking ability of the Supporters' Trust's ten per cent shareholding in the company was a clear detraction from making a full offer.'

'We said we could get some more shares for him,' explains Allen today, 'which would have taken him up to about 40-odd per cent. But he was worried about this ten per cent that Wednesdayite had got.' According to individuals that were close to the Trust, however, the former Everton man did not even make contact with them about the possibility of obtaining their ten per cent shareholding.

The Gregg withdrawal news had been part one of the press conference. Next up, Allen took the opportunity to get a few other bothers off his chest.

Glasses off, he ticked off the *Sheffield Star*, repeating their headline from an earlier article which had revealed the club was talking to Gregg, '"Gregg's the man",' Allen read, adding unhappily, 'All without getting proper confirmation.'

Allen castigated certain disgruntled Wednesday supporters who had taken to verbally abusing him at home matches in front of his family, along with one female supporter who had spoken out against him at a previous shareholders' meeting. '[T]here was one woman stood up,' Allen said in the press conference, 'the most venomous bitch I've ever come across in my life. She'd got three acid pages to read out about me… it was just absolutely appalling. Can't believe these people. Scum.'

The supporters' group Wednesdayite also would come in for criticism. Referring to the concerns raised in the Paul Gregg letter surrounding the group's shareholding, Allen said, 'These people [potential investors such as Gregg] would not be taken in and come in and purchase 30 per cent of the shares, knowing full well that Wednesdayite can, at the drop of a hat, bum [clicks fingers], like that, call an EGM.'

Then came the most memorable comments of the afternoon. 'These people,' Allen said, 'who call themselves fans are nothing but a bunch of *cretins*. And I hope you've got that word right, *cretins*, because that is what they are.' Quite a comment, coming right out of the mouth of the Sheffield Wednesday chairman.

Afterwards, the media coverage not surprisingly focused on two of the stronger words he had used, 'cretins' and 'scum'.

Wednesdayite's then vice-chairman, John Gath, remembers the day well. 'We'd been hearing snippets about what was going on and we thought he [Allen] was going to announce a takeover,' recalls Gath of what he'd been expecting from the press conference. 'Either that, or Gregg had pulled out. What we didn't expect though was for him [Allen] to go off on one the way he did. It really was a shock.'

Allen was questioned by the FA over his potentially 'abusive and/or insulting words', though ultimately would receive no punishment (the comments, in the FA's view, had not brought the game into disrepute). Today, he insists that the comments were aimed only at Wednesdayite and not the rest of the fans. 'The press didn't put it across right,' he says. 'I made them put that right. But, of course, it's too late once it's been headlined.'

The press conference seemed to be the writing on the wall for Allen and his time as the club's chairman, his reign at Hillsborough seeming to have run its course.

No matter, though. He'd just about had enough anyway.

One story is telling. 'We were having a good run, I was putting all this money into the club, and then, three rows down from me [at the ground] a kid stands up in a T-shirt saying "Fuck off Allen". I had my two grandsons there with me who were about eight or nine at the time. Disgraceful. "I could do without this," I thought.'

Another event would confirm to him that it was time to go. 'To run any business successfully,' says Allen, 'you must have confidentiality in the boardroom and trust in your fellow directors. Well, we used to have a board meeting down here [in the offices adjoined to the casino and next to Owlerton Stadium] on a Wednesday or Thursday afternoon. On Friday night I'd be in the casino on Ecclesall Road and people would be telling me what had happened in the boardroom meeting. Some directors were discussing it out of the boardroom. Disgraceful. Some of them just couldn't stop talking. I know who it was. After that I thought, "That's it, that's the final straw."'

It was four months after the press conference – November 2007 – that he left the club. '"I'm off, fellas," I said. I think a lot of people get involved in football for the wrong reason. They get involved for the kudos, which is the wrong reason and it can cost you a lot of money. And there were people there who weren't a lot of use to be frank… I'd prefer to finish it there.'

And that was that. Dave Allen had left the club.

'I went in there, took over as chairman and said, "I'll get the whole business right,"' he says. 'And I enjoyed getting them promoted into the Championship and enjoyed seeing us finish eighth in the league and doing okay. There were plenty of nice people there who I had support from, and to this day people come up to me and thank me for what I did for Sheffield Wednesday, which is very nice. "Thanks," they say, "you had a very difficult ride."

'But you know what? My wife never wanted me to get involved and I have to say: she was right.'

13

Dark Days

THROUGH the final few months of the 2006/07 season Brian Laws, as the new Wednesday manager, had taken a confident, exciting, well-performing side not far away from the Championship play-offs. There was optimism for the year ahead. Perhaps a tweak here and a tweak there might help push his team on. So far, the club which before his arrival had, in his own words, 'been chewing up and spitting out managers at the rate of nearly one a year', had been much kinder to him.

Sadly for Laws and the Owls, the six defeats in the opening six games of 2007/08 would dash all of that optimism. 'I feel like I must have run over a black cat,' said Laws. The bad luck had started with a disappointing summer in the transfer market.

Disappointment number one: Laws lost his best player, the talented and instrumental young Northern Irish winger, Chris Brunt, who was sold to West Bromwich Albion for £2.5m (rising to £3m). 'It was a no-brainer for me really,' explains Brunt today of the West Brom move. 'I wanted to further my career and felt I had to go. I felt a bit for Brian but I think his hands were tied. The finances were a big part of the club not being able to move forward and they sort of dictated everything.'

Some £1m of the fee would be paid back to the Co-operative Bank (who after that repayment were still owed over £20m).

Another £1m would be paid back to Dave Allen for the lending that was still outstanding to him (over £2m would remain due to him in remaining loans and accrued interest).

Disappointment numbers two, three and four in the transfer market that summer: Laws missing out on his three main targets for a new striker. Scunthorpe's Billy Sharp, Southampton's Kenywne Jones (whose seven goals in seven games had helped Wednesday to the League 1 play-offs back in 2004/05) and Grzegorz Rasiak (also of Southampton) were all dismissed as too expensive, either in transfer fee or wage demands. None of them was signed, much to the displeasure of Laws.

Disappointment number five: he lost Steve MacLean, the penalty-scoring hero of Cardiff 2005. A new contract had been on the table, but the offer, as Laws would recall, was 'so lame that it was obvious he [MacLean] wouldn't accept'. So he moved on to Cardiff City for nothing.

MacLean would be replaced by the often-injury-troubled former Everton and Arsenal striker, Francis Jeffers (£700,000). '[I]t looked a reasonable enough risk at the time,' Laws would recall, kindly. Alas, though, once signed, Jeffers would go on to break his ankle away at Stoke in October 2007, and make only three more appearances that season.

Despite the frustrating summer and awful winless beginning to the season, Laws, at least outwardly, remained upbeat. As his new goalkeeper for that season, Lee Grant, remembers, 'Brian did a really good job. He was up against it and had to stay really positive. If he had been coming in with a long face, it would have been very difficult for the players to pick themselves up and get motivated. But he was bright and bubbly, which I think was important. When you're up against it in the league or with other aspects of the club, financially or whatever, it's good for someone to be able to get a few smiles on faces.' And while the better results would come, it would take Wednesday until late October to move out of the relegation places.

January 2008 saw the derby with Sheffield United (the Blades' Premier League adventure having lasted only a year, with relegation back to the Championship followed by the departure of manager Neil Warnock) where, thankfully, marvellously, the Owls managed to find a way to win 2-0, much to the joy of every Wednesday fan.

After Marcus Tudgay had struck home the second, Laws charged down the Hillsborough touchline in ecstatic celebration. It looked like a man under immense pressure letting it all out.

Away from the pitch, it had been a similarly difficult period for the Owls. Ever since Dave Allen's departure in November 2007, there had been a leadership void at the top of the club. No chairman, no strong, prominent voice, it seemed. To some, it appeared the club's controversial chief executive, Kaven Walker, was going some way to filling that void. And that – in some people's minds, at least – wasn't good.

Walker had joined the club back in 2000, appointed in the last days of Dave Richards's chairmanship as commercial director. Previously, he had worked for Liverpool as retail/club-shop manager, then Derby County. In 2004, he was promoted in the place of Alan Sykes as Sheffield Wednesday's chief executive. By late 2007, after Paul Sturrock had been let go by the club and Allen, still just in place, had decided the club's next manager would have less day-to-day dealings with him (as he stepped back a little from the club to re-devote more of his time to his business, A&S Leisure), Walker's influence apparently increased dramatically. But he was not a popular character around Hillsborough.

Prior to Sturrock's departure, it is said that Walker had been talking down the Scot's abilities, claiming that he wasn't capable of managing at Championship level; Sturrock had confronted Walker over the comments and, before he had left the club, the pair had rowed and fallen out. Later, Sturrock's successor, Brian Laws, would also allude to the difficulties experienced with the chief executive. 'I had spoken to a lot of people who had warned me about the way Mr Walker worked,' Laws would recall in his autobiography. 'But I like to take people at face value and find things out for myself. Which I did! To say it became a challenging relationship would be an understatement.'

Apparently it would be a similar story for other club employees. One former club worker recalls a number of instances where they had watched Walker make life extremely difficult for certain other members of club staff, 'victimising and belittling them in public'. 'The club was not a very good place to work,' they explain of that time. Even the former Owls player, assistant manager, then manager Peter Eustace, who by now had been working as the club's chief scout, travelling up and down the country to take in first team, reserve and youth team games, had also apparently clashed with Walker. In April 2008 he would take Wednesday to an employment tribunal after the club had made him redundant from his £20,000-per-year job.

The tribunal heard from Sturrock, the last manager Eustace had worked for at the club, that despite Eustace being 'an exceptionally good judge of a footballer... Kaven Walker [had] repeatedly advocated his [Eustace's] redundancy, calling into question his value to the club'. Sturrock added, 'I believe Kaven Walker had a personal grudge against Mr Eustace.' Eustace lost the case in the end, but following Sturrock's comments, Walker did not appear to have come out of it looking too good.

'I don't think Kaven was a liked chief executive, I'll put it that way,' surmises Sturrock today of the man who was now so prominent in the club's operations.

It seemed even the local press suffered too, with journalists, such as Ian Appleyard of the *Yorkshire Post*, finding themselves banned from the ground after they had written something about the club which the management had seemingly not liked.

Also there was the ridiculous saga, apparently overseen by Walker, of the non-takeover of the club by the 'businessman' Geoff Sheard.

It had been in early 2008, a few months after Allen had left the club, when Sheard had tipped up at Wednesday with a letter from a consortium he was said to have been representing. The letter apparently showed $100m of proof of funding from the Dominican-based Private Capital Bank. It seemed genuine.

The supporters' group, Wednesdayite, previously cited for their 'potential blocking ability' of any such takeover, even met with Sheard in a Leeds hotel to show that they were open-minded to any party who could take the club forward and not be a block to them. There, they discussed Sheard's plans; namely, that an offer would be made for their 10.07 per cent shareholding. Weeks passed, however, and when no offer was made for anybody's shares, people began to speculate as to whether Sheard and his consortium were genuine or not. Perhaps, some even mused, he was a plant, put there to make Wednesdayite once again look like blockers to any potential deal?

Despite Sheard's stalling, Wednesdayite continued to play along, agreeing by member ballot that if Sheard produced tangible evidence of his funding and everything complied with the relevant financial regulations, the group would sell their shares to the consortium (thereby allowing Wednesdayite to demonstrate that they were an open and democratic organisation whose shareholding was not in fact a stumbling block to any potential takeover of the club).

Then it emerged that the original 'proof of $100m funding' letter that Sheard had provided to the club was, in fact, a fake. No deal would take place. Wednesdayite removed their conditional offer to sell. And Sheard shuffled away into the distance. A great big massive waste of time for everyone involved.

For Laws, trying his best to steer his Wednesday side through 2007/08 with all of that turmoil and trouble as the backdrop, it was not an easy season. Somehow, though, in spite of it all – in spite of losing players like Chris Brunt, Steve MacLean and, in March 2008, the youngster Glenn Whelan (the midfielder who over the past few years had developed into an excellent player, was sold to Stoke City for £500,000); and in spite of the apparent 'challenging relationship' with Walker – Laws' players just did enough to survive the always-threatened relegation from the Championship; a 4-1 last-day victory over Norwich at a packed Hillsborough enough to keep them up.

All matters considered, though, things didn't appear especially bright for the Owls.

14

Saloon-Bar Moanings

W HAT else for the football club? Nigel Short is a big Sheffield Wednesday fan. The kind who hates to miss a game; hardly ever does. The kind who over the years has helped raise thousands of pounds for the club, and for charity: bucket collections, sponsored runs and walks and cycle rides. For years he was secretary of the Wednesday Shareholders' Association; along with its chairman, David Coupe, he raised the money for the 100-by-50-foot Owls flag that appeared at the Wembley finals in 1993. He would go on to be chairman of Wednesdayite. 'Sheffield Wednesday,' he says, 'is in my blood.'

Like many football fans up and down the country, Short would sometimes make comments about the club he supported on an internet forum. Incredibly, those comments would lead to him becoming embroiled in a lengthy and distressing legal battle with his own football club: Sheffield Wednesday trying to sue one of their own fans. In a series of sorry episodes for the club around the time, this was the sorriest of them all.

* * * *

It was back in early 2006, before Paul Sturrock had been sacked by the club, before Dave Allen had resigned as chairman, before Brian

Laws had taken Wednesday close to the Championship play-offs, then steered them away from relegation the following season, that Short had taken to the lively and popular online message board, Owlstalk, to air some of his thoughts about the club and how it was being operated at the time.

He had been posting comments for several years under the pseudonym 'Grandad' (many knew that 'Grandad' was Short); more recent ones had focused on such things as a bucket collection that had recently taken place outside the ground for the benefit of then-struggling Rotherham United; a technical discussion about the intricacies of what exactly was required to become a member of the Sheffield Wednesday board; and an exasperated comment about the club's upper management, 'the club couldn't go forward while the Chief Exec [Kaven Walker] and Chairman [Dave Allen] remained in place,' Short wrote. He might also have on occasion referred to Kaven Walker as Karen; he wouldn't have been the first.

Tame stuff, one might think? The club didn't. In February 2006, Short received a letter from Wednesday's solicitors accusing him of having made multiple defamatory postings about the club's management. Unsurprisingly, he became very worried. 'I shit myself, quite frankly,' he says today.

In response to the letter, Short offered to make a public apology for any offence he might have caused to the club and Walker. Not wanting the club to be out of pocket either, he offered to pay Wednesday's legal costs (a few thousand pounds). Short, who had yet to receive any legal advice, 'just wanted the whole thing to go away'. His offer, however, was refused '…and,' says the man who would become Short's lawyer, 'I'm betting you they regret not taking the money.'

* * * *

Mark Lewis is one of the country's finest lawyers. He is the man who thought of and brought the first phone-hacking case in 2007 and who, through the summer of 2011, would play a role in bringing down the *News of the World* newspaper amid the phone-hacking scandal, acting on a no-win-no-fee basis for scores of victims. The newspaper published its last edition in July 2011, and three years later its former editor Andy Coulson was sent to prison for his role in the scandal. A fearless and dogged litigator, Lewis is certainly the kind of lawyer you would want on your side if the football club you loved was suing you for some things you had written about the people who were running it on an internet message board.

Short was put in touch with Lewis via one of Lewis's colleagues. A meeting was set up in Manchester (where Lewis was working at the time), where he and another sat with Short and read through the allegedly defamatory comments that Short had posted on Owlstalk. Laughing as they read, the lawyers dismissed the comments as not defamatory: nothing of the sort. The club, Short was told, didn't have a hope in hell.

'From a libel law point of view, it all sounded like an opinion to me,' explains Lewis today. 'Honest opinion is a defence to a libel claim and I think it was a pretty honest opinion to say something critical of a football club. So it became a question of saying to Nigel, "You've got nothing to lose. We think you can win. And you should fight this because this is an obvious case of somebody trying to bully you."'

Such was Lewis's confidence, he suggested taking the case on the basis of a no-win-no-fee style Conditional Fee Agreement (CFA). In this scenario, if the club were to lose the case, they might be liable for up to double Short's eventual legal costs. Lewis had never undertaken a CFA for a defendant before, but was incensed that legal big guns were firing at an individual who couldn't afford lawyers to defend himself.

After sending Short the first letter in February 2006, Wednesday waited a year before they issued proceedings against him (on the last possible day they could) for the alleged libel. They then waited a further four months (the maximum time allowed) before they actually served legal papers against him.

The delay was perplexing to Lewis. 'I'm not privy as to why the club didn't sue straight away,' he says. 'It could have been for all sorts of reasons. They might have thought, "Should we or shouldn't we?" To give them the benefit of the doubt, they might have thought that they didn't want to sue a fan. Or they might have thought, Sword of Damocles, "We'll leave it dangling over him so he's got a year to worry about whether we do sue him or we don't, then we'll sue him." I just don't know what was in their thought process. Ordinarily, though, if you were giving libel advice to someone you'd tell them to sue straight away. If someone is so concerned about a libel, you would think they'd want to act quickly to clear their name. Not, "Oh, we'll wait a year."'

For Short, the wait would be 'a year of hell'. The action brought against him had the ultimate potential of reaching the Royal Courts of Justice in London – the High Court. The case would only be Part One of the Sheffield-Wednesday-sues-its-own-fans story, however. Part Two came ahead of the 2007/08 season.

* * * *

Over a period of about 11 days through the summer of 2007, when the new season was approaching and talk of transfers and suchlike dominated the footballing discussions up and down the country, many more postings were made on the Owlstalk forum; this time by individuals other than Short. Some of these also caught the attention of Sheffield Wednesday as being offensive – postings again relating to the hierarchy of the club, specifically the board and its upper management, and to the manager Brian Laws.

Among them were comments like, 'When will there be some good news? All this transfer rumour is just pathetic.' And, 'This club is a disgrace at the moment.' There was also one exchange which speculated about what Laws and Kaven Walker might have been getting up to on a recent scouting trip to Holland, during which, it was joked, they 'blew all the [club's] money on hookers'; to which another poster would reply, 'It's not a hooker we need, it's a striker'; in turn prompting the devastating comeback, 'They wouldn't know the difference.' The club actually seemed to take this exchange seriously, apparently having more of an issue with the suggestion that Walker was unable to judge a competent player than the hookers bit.

In response to these comments, and others that had been posted, the club, in order to 'protect its reputation', moved to sue those who had made them, just as they were doing with Short.

This time around, the club needed to find out who the anonymous posters were (unlike with Short: despite his 'Grandad' pseudonym, he was known to the club, but the real names of the other posters were not). So the club and its lawyers requested from the operator of the Owlstalk site, Neil Hargreaves, the names, addresses, e-mail addresses – anything – of the 30 or more posters who were alleged to have made the 'false and defamatory' remarks about the club. Hargreaves, though, refused to give up that information, so Wednesday had to take him to court to get it.

Once again, Mark Lewis became involved. 'Because I was acting for Nigel, I then got to know Neil [Hargreaves],' Lewis explains. 'When he got the solicitors' letter he contacted me.' For Lewis, the whole affair was becoming somewhat inane. 'It was almost to the point where you'd expect people to be going around the ground handing out writs if someone shouted out something that the board didn't like. Something like, "Sack the board."'

For the benefit of those whose details the club had requested, a meeting was arranged in the upstairs room of the Park Hotel pub on Wadsley Lane, just up from the Wednesday ground. That evening, Lewis and his assistant went through with the posters the possible implications of the legal action and what the process would be going forward.

'I remember talking to them for about three and a half hours,' says Lewis, 'taking all their names and details. I remember speaking to people who were all very worried because of what was threatened to them.' Some present at the meeting had families and mortgages to worry about. One man had not even told his wife about the whole thing. That night, Lewis tried to reassure the people at the meeting that the club didn't have much of a case against them. 'I told them that the claims were what was known in legal circles as "bollocks."'

The case to obtain the details of the Owlstalk posters from Neil Hargreaves would be heard the following month, October 2007, at the High Court in London. Before that, though, Lewis had noticed one curiosity relating to the case.

'The claimants,' recalls Lewis, 'were Sheffield Wednesday Football Club Ltd., Dave Allen [chairman] and the rest of the board [Keith Addy, Ashley Carson, Ken Cooke, Bob Grierson, Geoff Hulley; plus chief executive Kaven Walker]. The eighth claimant was Brian Laws, the team's manager. So I put out a press release as soon as I saw that saying, "Sheffield Wednesday Manager Brian Laws Sues Fans!" Laws then said something like, "No, I didn't know I was suing the fans, I'm withdrawing from the case."'

'[W]hen I found out that I might be party to the action… I was furious,' Laws would later write in his autobiography. And, after the press release had filtered through the various news outlets, Laws demanded to be removed from the action. 'You can't have a manager suing his club's fans,' he would write. It would, then, just be Sheffield Wednesday Football Club Ltd., its directors and chief executive that would be involved.

'The [Hargreaves-Owlstalk] case was a situation where the claimants go along to the court and say, "These people are blogging about us, we want to know who they are,"' explains Lewis of the first court hearing. 'It's what lawyers call a Norwich Pharmacal application. We opposed it and the law was refined so that the club had to show that if they were to obtain the posters' details, any action that would later be taken against them was likely to be successful.'

In court, the list of the original 30-plus posters was reduced to 11 individuals whose details the club wanted. Between them, those 11 people had made a total of 14 allegedly libellous postings. The judge would consider each online comment in turn before ruling on whether or not a successful case might be brought against the poster, and whether their identity should subsequently be revealed.

'It is the Claimant's [Wednesday's] case,' judge Richard Parks QC began as he made his ruling in court, 'that the Defendant [Hargreaves] has permitted some users to pursue a sustained campaign of vilification against the Claimants.'

When things got going, nine of the comments were dismissed; Judge Parkes explaining how some of them 'border[ed] on the trivial… [were] barely defamatory or [were] little more than abusive or likely to be understood as jokes.' Some of the postings were dismissed as little more than 'saloon-bar moanings'. '[M]ore serious,' though, the judge went on, 'are those [comments] which may reasonably be understood to allege greed, selfishness, untrustworthiness and dishonest behaviour on the part of the Claimants.'

One such comment came from a poster named 'Vaughan', who, writing of the possible sale of the Southampton striker Grzegorz Rasiak to Wednesday, speculated how 'we never had any intention of buying him… you could hear the collective puckering of sphincters in the Wednesday boardroom from when Southampton said, "Okay, let's talk?" We then offer a ridiculous wage to ensure Rasiak would never be interested.' This comment, Judge Parkes remarked, 'arguably suggests that the directors have shown bad faith in negotiations for new players and damaged the club's reputation in consequence.' The real name of the poster 'Vaughan' would, then, have to be given up to the club.

So would those of 'DJ Mortimer', whose comments had, according to the judge, possibly questioned the trustworthiness of the chief executive Kaven Walker, along with two characters named 'Halfpint' (who turned out to be a grandmother of limited means living in America) and 'Ian', the pair having posted comments about the Wednesday's then chairman, Dave Allen. One comment, made by 'Halfpint', 'may suggest', Judge Parkes reasoned, 'that the Second Claimant is concerned only with his own profit, and not with the [best] interests of the club.'

So, in the end, Parkes would conclude that, 'the Claimants' entitlement to take action to protect their right to reputation outweighs, in my judgment, the right of the authors to maintain their anonymity and their right to express themselves freely.'

Four names, then – four Wednesdayites – would have to be revealed.

'But what happened next,' Lewis explains, 'was that they got that detail [and] then did *nothing* with it.' Just as Nigel Short had experienced, who having been served legal papers had still not actually been sued by the club, Wednesday sat on the information. Exactly what, then, had been the point of all that time and trouble and expense?

Adding to the whole farce was the strange tale of the then chairman of the fans' group Wednesdayite, Darryl Keys, who had also been threatened with a defamation suit from the club for comments he had made regarding the relationship between Wednesdayite and Wednesday.

Back in 2004, Keys had been banned from Hillsborough after he and another individual had organised a series of disaffection (with the club) induced Black Balloon protests at the ground (a ban which was cannily got around thanks to a disguise of glasses, baseball cap and two-day stubble). More recently, though, Keys had claimed that he, as chairman of Wednesdayite, had had some dialogue with one of the club's directors: in the interests of improved relations, and to show that the fans' group had nothing to hide, an offer was made for the director to join the Wednesdayite board.

But thanks to the strained relationship between Wednesdayite and the club, the latter party's directors were apparently not meant to be speaking to the group – at all. So Keys mustn't have been telling the truth when he said that he'd been speaking to a board member, right? Wrong. He had, to one director at a supporters' event. There had been follow-up e-mails and text messages too.

But after Keys publicly mentioned their conversation, he was threatened with a defamation suit for having claimed that the forbidden club-director-and-Wednesdayite dialogue had taken place, when in theory it should not, because the board apparently had not been permitted to speak to the group.

'Trouble was,' explains Lewis, who also represented Keys, 'Darryl *had* spoken to a board member, so he was effectively accused of lying when he was telling the truth.' The club would drop the action when they realised this.

'The club got caught out because in one of the defence letters I'd actually told them certain specific inside information on the club,' explains Keys today, 'information which I could only have got from a director of the club.'

* * * *

Considering everything that had been going on with the club around that time, the Nigel Short case, the Owlstalk case, the Darryl Keys hoo-hah, an aside: what of the commercial arguments for a football club spending its own money to sue its own fans – its own customers?

Talking of Short's case specifically, Lewis considers, 'If you think of Sheffield Wednesday as a business, it sells a product: watching football. In suing Nigel Short, it decided to sue one of its good customers. If you win the case, you'll lose Nigel Short as a fan forever because he ain't going to be going back into the ground afterwards. Also, a number of other people will not be going back into the ground either, because they'll think, "They sue their fans..." There's a matter of principle there. How do you get fans in? By winning. How do you win? By making sure you've got the best players. How do you lose fans? By suing them and by not having the best players because you're spending your money on lawyers.

'So eventually it became more about Sheffield Wednesday suing Nigel Short than the things he had actually said. They said that he had damaged their reputation. But Sheffield Wednesday should have been looking at the business consequences, because suing Nigel Short did them more damage than any of his words did.

'Also, at the very beginning of the case I think Nigel offered them £2,000 to settle. If the club had come back to him on his offer and said, "We'll take £5,000 instead," I think Nigel might have said, "Look, I haven't got £5,000 to give you. But I might be able to give you £2,000 in a down payment and £500 or £250 a month for the next few months." Cases are very stressful, so if as a lawyer I say to you, "You know, you shouldn't pay £5,000, but if you do pay you won't be worried for the next two years over what the outcome of the case is," you'd be paying for peace of mind. A lot of clients will take that peace of mind.

'However, if Nigel had been willing to pay them £5,000, he would have had to pay my legal costs as well [as part of the Conditional Fee Agreement that was in place, his costs would have been due had Short ended the case before it was actually contested in court].

'Now, a libel case would cost much more than Nigel Short was worth and Sheffield Wednesday, if you look at it from a business point of view, went into a case knowing that if they fought it to trial and *lost* they would have to pay their own costs and Nigel's costs, along with a CFA uplift on those costs. This could have been up to £400,000.

'If the club had *won* they still would have to pay their own costs, probably a few hundred thousand pounds. Plus, they probably would have got a little bit from Nigel, but not much. That sort of money could have bought Sheffield Wednesday a new player. And doing that would have achieved two things: it would have got people more interested in the club and it would have stopped them doing this stupid thing of suing fans, which again would have improved the reputation of the club and probably would have stopped the people saying what they were saying in the first place.'

Through November and December 2007 two things happened regarding Sheffield Wednesday, its board and the various legal actions that were, or were not, being taken against its own supporters, Nigel Short and the Owlstalk Four. One, at the club's

AGM one board member and claimant in the cases, Ken Cooke, expressed a wish for the ongoing saga to be brought to a resolution. Two, Short was diagnosed with throat cancer.

'I was given a 30 per cent chance of living,' says Short today, sitting in a quiet corner of a pub near his home on the outskirts of Sheffield.

Following an operation to remove the lump from his neck, Short endured a seven-week course of radiotherapy (35 doses) followed by two doses of chemotherapy for a second lump on his tonsils. From March 2008, from about which time his friend Daryl Keys had taken on the case along with Short's lawyers, he 'focused now on living'.

Before his treatment had begun, he had received an offer from the club: pay your own legal costs – which had by now amassed to around £50,000 – and the club would drop the case.

£50,000.

Perhaps the 'generous' offer, which would have bankrupted Short, was a way for the club to get out before a defeat in court. Who knew? Either way, it was refused. As Lewis explains, 'One, Nigel didn't have £50,000 in his back pocket just to give them. Two, we still believed that the merit of the case was completely the other way. We were going to carry on and beat them.'

So the threat of the potential day in court went on for Short, just as he prepared himself for a gruelling seven weeks of treatment and months of painful recovery afterwards. The 'Owlstalk Four' were left dangling too.

The months rolled on. Short, having completed his treatment in April 2008, spent those months recovering. The sickness gradually alleviating; the painkillers required less frequently. Though he found it massively draining, he had even managed to make it to Hillsborough for the last game of the season: a stay-up finale against Norwich City; the 4-1 win making sure Wednesday weren't going back down to League 1.

Happily, in early September 2008, on the third day of the month, Short would then announce on his blog (which had been keeping his family and friends up to date of the progress of his treatment) the good news, 'And now for the moment we've all been waiting for,' he would write, '...complete remission.' The all-clear. Brilliant news.

And then, a few days after that, Wednesday, just like that, dropped their case against Nigel Short. Two and a half years on from sending him the first warning letter about his online comments it was over. Time had been booked into the Royal Courts of Justice in London to hear his case. That is how serious it had been. That is how close it had come. But with the click of a finger from the club, that was it. Years and months of worry, over. The other actions against the Owlstalk Four would be dropped too.

Over.

* * * *

Lewis says, 'In libel law, you should only ever pursue a case if you're prepared to fight it all the way to trial. You're supposed to have that in all cases, but in libel law particularly.

'At this point I think Sheffield Wednesday realised that it wasn't wise to keep on suing people, that the last thing they wanted was for this to carry on. I suspect at this point somebody had said to them, "What are you doing here?" because suddenly they realised – a football analogy – that they had scored a massive own goal and needed a way out.

'I have to say overall that I didn't think much of the cases. I don't think they should have been pursued. They were examples in the movement of libel bullying where organisations threaten to sue an individual to get them to change their view [later, the *Guardian* columnist George Monbiot would refer to the whole affair as 'the worst example of legal bullying I have ever seen']. The cases were synoptic of a concept of libel bullying that lots of people were doing, saying, "I don't like your opinion, I'm going to serve a writ on you because you don't have as much money as me, so I'll teach you a lesson." And I think they should have been thrown out because that's what football fans say anyway. It was abysmal really.'

* * * *

Owlstalk-Hargreaves would become a reported case and is now even taught to law students at universities, both as an example of the application of a Norwich Pharmacal order and of anonymous internet defamation.

Meanwhile, for Nigel Short reflecting today, he still feels the pain from the whole sorry saga. 'It was scandalous,' he says. 'It had a massive impact on my life and caused all sorts of worry for my family, friends and my partner at the time.' Short, who would go on to become chairman of Wednesdayite, is still a season-ticket holder on the Kop and is as passionate as ever about the club, *his* club.

In June 2009, he and Wednesday would reach an agreement on his outstanding legal costs. As the case never got to court, the no-win-no-fee CFA that had been in place was not applicable and so in the region of £80,000, it is believed, would be paid over for Short's costs. Added to that would be the club's own legal costs.

For Lewis, after helping the Wednesday fans defend themselves against their own football club, he would go on to bring to court the phone-hacking cases that would ultimately play a role in bringing down the *News of the World* newspaper. He is considered one of the country's finest lawyers.

'My profile is different now because people have heard of me,' says Lewis, 'which wasn't my point, wasn't my decision. But I guess that when you get older and more experienced you learn and Nigel's case was part of a thing that led to the *News of the World* closing down. Both were about trying to make people realise that if they took me on, it would be a fight. I wasn't just going to roll over.'

As Short says finally, 'Mark never let go.'

As for those directors and the chief executive, who on behalf of the club had brought the action against Wednesday's own supporters, all of them would, within a few years, be out of the door and out of the picture.

But that, is another story.

15

Lee Strafford: Wednesday Man

For you, the months have rolled by and the project,
the book – this Wednesday story – goes on still.
The e-mails and letters, the phone calls and the big
meetings. More questions and more answers as the
story gets deeper and you work to bring it all together.

Sometimes, you think of your mate Jim's dad's poem,
the one with the line, 'These are things I know.'

I N September 2008, Brian Laws's Sheffield Wednesday were doing averagely in the Championship. After four league games in to the 2008/09 season they had won only once and sat 14th in the table. The main signing that summer had been the combative midfielder James O'Connor, free from Burnley, And over the previous year and a half or so Laws had lost Madjid Bougherra, Chris Brunt and Glenn Whelan.

Off the field, too, the club was in a mess, had been in the process of maybe suing its own fans, and leaderless since the previous November when Dave Allen had departed the club (the void filled to some extent by the chief executive, Kaven Walker). Drifting and in need of something new at the top, along with outside investment – finances still were desperate – something drastic had to happen. A positive change was needed.

It would come in the form of the entrepreneur and Wednesday fan Lee Strafford.

* * * *

Strafford is a Wednesdayite born and bred. For a time as a youngster he lived on the vast Parson Cross estate – thousands of houses sitting a couple of miles up from Hillsborough. At weekends, Strafford would walk down the hill to the match; sometimes, in the days of two-pence fares, taking the bus. He would also spend time living abroad. His father was in the army and for years the family's home was Germany or Cyprus.

A while after Strafford senior had left the army, he set up a telecoms company which offered 'structured cabling services' (specifically, a single-wire solution for telephone, data and video, where before there had been three) to government and big businesses in London. Then aged 14 and disillusioned with school, Lee Strafford went down to the capital to work for his dad. As he worked his way up over the next several years, he showed a talent for tackling complex problems and marshalling a team of workers. 'It was fabulous,' Strafford says of his time in London. 'No responsibilities. No liabilities. Plenty of work. Young and independent. Good times.'

The fallout from the early 1990s recession would, though, kick the business into liquidation, leaving Strafford on the dole. And worse still, his wisdom teeth were breaching. That was 1993, the year of Wednesday's cup-final defeats. 'That was a nightmare,' he says, 'having to watch the finals on television because I couldn't afford to go to Wembley. Andy Linighan, Chris Woods's slippery hands and wisdom teeth is what I remember from that time.'

Strafford would move back to Sheffield, spending a few tough years on the dole before managing to get back on his feet and set up his own telecoms company. Later, he co-founded PlusNet (operating initially under the Force9 Internet brand) as an offshoot of the computer components wholesaler. In 1998 the wholesaler was sold, along with PlusNet, to an American company, Insight Enterprises. Strafford held on to his five per cent of PlusNet shares and would build the company up.

The company ethos, devised and driven forward by Strafford, was to put the customer first, listen to their concerns and address them quickly (technical problems would be tracked via the company's website, for instance). Be open and reactive, honest, respectful and well-governed was the way – get people to *want* to work with you.

In 2004 the company became a great success story of Sheffield's developing technology industry as it floated on the Alternative Investment Market. In 2007, with annual revenues surpassing £50m, PlusNet was bought for £67m by BT. Strafford's share of the sale was £3.2m. If he didn't want to, he never had to work again in his life.

During the rise of PlusNet, the company had taken a hospitality box at Hillsborough for the use of its staff. Between 2005 and 2009 it would sponsor the team strip (£250,000 a year in the Championship, according to Strafford), during which time Strafford was able to build up a good idea of what might be happening behind the scenes at Sheffield Wednesday.

'I was in the corporate area,' he says, 'but I didn't fraternise much with the Ten-Bob Millionaire Mafia – the hangers-on from the Establishment and the old manufacturing era. Not much substance and not much real money. Instead, I'd be speaking to the club's staff. I'm a transparent person and I was always nice and respectful to people, so the staff there would start telling me things: "It's not good, this place," that sort of thing.

'At first, you think it's just gossip; people who are always unhappy in their working environment. But eventually the stories built up into patterns. Above this had also been the Geoff Sheard fiasco and the whole suing the fans thing. I felt I needed to do something.'

Strafford believed that if positive change could be instilled at the club, and if Wednesday were readied ethically, financially and governance-wise for a serious investment process, then new owners could be found for the club.

He offered his services and in September 2008 the lifelong Owls fan and newly-made millionaire, fresh out of the modern and forward-looking, customer-facing business that was PlusNet, was brought on board at Sheffield Wednesday.

We meet in Sheffield, in the middle of town, in the bar of a hotel joined to the Winter Garden development, to talk of how he became involved with the club. Though speaking without much pause, Strafford always speaks in a considered, technical and businesslike way.

'"What are you doing?" I was asked by the directors.

'"Well," I told them. "I'm a fan. I've gone from the dole to having made enough money to never to have to work again. I can put the time in and I've got the connections to help change things – the ownership – and get us somebody new in."'

The board seemed receptive: a new face who might at last be able to help bring investment to the club. Good stuff.

And so Strafford, along with Nick Parker (an experienced finance professional Strafford brought in to work alongside him) got to work trying to improve things at the club.

The first step was to ask Howard Wilkinson to help out on the football side. Everyone knew that Wilkinson cared about the club – his club. He was a popular and respected figure and having more recently worked in the game's political arena (with the FA and as chairman of the League Managers Association), Strafford believed him to be the ideal man to help.

'I actually asked Howard to be chairman,' recalls Strafford, 'and after a stern interrogation of my intentions and our plan, he agreed to work with us. In the end he couldn't be chairman as it might have conflicted with his role with the League Managers body, so he joined us as technical advisor on the footballing side.'

Action would be taken to re-engage the fan base – former players were brought on to the pitch and a big flag was made for the Kop ('Forward Together' it read) – and the club's own staff. Strafford took the time to talk and listen to the people who kept the club running day to day. He got smiles back on people's faces; everyone working towards the common cause.

A suggestion would also be made regarding the legal action still looming against the internet-forum posting fans (Nigel Short and the Owlstalk Four). 'I'd built up PlusNet transparently with my customers,' Strafford says, 'talking to them online. I then watched my football club sue its customers. Now you *can't* threaten your customers, and suing a bunch of fans is suing everyone. It's saying to everyone, "This is not your club and we will take your livelihood away from you." I was just dismayed and appalled by it and it wasn't good for attracting investors.' The legal actions would be dropped.

In Strafford's words, he and Parker then began 'updating everything. There'd been no appetite for developing things in the long term at the club. It was clear, as one example, that a strategy was needed for season tickets, how they were priced and marketed. There was no sensible plan for families, for bringing younger fans through. They'd followed the same processes for the past 20 years.'

A new ticketing strategy would, then, be introduced, along with things like new catering arrangements ('You're supposed to provide a decent catering experience and make some good money out of it, but we weren't') and plans for a better kit-manufacturing deal ('We'd had a product that kept getting worse and worse'). Later, sponsorship of the shirts would be given away to the local children's hospital. 'I was certain that replacing a crap product with a good product that was linked to a charitable brand would not only drive sales of shirts but also become part of the healing process of the club,' Strafford explains. £1 per shirt sold would go to the hospital.

'There were also some unprofessional practices around the playing side as well,' remembers Strafford, 'around the recruitment and due diligence of players, medically etc. But we'd had no real detailed understanding of these issues until we were in a position of authority. It was mind-blowing how much had to be overhauled.'

Significant effort would also be made fostering a good relationship with the club's biggest lenders, the Co-op Bank. 'We went off and spoke to them,' Strafford explains. 'We told them that we were looking to bring in some new investment or carry out a restructuring, and there was palpable belief from them. "We've checked you out," they told us. "You and Nick [Parker] have the ability to sort things out. And Lee, you care about the club."'

An initial business plan would be developed, informed by answers to questions Strafford and Parker had previously asked about the club's finances, to present to those potential investors.

After that initial work, just before Christmas 2008, three months after they had first become involved with the club, Strafford and Parker were formally co-opted to the board of Sheffield Wednesday. Strafford became chairman.

* * * *

On the investment front, a promising four-party group soon emerged. There was talk of £20m: £5m each in the form of fresh investment, debt restructuring (which included getting the bank onside with a £2m repayment) and a share-dilution exercise. 'They were credible people with letters of intent,' Strafford explains of the group. The four parties, Strafford says, were: Tim Crown of Insight Enterprises (who had backed PlusNet), the Hero Fund (backed by the Emirates Bank), Spice Group (an Indian funder of the A1 Grand Prix series) and the venture capitalists Clearbrook Capital.

Up to that point things had seemed positive and forward-moving, but one issue remained: the club's chief executive, Kaven Walker. 'There were questions that came to our attention,' explains Strafford, 'over things like kit deals. Plus there was the Geoff Sheard thing, and Kaven had been central in the suing the fans episode.'

In fact, Strafford had had concerns about him stretching back to the pair's first interactions when PlusNet had first taken on sponsorship of the club's strip – one 'shocking' meeting in particular that, as Strafford recalls, became 'seared into my memory. "Oh God,"' he remembers thinking that day.

Despite a charm offensive from Walker begun around the time Strafford arrived at the club, the latter felt that the former had to go.

'I approached some of the older board members and said, "Look, Kaven wasn't really part of the plan going forward anyway. He's got to go now."

'We then spoke to Kaven and basically said that he couldn't continue in his role. Initially, he couldn't believe what was happening. Then he started being quite disruptive, saying a few things that referenced quite an aggressive stance, to which we said, "Look, you're better off keeping things as clean as possible."'

Walker would leave in December 2008 with a settlement of around £300,000, a detail Strafford was not happy about. 'I actually wanted him fired,' he says. 'I didn't think he would contest it. But in the end, I was a single vote against everybody else.' The announcement made after he left would explain that the departure was by mutual consent.

'Right up to that very point there had been a really, really nega-tive atmosphere at the club,' says Strafford, 'but a cloud lifted after that.

'We'd actually asked Brian Laws and Sean McAuley in for meetings immediately after that, so they had been sat outside the office waiting. Brian was first to come in. We sat down and, well, there was a bit of humour in it, because he was sat there thinking, "Well I'm going to get fired now too," and I should really have stayed professional, but a smile broke out on my face. Then Brian [who had endured what he would describe as a 'challenging relationship' with Walker] relaxed and started chuckling. He reached over, patted me on the shoulder and said, "It doesn't matter what you do going forward, nothing will be more important to this football club than what you just did." That was pretty big.'

Since Strafford's arrival at the club, the belief of his manager Brian Laws had been building steadily. He was, it was said, openly more relaxed and seemingly happier; a new man who hailed the Strafford period as a 'new dawn'.

Results on the pitch were more positive too – Marcus Tudgay's belting 25-yard strike securing a 2-1 win at the Lane against Sheffield United; a 4-2 win coming at Burnley; plus a few good home wins with some nice football being played.

Wednesday would finish the season 12th and there were feelings of optimism about what could happen both on and off the field in the future.

Following Walker's departure, Strafford had to go back to the four-party £20m group to alleviate any concerns that may have arisen from that parting of ways between the club and its chief executive, and any due diligence issues which may have related to that.

'I went off and spoke to them,' recalls Strafford. 'The Americans, Tim Crown; he'd worked with me previously at PlusNet, so he trusted me. I told him that the situation was fixable, that we'd sort it out. Give us some time. The venture capitalists told us to work it out, demonstrate that we'd sorted the issues out, then come back and talk to us again.'

Sadly, the other two parties weren't as positive or as patient. 'So at that point we were in a position where we didn't have all the investment committed anymore. We needed to rebuild.'

In May 2009, Strafford took a trip to America to seek out potential alternate investors. 'We'd some great meetings lined up,' he explains. 'Meetings with people who owned sports assets over there, plus pretty much all of the key intermediaries that do the deals in US sports, whether that's for stadium financing or team trades. One big group involved in that was Inner Circle Sports (ICS).'

ICS was a 'boutique investment bank focused on the global sports industry' that had helped broker George Gillett's and Tom Hicks's takeover-turned-sour of Liverpool, then New England Sports Ventures' subsequent takeover of the Reds.

'I thought ICS were too big and that there was no way they were going to take our deal on,' says Strafford. 'The only reason I wanted to meet them was so that they would recommend our deal if they were asked by someone else about us. But once I'd outlined the deal to them – potentially massive club, assets intact, stadium needs some development but the club had a plan to be run properly – they in fact turned round and said that *they* wanted to help do the deal. I was blown away.'

As matchmakers in any deal, ICS would have been due up to £1m in success fees.

'We then did a whole bunch of due diligence work with ICS. Nick [Parker] worked with Paul Johnson [the club's day-to-day accountant] to answer all of their questions, and the answers that came back were that the club was cash neutral; that it spent what it earned.'

While the club had posted profits of £1.4m in 2006/07 and £2.2m in 2007/08, helped by the sales of Madjid Bougherra for £2.5m and Chris Brunt for £2.5m plus add-ons, 2008/09's figures, to be released in early 2010, would ultimately show a different picture: a £3.7m loss, even after the £500,000 sale of Glenn Whelan.

'After that,' says Strafford, 'Inner Circle started marketing us and the belief that something could happen was building.'

* * * *

Added to Strafford's feeling of optimism and positivity around the whole project was the club's possible involvement in England's bid to host the 2018 World Cup.

The Football Association had decided that it was going to put its name in the hat to host the tournament, going up against such other nations as Russia. Later in 2009, the FA would choose which clubs' grounds it wanted to be part of its bid.

What with the challenges Wednesday were trying to work through at the time, the club were not ideally set up to put together their own bid to be considered. For Strafford, however, who was conscious of Sheffield United's intention to have Bramall Lane included on the initial list of possible venues, Wednesday simply had to be involved. Sheffield and Hillsborough had successfully hosted games during the World Cup in 1966, and the European Championship in 1996, and he thought they should do again.

'So we put together our bid, doing it the way I did all of those things – I got a load of people together and asked them to work for nowt, to work for the good of the city and the club. The result was that a whole bunch of Sheffield Wednesday supporters that had the capabilities applicable to a bid helped out and were brilliant.'

The plans released for a redeveloped Hillsborough World Cup venue were impressive. An increase in its capacity to over 44,000, brought by the infilling of the corners between the Kop and North Stand and West and South Stands; a row of new executive boxes on the North; new roofs for the Kop and West; plus the creation of associated educational, community and business facilities around the ground. The development would cost over £22m; funded, says Strafford, by community and government grants and future extra revenues.

In late 2009, the FA made its decision. The preferred venue for Sheffield would be... Hillsborough – and not Bramall Lane. Hooray! Naturally the Blades were annoyed and tried to apply for judicial review against the council for showing bias towards Wednesday (specifically, for the speed at which the Owls were awarded planning permission for their proposed development). But the attempt didn't get very far.

Of course, however, as FIFA would controversially choose Russia ahead of England to host the Cup, the whole point became moot anyway.

According to Wednesday's accounts, a total of £410,000 would be spent on the bid (£202,000 in 2009/10 and £208,000 in 2010/11). 'In the end, we couldn't do the plans for nowt,' admits Strafford.

Though he does doubt that the total costs, of which £208,000 was incurred between June 2010 and May 2011 (after the FA had selected Hillsborough as the Sheffield option), were really that high. 'I just don't see what those second-year costs are,' he says.

The city council's reputed payment to the FA to be part of the bid was £250,000.

* * * *

For the 2009/10 season, a bold budget had been set for the club. 'The initial due diligence which had been done showed that the club was cash neutral, cash break-even,' explains Strafford. 'We'd got the help of the uplifting of the TV money as well. That was a couple of million quid and gave us the opportunity to bring in some players. And subject to the season tickets and everything else coming through on target [the aim for season ticket sales for 2009/10 was 16,500 versus the 12,000 sold the previous season], that should have given us enough to plan for a mid-table finish, maybe even sneak into the play-offs. That would have given us the platform to be able to get a deal done on the club.'

In the end, the season tickets didn't come in on target. Although increasingly supportive of the changes that had been made under Strafford so far, Wednesday's fan base was still fairly bruised from the various 'events' of recent years and take-up on the tickets was not as good as had been hoped. This shortfall would lead to the budget being adjusted down by around £300,000, which in turn would cause Brian Laws's recruitment to be paused following the free-transfer arrivals of the experienced defender Darren Purse and midfielder Tommy Miller. Marcus Tudgay, Lee Grant and Tommy Spurr would, at least, be secured on new contracts at various points over those months.

Disappointingly, as the season got under way, Wednesday would manage to win only three of their opening 11 league games. Defeat would also come at Port Vale in the League Cup, with Francis Jeffers contributing to events by getting himself sent off for headbutting an opponent.

More positively, on the investment front, Inner Circle Sports continued to shop Wednesday around, hoping to attract an investor to the club.

But then, a problem would emerge with the finances and everything hit the fan.

This is how Strafford tells it:

'Nick Parker had been working really closely with Paul Johnson on the numbers and we were there or thereabouts on the budget – just a few hundred grand out because of the season tickets. Then, one day, Nick turns around and says that the numbers are looking off, that there was a gap appearing in our finances.

'The first question from me was, "How big is this gap?"

'"A few hundred grand," he said.

'"Okay," I said. "Do we know how big this gap is going to get?"

'"I don't know yet, I haven't finished digging."

'"Okay. You carry on digging and we'll find a few hundred grand."'

The result of this was Richard Wood going out on loan; sent to Coventry, at first on loan, but later the move was made permanent for a pre-agreed £300,000.

It was Strafford who had to break the news to Laws that there had been a problem and one of his better players now had to go. 'There's been a problem,' Strafford explained to Laws. 'The numbers have been screwed up and we're digging into what's going on. But, bottom line, we need to raise a few hundred grand and someone needs to go.'

'Unfortunately,' says Strafford, 'all of the confidence that Brian had been showing up to that point fell apart on the back of that blow.'

Strafford also now had to inform the bank of the problem. 'We were transparent with them and they said, "Well, yeah, sell a player and it'll be all right."'

But the plot would thicken.

'As we went into Christmas [2009], the picture building was that there was actually a bigger hole than we first had thought, more like £1.5m. Basically, the cash profile of the business looked very different to the model that we'd been given originally when we had put the original business plan together. The club was burning £1.5m every year and was only cash neutral after player sales. It hadn't been my job to look at the numbers, but Lord I wish I had. The process had found that we [Strafford and Parker] had been misled.

'Nick was really angry when he was talking to me and I was saying to Nick, "This is going to compromise our ability to do a deal. All the work we've done to get to this point will have been a waste."'

Nick Parker would go on to tell the board, 'The management accounts did not tie in with the budget that had been presented to the club's bank and are not what [investment brokers] Inner Circle Sports are working from.'

Later, he would also say, 'The club has been cash negative not just this year but in previous years and it would have been better if that had been made clear before now.'

Further on in the year, though, he would curiously change his stance, reputedly remarking how 'The infamous hole in the accounts is rubbish' and blaming any shortfalls that had emerged on 'a very ambitious budget... that wasn't achieved'. When asked to contribute to this book, Parker politely declined.

'Look,' Strafford would explain to the board, 'this club isn't investor-ready. We've told the investors it is, but it isn't.'

There are strong suggestions that other members of the board might have been aware of such a shortfall. Later, when the minutes from a heated board meeting were published in the *Yorkshire Post*, a reference to the £1.5m gap in the finances was made in them; the minutes noting, 'that he [Bob Grierson, Wednesday's long-serving finance director] chose not to say anything [about the gap] because if we [the club] had hit the revenue numbers there would have been no problem'. Such a revelation would prove hard to take for Strafford.

Strafford also had to explain the situation to the Co-op Bank. '"Look," we said to them,' Strafford recalls, '"we did a budget based on the numbers we were given, we then uplifted that budget based on the uplifted TV income, but we've been misled about the figures." At that point, they were still supportive but obviously concerned.'

He also informed Inner Circle Sports who, according to Strafford, now became worried that the work they were doing on behalf of the club would damage their reputation. Interest in the club then seemed to cool.

One party, Club 9 Sports, a Chicago-based subsidiary of a banking firm, had been on the scene. Brought to the table by ICS, there had been talk of a £20m investment from them. But when the group's main backer detached himself from the group, things fell away. In subsequent months Club 9 would return to make lower and lower offers for the club, at one point offering £2m for 40 per cent of the shareholding while taking over £400,000 per year in 'management fees'. They would be told to get lost.

To cope with the shortfall in the finances – the £1.5m 'hole' – the club briefly stopped paying its creditors and even borrowed against future season-ticket sales. Meanwhile, Laws would be told that at least another one of his better players would now have to be moved on.

This further blow seemed to signal the end for Laws. With his team having not won since mid-October and now sitting in the relegation places, in Strafford's words, 'Brian had just crumbled, basically. His fire and imagination and self-confidence went. His ability to get the team to perform had gone.

'Everyone can recognise when someone has lost the fight, whether they're conscious of it or not,' explains Strafford. 'They're either there, with the energy and the ideas, or they're not. And there was a difference now in Brian. It was a nightmare. We knew he wasn't going to be able to inspire the players to give the performances that were needed to keep us up.'

Laws had continued to do his best to turn the results around, keeping positive in front of the players. 'His relationship with us never changed,' remembers defender Darren Purse. Yet as goalkeeper Lee Grant recalls, 'I think deep down at that stage he would have had huge questions and reservations over where the club was heading.' With the defeats piling up, decisive action would be taken.

In late December 2009, the Owls turned up at Milan Mandarić-owned Leicester City and lost 3-0. Afterwards, Brian was sacked as Wednesday manager.

It was a very difficult moment for Strafford. 'I had a brilliant relationship with Brian,' he says. 'I had so much respect for him, considering what he'd had to deal with off the field. But I was sat there thinking, "He's got to go. It's just not recoverable, this." It was such a shame because if we'd had a real budget, based on real information, we could have done a deal with an investor and everything would have been all right.'

'I was drained physically and mentally,' Laws would recall of himself following his dismissal. And he was gone.

Thoughts now turned to his successor.

'We had a plan for two sets of circumstances for a new manager,' explains Strafford of the plan to find Laws's successor. 'One with investment and one without investment. And the reality at the time was that because there hadn't been any deal yet, you had to hire against the no-investment option.

'We had to go for a manager who not only could understand the big historical context of the club and the pressure of working in that situation, but who also was willing to come in and work under the restricted budget and [on] the basis that investment might never happen. Also we wanted a proper technical football manager and ideally someone who had experience of a relegation battle. On that basis, a big long list of potentials then turned into quite a short one.

'Loads and loads of people still applied for the job [28 apparently showed some interest]. Some applications were hilarious. Some were unsurprising. Some weren't. Some of those who applied shouldn't have been applying because they were already in jobs.'

Then, out of the blue, the promising Preston North End manager Alan Irvine (once David Moyes's assistant) was sacked. Despite the firing, Irvine was still a rising and well-regarded manager who had recently taken Preston to the play-off semi-finals, and Wednesday were interested. Irvine was interviewed. The Owls liked what they heard and Irvine was appointed.

'I am delighted to take up the position,' said Wednesday's eighth manager in a decade. 'It is a club with great traditions and a brilliant outlook for the future.'

Five wins from his first seven games made people believe things would be okay, that the club might avoid the drop. As Irvine's assistant, Rob Kelly, explains of the initial turnaround, 'We freshened it up, gave the players a different kind of organisation and took the pressure off them really. A different approach. Something new. We concentrated on individual and collective performances and we got a good reaction.'

Irvine won the Championship Manager of the Month award for January and, going into the Nottingham Forest away game in early February 2010, Wednesday were out of the relegation places and looking upwards. Things seemed to be going well.

Time, then, for some more off-field drama to disrupt things, this time revolving around an impromptu Wednesday board meeting scheduled to be held at Forest's City ground.

* * * *

Since becoming involved with the club, Strafford and Nick Parker had been getting on well with the ethical Manchester Co-operative Bank. And, up until being told about the £1.5m-hole-in-the-budget issue, the bank had appeared to be largely satisfied with what they were trying to achieve.

The week after the Forest away game, a meeting was due to take place in Manchester between the club and the bank to discuss an upcoming £500,000 interest payment on the club's loans. As chairman of the club, Strafford expected to attend. However, according to him, the club's finance director Bob Grierson didn't want him to go and instead wanted to attend himself, along with Parker. Remarkably, again according to Strafford, a discussion over who would be going to the meeting was now scheduled to take place at a specially arranged board meeting... to be held at Nottingham Forest's City Ground!

'Apparently,' recalls Strafford, 'they [various members of the board] had been talking the day before the game and had decided that they were going to organise a room at Forest. I couldn't believe it. There we were trying to stay in the division, trying to show the new manager that the club was being run properly, and then they go and do this.

'The first thing that went through my head was, "Why didn't Nick [Parker] tell them to fuck off?" So I asked him and he goes, "Ummm, I don't really know what to say."

'"God, get a backbone," I thought.

'The second thing that went through my head was that this was going to get into the dressing rooms. If you're going to hold a board meeting [at Forest], you've got to ask Forest if you can do that, and it would not be in their interests to keep that a secret. And if the opposition know this kind of disruption was going on it could help them.

'So I got to Forest and told Nick that there was no way there was going to be any board meeting. Nick said that Howard [Wilkinson] had talked them into cancelling it, so it never happened. But the damage had already been done.

'Now, I'd been in some scrapes as a lad. But that was the closest I came to forgetting who I was, where I was and the role that I had as chairman of Sheffield Wednesday Football Club. Bunch of old farts. Organising a meeting like that at someone else's club. Absolute disgrace to our football club. And did we win that game? No, we didn't.'

Wednesday lost 2-1.

When everyone had returned to Sheffield, it was agreed that Grierson would go with Parker to the meeting at the bank (during which it would be agreed that Wednesday could defer the £500,000 interest payment that was due to the bank – the 'special relationship' the club seemed to enjoy with the bank continuing nicely). But, in addition, that there would be a second meeting that Strafford would attend during which he would, in his words, 'discuss the issue around being misled on the finances'. Not long after that second meeting with the bank, things would turn quite unpleasant in the Wednesday boardroom.

For it was during the March 2010 board meeting that Grierson would go on the attack against Strafford. Focusing on the commercial direction that the club had taken under the new chairman, and his inability so far to bring any investment into the club, Grierson pretty much laid into him and heavily criticised Strafford's performance since he had become involved with the club.

The attack, made on the record in the Hillsborough boardroom and subsequently published in the *Yorkshire Post*, makes compelling reading.

'You have consistently said you had unearthed new revenue streams that was [*sic*] funding the increased player budget,' Grierson said. '[But] the accounts show that far from finding new revenue streams you have destroyed existing profitable cost centres.

'You have been pleading with fans to renew season tickets… saying it was in order to enable you to ascertain the player budget… [But] the facts are that the money was needed desperately to shore up the cash-flow.

'You turned down £100,000 in shirt sponsorship, deciding to give the sponsorship to the Children's Hospital for nothing.

'You have decided to change shirt supplier, which could cost us £300,000 in breach of contract [though, according to Strafford, it didn't – the new manufacturer Puma paid for it].

'You decided to bring the concourse catering in-house, costing the club £250,000 for breach of contract.

'You have lied to the fans and are still doing so.

'I could go on.'

Strafford would refute the claims, labelling the comments 'a completely unfair and baseless character assassination'. A long statement would be issued in which he defended himself, noting how in light of the alleged £1.5m gap in the accounts, he and Parker 'had had no visibility as to the [club's] true financial model'; he added that Grierson had told him 'the club was cash neutral… and was clean in terms of due diligence issues' but that 'neither of these statements [was] true'. He concluded there was 'no doubt whatsoever that it will be shown that the net shortfall in cash correlates more to the missing £1.5m… than [to] any mismanagement by myself and Nick Parker'.

Indeed, when released, the 2009/10 accounts would show an increase of £2m in matchday receipts and associated turnover, from an increased average attendance of 1,638, plus an extra £695,000 in revenue from commercial activities.

Strafford would also point out how, during Grierson's tenure as finance director, 'controlling finance' at the club, Wednesday had moved 'from cash-rich at the top of the Premier League to debt-burdened and in the third tier of football'.

Amid the Owls' vital run-in to the end of 2009/10, all of this off-field infighting was casting an unwanted shadow over the club. It was the last thing the team needed, as despite an excellent initial run under their new manager Alan Irvine, a drop-off in results had meant that relegation was becoming a more and more realistic potential outcome to the season. After a win over Watford at Hillsborough in March, form became desperate and Wednesday now found themselves in real trouble.

Darren Purse offers a candid insight into why things had gone wrong. 'With the squad of players that we had,' says Purse, 'we should have been in the top half of the table, trying to get in the play-offs. But we suffered from a lack of work ethic and that's why we were down there. It wasn't because we weren't good enough.

It was because we didn't work hard enough. And that's one of the worst things you can say as a footballer.'

Once again, for the second time in three seasons, Wednesday would have to endure yet more last-day-of-the-season drama as they scrapped with Crystal Palace for survival.

Going into the final game, Palace sat 22nd in the Championship table (there because they had received a ten-point penalty for entering administration that season): one position and two points above the Owls. The scenario for the last-day showdown, then: Wednesday needing a win to jump over Palace and stay up, with any other outcome condemning them to relegation to League 1.

As ever for such an occasion at Hillsborough, over 37,000 fans would be there in the ground, along with the television cameras, for the big nervous season finale.

Making the 30-minute journey from his home to the ground, Strafford, despite everything that had been going on behind the scenes at his club in recent weeks and months, was feeling positive about the win-or-nothing game. 'I was feeling optimistic. There was a fabulous energy from the fans leading up to the game and at kick-off,' he remembers, 'what an atmosphere it was. And that created a confidence in everybody. There was a determination.'

There would, though, be no happy ending for Wednesday. The game finished 2-2 and the Owls, having twice trailed and twice come back, were relegated. Down, down, down... back to the third tier.

In the stands there were tearful eyes and bowed and shaking heads. Down on the pitch, players laid on the grass, dejected, heads in their hands. Strafford, watching on, was feeling a similar pain. Wednesday were down.

* * * *

Through the fallout and the heartbreak of relegation, Strafford had decided that the only thing for him to do now was to take some win-or-bust action of his own: he would try to get Bob Grierson removed from the Wednesday board. It was a move that Strafford saw as absolutely necessary if he was to carry on as chairman.

'There was a conversation that needed to happen,' he says. 'So we [he and Nick Parker] sat down and talked with representatives of one board member. Going into that meeting, I had said to Nick, "If you don't say the right kind of things in this meeting, then it's done with." The articles of the club dictated that all board members have to vote to get rid of one board member, so if Nick stood by me we would be able to see this through.

'But he didn't say the right things.

'So, they turn up, and started ripping into what we'd done over the last few years. I couldn't believe it. Then they turned to Nick and said, "Well, either Lee goes or Bob [Grierson] goes, what's your plan?" And Nick says – and I'll never forget this – "I serve at the pleasure of the board." He turns to me and tells me, "You need to go, Lee." My world fell apart at that moment. Never in my wildest dreams did I see that coming.

'I told them, "This is a crazy decision. The fans are not going to support you guys going forward. But I will go."

'So I went.

'There was one last board meeting and the agenda was: What's next? What is the plan for League 1: follow a promotion budget backed by the Co-op or cut costs? I sat in on that meeting, then drafted my resignation.' After such promising beginnings, it was a sad end for a good Wednesday man.

For Strafford, however, although hurt and betrayed, misled and 'screwed' by those still in power at the club, other things could take his attention. He had a young family, enough money never to have to work again, and other technology projects in Sheffield and further afield to help out with: he'd be fine.

Among other projects Strafford is now working with the city's emerging technology community, imparting his knowledge and experience to mentor emerging tech entrepreneurs whose businesses are helping the city to find its new economic identity.

'It's all about digital-led innovation,' he explains more enthusiastically after hours and hours of talking about his Wednesday experiences. 'In Sheffield, we've got a track record of hundreds of years of innovation in steel and manufacturing. No question there's always going to be a place for high-value manufacturing in the city. And a large conurbation is always going to support a good services industry. But the driver in an economy is digital. So we've set about building an ecosystem that will help people build technology businesses in the north. We've had fantastic support and it's been incredibly rewarding. Not financially – I've not had a wage packet in years – but it's been brilliant.'

Following his experiences of life at the helm of Sheffield Wednesday, Strafford is glad to have found something more rewarding; an arena where his help is more appreciated; somewhere that he is able to make more of a difference.

And still, as he walked out of the club in May 2010, he wasn't quite finished with Wednesday yet. He still had a significant part to play in the future of the club… *his* club.

16

Wind-Ups

THROUGH the past three decades, Howard Wilkinson has been a well-known figure in the game. As a manager he was a First Division championship winner with Leeds United. As a footballing politician, technical advisor to the FA and chairman of the League Managers Association.

Wilkinson grew up a mile out of the city centre and as a youngster would travel to Hillsborough by tram, then be carried through the Kop turnstiles on the shoulders of his father to watch his heroes play: Jackie Sewell, Albert Quixall and the loyal club servant Redfern Froggatt.

And Wilkinson became a decent footballer himself. A winger, he was offered terms by Don Revie's Leeds but instead went with his heart and chose Wednesday, even though the offer was for less money. 'I never did have much sense,' he says today, sitting, relaxed, in his living room in a leafy Sheffield suburb, a smile creeping across his face.

Later, following playing spells with Brighton and Boston United, then his swift ascendance as a coach for Notts County, Wilkinson returned to Hillsborough in 1983 to take over from Jack Charlton as Wednesday boss, lifting the club back to the First Division.

Howard Wilkinson: Sheffield Wednesday fan, Sheffield Wednesday player, Sheffield Wednesday manager.

From March 1984 to 12 months later, when the miners' strike raged in Yorkshire and beyond, Wilkinson, whose father had been a miner, was vocal in his support for their cause. 'The chairman [Bert McGee] gave me a very serious talking-to for some of the things I was saying in public,' Wilkinson recalls, 'all pro-miner stuff. But I'm a Sheffield lad. I'd come back to Sheffield to manage a Sheffield club. We'd got a lot of fans from around the area. A lot of them were miners. So I didn't want to stop what I was saying.' He cared about them and he cared about their fight. 'It was about more than just jobs. It was about communities and a way of life.'

After Wednesday, had been Leeds, before his career had taken a predominantly political path (save for a few more brief managerial stints at club and international level), most notably with the FA, where Wilkinson would hone his footballing administration skills. Then, in the summer of 2010, when his club, the club he cared about, needed him, he became at age 66 interim chairman of Sheffield Wednesday.

Howard Wilkinson: Sheffield Wednesday fan, player, manager and now, Sheffield Wednesday chairman.

* * * *

Wilkinson had been working with Lee Strafford and Nick Parker on a technical basis since January 2009 and now, following the last-day relegation of 2009/10 and Strafford's departure from the club, with Wednesday again finding itself chairman-less and rudderless, Wilkinson was asked to step forward and step in (the League Managers Association, the body which he also chaired, would agree that under the circumstances he could carry on in both roles).

'The board asked me because they thought I was the best person to deal with the situation at the time,' he explains. 'Obviously we had got relegated to League 1 and it had become very apparent to everyone that the next season would be a problem. I knew from day one that the financial situation of the football club was precarious [the club's debt, comprising both bank borrowings and directors' loans, now stood at over £25m]. But we had to get on with everything, focusing especially on trying to sell, and therefore save, the club.'

Despite an expected £2m–£3m drop-off in revenue for the upcoming season due to the relegation (a drop that ended up being more like £4.4m) Wednesday were still set to follow an aspirational promotion budget for the upcoming season, with significant sums still to be spent on player wages. It was an approach that would give manager Alan Irvine a good chance of returning the club to the Championship at the first go.

Early in the summer he'd been busy revamping his team, with big-earning Francis Jeffers and Michael Gray leaving the club, along with Leon Clarke, Etienne Esajas, the youngster Sean McAllister and the much-liked though now injury-troubled American defender Frankie Simek. In their place came eight new players, all of them free transfers, among them the Scottish winger Gary Teale, Chris Sedgwick and the promising midfielder Giles Coke. Later, Neil Mellor, once of Liverpool, would also be signed on a season-long loan from Preston North End.

[Louis Clay]

On paper, the group Irvine had assembled looked capable of making good strides towards the top places in the League 1 table. 'We were given a competitive budget,' recalls Irvine's assistant, Rob Kelly. 'We'd got some people in who we thought could cope with wearing a Sheffield Wednesday shirt. We tried to go with solid citizens, people who could handle it.'

The opening few games of the season would see Wednesday playing confidently, purposefully and, most importantly, winningly – three victories and one draw from the first four games.

* * * *

Off the pitch, however, there'd been trouble at the club.

Through the summer cash had generally become tighter and tighter, with creditors such as the Sheffield Children's Hospital (who were owed money as part of the arrangement to have its logo appear on the Wednesday strip and £1 to be paid to the hospital for every replica shirt sold) and HMRC, owed £550,000 in PAYE, not being paid. HMRC, not covered by the Football League's football creditors rule (which saw other clubs, players and managers etc. paid before creditors, such as HMRC), was now ready to push hard for its money.

Through 2010, Wednesday and a number of other football clubs had chosen to delay VAT and PAYE payments that were due to the tax authorities, effectively using HMRC as an unofficial overdraft facility. Now, though, HMRC was coming down on clubs for delayed or non-payment and, in order to push them into paying, several of these clubs were issued with winding-up petitions (essentially, requests to liquidate an insolvent company). Sheffield Wednesday was one of them. This was serious: the company, the football club, could be put out of business. 'I think at that point [the] government said, "Enough is enough as far as football is concerned,"' recalls Wilkinson of the situation. 'And I knew then that we'd got a problem.'

Upon the announcement of the petition in July 2010, chief executive Nick Parker would come out with this surprising comment, 'As part of our ongoing pressure on cash-flow, we have decided to adopt the same approach as other clubs to HMRC [that is, to not pay them]. A consequence of this has been this court order, which is similar to those received by Preston, Cardiff and many other clubs.'

The winding-up petition was due to be faced in court on 11 August 2010. Cash, now, was needed to make the problem go away.

A bid 'in the region' of £1m (though probably less) was received from Burnley, now managed by Brian Laws, for goalkeeper Lee Grant and reluctantly accepted. 'It would be wrong of me to say that I was looking to get out of Wednesday,' says Grant today. 'I was sad to leave. But with the winding-up petition it was pretty clear why I had to be sold.' The fee received for him would temporarily ease the club's cash-flow problems, HMRC received a 'substantial' payment towards the amount it was owed, the hearing for the winding-up petition was adjourned until 8 September – breathing space in which to find more cash – and the club's transfer embargo lifted (for now). Nicky Weaver, the former Manchester City man and keen Wednesdayite, was brought in on a free transfer to replace the outgoing Grant.

It was a close shave – the winding-up petition temporarily averted. But Wednesday were by no means out of the woods yet.

By the time of the club's adjourned court date on 8 September, Wednesday, despite having made the 'substantial' payment to HMRC following Lee Grant's sale, now owed it £1.1m. Some £703,000 of this was due immediately, meaning that unless they paid up, the club either was about to be wound up and put out of business, or put into administration, which would bring, among other things, a ten-point deduction in League 1.

And with no buyer or investor even on the horizon at that stage, the Co-op Bank was left as the only party that could, it seemed, help the club. Chairman Howard Wilkinson knew that well, so he got on the phone.

'We had reached the 11th hour. We were about to be wound up. You clutch at straws, you know,' recalls Wilkinson of that time, 'and I had to use imaginative ways – which we won't talk about here – to persuade them [the bank] to help. I'm not going to go into what I said, but my arguments to persuade them to help us out and pay HMRC were verging on blackmail looking back.

'I've never been in that situation before in my life but at that moment I was desperate and using anything I could do to fight. I'm sorry about it, but that was the situation. Fortunately, they did come back at the 11th hour, plus 59 minutes, and said, "Okay, this time we'll do it." So they lent us a bit more and paid HMRC for us.'

It was the night before the rearranged petition was due to be heard that the bank agreed to step in and stump up the £703,000 (or £780,000 once associated fees were included) that was required for HMRC. The 'special' relationship between bank and club kept on giving.

With the payment, the winding-up petition was delayed. 'But,' Wilkinson explains, 'we were still on death row unless we could get a big injection of funds.' The message from the bank now being: go away and get it sorted.

But that was easier said than done. Wednesday had been trying to attract investment for a long time and up to now nothing had materialised. And as Wilkinson recalls of the reality of the situation at the time, 'Nick Parker sat through meeting after meeting with people who said they were seriously interested and had serious money. People you just had to listen to just in case.' But invariably nothing would come of those meetings. 'It was like trying to push custard uphill,' he says.

Unfortunately, back on the pitch, after the bright beginnings of the season, things had also begun to deteriorate for Alan Irvine's men.

Though in early September the Owls were unbeaten and sat at the top of the table, at Brentford, against the division's bottom side, Wednesday were awful, dominated by the home side to lose 1-0. The high-flying Owls had dipped, and were destined to dip further still.

Had something to do with the club's day in court to face the ultimately averted winding-up petition, as it was then only days away? There was a general cloud of uncertainty hanging heavy over the club for at that point it wasn't known that the Co-op would come to Wednesday's (temporary) rescue. Administration had seemed a realistic option. As the defender Darren Purse recalls, the team perhaps were affected by the off-field events. 'Players always say that they aren't aware of things like that,' he says. 'But you knew what was going on. When you're involved in that situation you try to say all the right things to the press: "We don't know what's going on. We just want to concentrate on the football." But of course it's going to affect you. You're always aware of it.'

Irvine would insist that his team were unaffected by what the club was going through. 'We don't talk about it,' he said. But as Purse's comments demonstrate, it very probably did have an effect. The players were not in a bubble and Wednesday's form after the Brentford defeat would read LLLD; the continued uncertainty even after the Co-op Bank's intervention perhaps still hanging.

The limp home defeat to Southampton at the end of September was a low point and after the game a group of seriously fed-up fans gathered under the South Stand. They wanted someone from the club, from the board, to come out and speak to them about exactly what was going on. Wilkinson stepped forward.

'Well, we were in the boardroom,' he remembers, 'and someone said there was a crowd outside the front door. I was being told that it wasn't safe to go out etc. But I thought, "No. Why shouldn't I go out? Am I going to get shot? Am I going to get assaulted? What's the worst that can happen to me?" I think that if you're the leader there are times when you've got to go out and face the music. So Nick Parker and I went out.'

The meeting that followed, captured on camera phones and later posted online for all to see, showed Wilkinson and Parker trying to explain to those fans what was going on behind the scenes at the club. Despite Wilkinson having to speak against a backdrop of interruptions and swearing from some of the gathered crowd, it nevertheless provided an opportunity for the pair to spell out the gravity of the situation and confirm how influential the bank was in the whole affair, before offering a pledge to keep at it until a solution was found.

* * * *

Howard Wilkinson – The facts are that this club is in trouble and has been in trouble for a very long time… the only thing that is going to sort this situation out is getting somebody with some money to the table.

Nick Parker – The people that run this club is the Co-operative Bank.

Wilkinson – At the moment we're fighting for our lives, and we'll keep doing it... We'll keep working at it and trying to make it happen.

* * * *

'I was glad I went out,' explains Wilkinson today. 'The leader has to be visible and prepared to listen.'

* * * *

The Co-operative Bank's earlier rescue had covered the HMRC demand and helped the club avert immediate disaster. However, at the end of September 2010 a *second* winding-up petition would be announced by Parker. Again it was from HMRC and related to an outstanding PAYE bill of £600,000. This time around, with the last card having been played with the bank, many believed that at least administration was ahead, maybe worse. The end of days?

As 17 November neared, the date of the hearing of the second petition, furious work was going on behind the scenes by Wilkinson and Parker as they spoke to a number of parties in an attempt to try and get an investment deal done. But hardly anyone *could* help, or was ever intending to, and it was difficult. As Wilkinson explains, 'We had so many people wasting our time. You can never be sure that the next one will be the one. And each time you would sit there thinking, "This is the one." People all with great ideas, but ideas which came to nothing.'

One notable false alarm was when a Middle East-based consortium, headed by former Wednesday goalkeeper Chris Turner, was apparently close to doing a deal. Wilkinson believed the group was genuine. Apparently £2m was being offered for short-term cash-flow – to pay HMRC and swerve administration – in advance of completing a full takeover that would bring a supposed £13m–£15m investment. Wilkinson was so confident that it was going to happen he took to the BBC's *Football Focus* programme to spread the good news. However, as the weeks dragged on with no payments forthcoming, the potential deal collapsed.

'From then on, I just didn't allow myself to get too excited,' says Wilkinson. 'In the first four weeks of dealing with them [the consortium] I was becoming very engaged with them and the plan.

But after that I just realised you can't allow yourself that luxury. You must not allow yourself to assume anything. It's a bit like selling your house really. Until they've signed the contract, it's still your home.

'We quickly learned to say, "Okay, we hear what you have to say. Meeting over. Now put the money in the bank as a sign of serious intent. Then we can do something."'

The uncertainty of the whole situation was surmised brilliantly by another Wednesday board member, Geoff Hulley, who, when asked, 'What's the latest on the takeover?' during a radio interview, replied, 'I don't know myself. I'm anxious to find out.'

* * * *

The club's second day in court to face the second winding-up petition arrived. Wednesday 17 November 2010. A huge day in the recent history of the club.

Nick Parker would be attending for the club and that morning he and the rest of the contingent from Sheffield (which included members of the local press) piled on the early trains south to London to watch the day unfold. The *Yorkshire Post* and *Sheffield Star* would provide running updates online of the day's events.

Matt Slater, a journalist seasoned in reporting on such events for the BBC, was there as well. He remembers the day. 'In the space of a year I'd been to the High Court about ten times with cases like Portsmouth, Southend United and Cardiff City,' he says, 'and other high-profile insolvency cases involving football clubs.

'Wednesday were quite an interesting case study at the time as they were one of the bigger clubs that had fallen on hard times. And one which, like a lot of other clubs, had a big debt.

'On the day I was aware that this was obviously a big and important story in Sheffield. A club which had been so poorly run with so many bad decisions going back years and years, which had now found itself in this crisis moment.'

It was in the Companies Court, court 55, at the Royal Courts of Justice in London, past grand main hall, with its statues and portraits on the wall, that the case would be heard.

'Insolvency courts have a kind of language and rhythm of their own,' explains Slater. 'Once you're inside you have to work out which bits of the case are interesting, or mean anything to what you're there to report on; and because there are so many cases being heard on any one day, if you aren't paying attention the football club case could be up before you know it. There'd be hundreds of companies on the list and the judge would sort of race through them: that one's gone, that one's gone etc. Then the football club would be mentioned.'

By the time Wednesday's case did come up, the club owed HMRC £1.4m in PAYE, VAT and interest. They were skint and the Co-op Bank would not be helping out again. Yet, miraculously, apparently the Owls seemed to have a solution up their sleeve.

The club would request a 28-day adjournment. Claiming they were 'on the verge of a takeover deal with a consortium of local businessmen', and that supposedly the deal would 'be able to proceed very quickly', they made their case and crossed their fingers.

The tension built. The judge said this, 'You are clearly trading insolvently and you are very probably doing so using HMRC money.' Nonetheless, apparently persuaded by the claim that a buyer – the group of local businessmen whom to that point had not managed to conclude a deal with Howard Wilkinson, but who apparently now were ready to make one – was ready to go and make a deal happen, he granted the adjournment.

'I never really felt there was a crisis with Wednesday,' observes Slater today, 'that the club were really on the brink. As so often happens with football clubs, I always felt that there was a way out and that someone would pick up the pieces.'

At last, it seemed as though there was.

Afterwards outside the court, an emotional Parker faced up to the press. 'I am very relieved,' he said, 'but more importantly I am very, very angry. This club should not be where it is today.'

Condemning the tyre-kickers and the time-wasters that had shown interest in the past but had lacked proper substance, he went on, 'There are people out there who say they have money when they do not,' before remarking of those that *did* have money, 'It is now time for those people… to step forward and in private do a deal. A deal can be done in days. I know that there are people who are out there who can do it.' (Presumably he was talking about the 'consortium of local businessmen'.) Strong words from the chief executive.

The date of the reconvened hearing was due to be 15 December. The real deadline was 1 December, however. This was the hearing date of *another* winding-up petition, again brought by HMRC.

* * * *

Two weeks to D-Day. The time was now for someone to step forward to do a deal and rescue the club.

Despite what had been said in court about there being a specific consortium of local businessmen ready to move on the club, it seems that at that stage several different groups were in the picture (and not all of them matching the description of a consortium of local businessmen).

Was the consortium that of Spencer Fearn? A Wednesday fan who had founded the training business Life Skills Solutions (that season's sponsors of the South Stand at Hillsborough), Fearn had owned the uncelebrated Scottish club East Stirling. Back in the summer of 2010, Fearn had become attached to the group 'Wednesday Forward', which hoped to bring potential investors of varying wealth, from home and abroad, together. Following the club's day in court, the group apparently were having talks with the club and the bank; it was suggested an initial £5m would be put in for cash flow, followed later by another £5m.

Was the consortium the 'Save Our Owls' 'coalition', a group behind the 'One Wednesday Fund' that aimed to gather finance from a range of Wednesday fans willing to put up individual donations of between £100 and £500,000 (or more if they had it)? The coalition, fronted by local businessman Garry Scotting, had spoken to the Co-op Bank and apparently received from it 'informal approval' for its offer to invest £6m into the club. £17m of the debt would apparently be written off; indication, perhaps, of the bank's willingness to accept about only £6m of the £20m-plus owed to it at the time. After all, how much of the debt had been written down in the bank's books already, possibly back in 2006, when the parked debt agreement between the club and the Co-op was agreed? The remainder of the debt would be paid off in structured payments over the next few years. Not long after the club's temporary amnesty in court, it is said that pledges to the 'One Wednesday Fund' had reached £2m.

Or maybe the consortium of local businessmen that was 'on the verge' of a takeover was the one believed (at least by the *Yorkshire Post*) to have involved the former Wednesday director and steel-recycling man, Mick Wright?

It's believed that Wright, who had left the Wednesday board back in 2005, along with another former board member, Ken Cooke, were fronting their own group – their very own 'consortium of local businessmen', perhaps. The rumour (unconfirmed) was that the group also included existing board members Bob Grierson and Geoff Hulley, along with former director Keith Addy. It's unclear what kind of offer the group had up their sleeve. Though, if they were the group which had been referred to in court, presumably they would 'be able to proceed very quickly' towards a deal. If these individuals *were* involved, why hadn't they stepped forward at any stage before?

There was one other party in the running. He was not a 'consortium of local businessmen'; rather a 72-year-old Serbian-American multi-millionaire and former owner of Portsmouth and Leicester City. At the time he was said to be worth upwards of £75m, if not significantly more; a later *Sunday Times* Rich List would state his worth at £102m. Milan Mandarić was interested.

* * * *

'The first contact we had with Milan Mandarić was before the away game with Brentford [earlier in the season, September 2010],' recalls Wilkinson. 'Nick Parker and I were driving down in the car and we got a phone call. The caller didn't name him at the time, but the person on the phone represented Milan.' As time went on, the businessman would become more and more interested in the prospect of owning Sheffield Wednesday.

A few months after Wilkinson had received that call, just *before* the club's big day in court, a formal bid had in fact come in from Mandarić (at that point, he was the only one of the interested parties actually to make such a bid). But he had been rejected.

Reportedly, he had offered £8m to the Co-op Bank for the circa £20m-plus debt the club owed to it. And while the bank was apparently open to this bid (it was, of course, higher than the 'Save Our Owls' group's £6m offer), they were not the only party to satisfy.

Between them, some of Wednesday's current and former directors were owed several millions of pounds in loans and interest tied up in the club. One, the former chairman Dave Allen, was due around £2.4m. But when an offer of only £250,000 was made to him by Mandarić's representative, Allen rebuffed it. 'It was a derisory offer,' Allen said at the time. 'I wasn't prepared to listen to it.' Initially, then, Mandarić's offer had been rejected.

The other loan-note holders, Bob Grierson, Geoff Hulley, Keith Addy, Ken Cooke and Mick Wright reportedly received similar cut-price offers for their shares. As the *Yorkshire Post* would report, only *some* of them had been/were 'receptive' to Mandarić's bid.

'My offer is still there, but the loan-holders did not want to go for it,' Mandarić would say afterwards, adding, 'It's the end of the deal, I think. What can I do? It's not my decision, it's the decision of those people still involved in the club... I just hope they have a plan B and that they don't go into administration.'

It was winter and cold and difficult for everyone involved with the club. Who knew what was going to happen? Would a resolution ever come?

As the clock ticked, one worry now became that even if a deal could be struck with the club, the bank and some of the loan-note holders, there might, as some reporting had suggested, still be a blocker in the form of another party, perhaps the consortium supposedly headed by Mick Wright (and which potentially contained several of the loan-note holders).

Could the bids of other parties be blocked by a member or members of this consortium, in turn putting that group in prime position to get hold of the club?

Further complicating the mix was the thinking that the Co-op Bank might be supportive of that other party – or others similar to it – but that, going forward, this might not be in the best interests of the club (especially considering the position Wednesday were in, how they had got there and who had been guiding the club through that time from the boardroom).

One man believed this scenario might well be the case. He believed that something had to be done to persuade the bank that a change in ownership of the club that was positive, in Wednesday's best interest, had to take place in favour of one that was not. That man was Lee Strafford, former Wednesday chairman.

* * * *

After he had left the club back at the end of the 2009/10 season, Strafford had embarked on a process that he hoped, ultimately, would help force through what he considered to be a change for good at the club. After everything that had happened at Wednesday, particularly during his turbulent time spent as chairman, Strafford wanted to see the right change made.

Therefore, in light of any future deal for the club – and inspired by everything that he had experienced when he was chairman; everything he'd seen and been put through – Strafford had decided to make contact with the club's biggest lenders, the Co-op Bank, to whistle-blow on what he terms the long-standing 'corporate misbehaviour' within the club. 'I felt there was something I could do,' he says, believing that the outcome of his actions could lead to the 'right', not wrong individual(s) taking control of the club.

Strafford's initial contact, back in the summer, had led to a phone conversation with an individual who dealt with matters like these at the bank. During this call, he outlined in detail the nature of his concerns – the problems he had encountered, the fact that people still involved with the club *might* be trying to get hold of it outright – after which the bank initiated a full investigation. He then provided an evidence pack of club budgets, management accounts and his own testimony. All of which, he says, supported among other things, the datum that before he and Nick Parker had joined the board they had been told the club was cash neutral, and that upon subsequent discovery it was found to have not been. After reviewing the pack, the bank requested a follow-up meeting during which they could find out more.

So, in June 2010, Strafford travelled over to Manchester, to the Hilton airport hotel, to a quiet, discreet room for a face-to-face meeting with the bank. Its Manchester city centre offices were not considered an appropriate venue for such a clandestine event; the risk of people involved in Wednesday's account noticing the former Wednesday chairman strolling in to the offices was too great.

When the meeting finished, after Strafford had told all of his rollercoaster ride as chairman of the club, the bank thanked him for all his help. They had everything they needed for now and said they would get back to him if they needed anything more. 'I left them reflecting on the end of my report,' explains Strafford, 'which included a note of one last conversation I had with Howard Wilkinson after I resigned, where I said that he must get confirmation from the Co-op that they were backing a plan to lose £2m in order to go for promotion. And that if that was not the case, the club could be in deep trouble.

'The bank told me I had to trust them to do whatever it was that they were going to do next,' Strafford says today. 'They'd decided on a course of action. I take some comfort in the fact that it did end up influencing how the Co-op dealt with the club from then on.'

Strafford's actions would lead to the big change that needed to happen at Wednesday before the club could move forward.

* * * *

Late 2010. The bank was the major player in the club's future direction. As of May 2010 it was owed over £20m by Wednesday and the big decisions involving the club, such as whether it would be lent more money to avoid being wound up in court, or to whom the club would be sold, were pretty much the Co-op's to make. And now, perhaps after what had been learned from Strafford during his whistle-blowing exercise, a shift in the bank's stance from being supportive of Wednesday and the club's leadership (that long-standing 'special relationship' between bank and club) to not being so supportive, seemingly took place.

Over in Manchester at the Co-op Bank, with the clock ticking towards 1 December 2010 when Wednesday would face the latest winding-up petition, it is understood that a series of meetings took place between key parties at the bank and at the club, which would confirm the direction the bank would now take when it came to the Wednesday overall and the identity of any potential new owners. Going forward, the 'special relationship' would not be quite so special and other, non-Sheffield-based parties, would seemingly be favoured by the bank.

The bank, it seemed, now favoured an outsider, such as, say, Milan Mandarić. It was a massive moment. The other parties were about to be shifted out of the way. A big change at the club was about to take place.

So, all of a sudden, with the apparent backing of the bank over the other parties, the Serbian-American former owner of Portsmouth and Leicester City now simply had to come up with a more agreeable offer to the loan-note holders and Sheffield Wednesday would be his.

'During the last knockings, if you like, it became very, very clear that Milan Mandarić was in pole position to acquire the club,' recalls Wilkinson of the situation at that stage in late November 2010. 'Certainly, as well, once he'd publicly thrown his cap into the ring, my attention narrowed.

'Basically, Milan wanted the club. But of course he had a price he was willing to pay and it was about getting other people to understand that they were going to have to agree a price to sell at. The question was: how much?'

Thankfully, an agreeable price would be found. A deal to rescue Sheffield Wednesday would be done.

Mandarić came back with another offer to clear the £23m of loans now outstanding with the Co-op Bank (by offering £7m to clear them, with an additional £250,000 if and when the club achieved promotion from League 1 and a further £750,000 if a Premier League return was reached by the end of 2020/21), before making revised offers to current and former directors for their loans. A key man in proceedings now was the club's former chairman, Dave Allen.

When Mandarić called up Allen and the pair spoke, in Mandarić's words, 'one businessman to another', an agreement between them neared and, following their lawyers' late-night talks, an agreement was eventually reached.

For his shares and loans, Allen would take £750,000 now and £750,000 if and when Wednesday made it back to the top tier (much better, of course, than the 'derisory' £250,000 offer Mandarić had made earlier.

For Allen, along with giving up his shares in the club that he had acquired in 2001 for £500,000, he would also be foregoing the £900,000 in accrued interest that he was still owed from the loans he had made to the club. The papers would be signed at Allen's Napoleon's casino. It is believed less generous deals were also reached with the other loan-note holders, Bob Grierson, Geoff Hulley, Keith Addy, Mick Wright and Ken Cooke. According to the *Sheffield Star*, this group took around 20 per cent of what was owed to them collectively.

Mandarić would also pay the £1.4m that was still outstanding to HMRC, making the winding-up petitions go away. The club would not now be required to turn up to court again to face that petition.

In all, Mandarić agreed to pay out around £10m upfront for the club, plus a potential further few million dependent on the club's future success, plus £1 for all of the club's shares. Ownership would be held via the Delaware-based UK Football Investments, LLC company, which had owned Leicester City. The debt was removed from the club – nothing, for now, owed to a bank or past or present directors.

After all those years, change was just about here.

A new era ahead.

* * * *

On 11 December 2010, the club's new owner-elect would be at Hillsborough for the Bristol Rovers game. Wednesday, sitting fourth in the table before kick-off, won 6-2. As he looked on from the directors' box, Milan Mandarić received a warm reception from the crowd.

Then, a few days later, on a chilly December Tuesday morning, the takeover would be confirmed.

Ten minutes was all it took for the club's shareholders to pass the deal through. In the Jack Charlton Suite in the South Stand at Hillsborough, 99.7 per cent of them were in favour of giving up their shares and handing them over to the new man in the hope of better times. Earlier, the supporters' group Wednesdayite, recognising that Mandarić represented the 'only realistic opportunity to see the Owls survive the short-term difficulties' the club faced, had quickly balloted its members and approved the handing over of their ten-per-cent-plus shareholding.

After the years of waiting, the countless rumoured takeovers and non-takeovers, the deal was done. It *had* happened. Out with the old and in with the new. The Owls, so close to the brink, had been saved.

'Sheffield Wednesday is one of the most famous names in football,' Mandarić would say. 'I give supporters and everybody who cares for this club an assurance... [that] I will do everything in my power... to again make Sheffield Wednesday a real force in English football.'

For Wilkinson, ready to hand over the reins to Mandarić after a draining, up-and-down six months as chairman, the long journey was over. It was a great relief for the man who had always done his very best for the club: he could see a brighter future. 'People in Sheffield are used to bad weather,' he would say. 'But this is a sunny day.

'When Sheffield Wednesday needed someone to step up and deliver – Milan was that man. The only way is up.' Well done, Mr Wilkinson.

For Strafford, who had gone to the Co-op Bank in the hope of helping bring about some positive change at the club, his decision and his efforts had at last been vindicated. 'I have no doubt that if I had not whistle-blown to the Co-op they would not have managed it in the same way,' he says today. 'And that could have resulted in the old guard buying the club outright.' Well done, then, Mr Strafford too.

A new era for the club could now begin.

Act III
Return?

[Louis Clay]

17

Enter Milan

I

THE city of Novi Sad lies in the Serbian province of Vojvodina, about one hour north of the capital Belgrade, and sits along the great and wide Danube River; its waters linking the city north to Budapest, Vienna and Germany.

In the 1990s, following the break-up of Yugoslavia, Novi Sad was a battered and broken place with NATO's 78-day bombing campaign during the Kosovo war having destroyed the city's oil refineries, roads and three bridges that crossed the river. Thousands of miles away, the man who in 2010 would come to the rescue of Sheffield Wednesday, cried as he watched on television the destruction of the city where he had grown up.

It was to Novi Sad that following the Second World War, Milan Mandarić, born in 1938, had moved from Vrebac, a small village in the region of Lika in what today is Croatia. Before that, in 1941, when the Nazis and their allies had brutally occupied Yugoslavia, his mother, Milica, had fled with Milan and her baby daughter Smiljana to the Croatian mountains, 'hiding from the enemy', while her husband Dusan was sent to an Austrian concentration camp (he would survive). 'When we returned [to Vrebac],' Milan would later tell, 'our village was destroyed.'

After the war in Novi Sad, Dusan opened a machine shop and later, when grown up Milan graduated from the city's mechanical engineering facility, he took it over from his father, building it into one of Yugoslavia's largest businesses; its numerous factories across the country exporting automotive parts around the world. Aged 25, it is said that Milan Mandarić was the country's wealthiest businessman.

Then things changed.

A swerve of approach from President Tito's Communist regime and Mandarić, having by now (the late 1960s) built up such wealth, was asked to leave the country.

Separated from his home, his business and his money, he first moved to Zurich before, in 1969, to the west coast of America, where he found work making components for the nascent computer industry.

In 1971, Mandarić set up his own circuit-board business, Lika Corporation, which in five years became the biggest manufacturer of computer components in America. In 1980 the Tandy Corporation purchased the company for $4.5m in cash and shares, after which Mandarić set up another computer components manufacturer, Sanmina Corporation (named after his daughters, Alek*san*dra and Jas*mina*). Much like his previous ventures, Sanmina would go from strength to strength.

Mandarić loved football too though, 'lived and breathed it', reckoned one observer. As a youngster in Novi Sad he had almost made it with his hometown club, FK Vojvodina. And although life as a player would not be his path, when in 1974, the opportunity arose to bring a new North American Soccer League (NASL) franchise to the west coast of America, Mandarić wanted to play a part.

Some $300,000 later (the amount required to set up the franchise; Mandarić would be the largest of five investors) and the San Jose Earthquakes were up and running; the franchise's co-owner Mandarić demanding high levels of professionalism and effort from all of his players, telling them before one game, for instance, 'You must give everything you've got of yourself, your heart, your blood.'

After three years Mandarić sold up and moved on, reportedly having spent the equivalent of £2.5m today on the project. He bought another franchise, the Connecticut Bicentennials, moved them to Oakland and renamed them the Stompers. Three years after that he returned to San Jose and the Earthquakes.

When the NASL folded in 1984, Mandarić looked to Europe for his next footballing fix, acquiring a 50 per cent stake in Belgian club Standard Liège for £1.25m. Things didn't turn out too well, though, and when he couldn't get hold of the other 50 per cent of Liège, he left.

In 1997 he would return to European football, purchasing a majority share of Ligue 1 club OGC Nice. In Mandarić's first year with the club, Nice won the Coupe de France... and got relegated.

When he sold up and moved on not long after that, he apparently broke even on the £400,000 he had originally paid for his share of the club, and the £1.6m he had subsequently invested. After Nice, came Belgium (again) with a brief involvement with Sporting Charleroi. Then, in 1999, he purchased struggling English First Division outfit Portsmouth.

Pompey had been a struggling club fighting with administration, but with £5m would be saved by Mandarić who, having gained control of the club, began working to steer it away from the abyss.

In England Mandarić would become known as a hands-on owner, attending all of Portsmouth's games and, it is said, talking every day on the phone to his manager. Over the next few years he would replace several of those managers – Alan Ball, Tony Pulis, Steve Claridge and Graham Rix – before settling on the former West Ham boss, Harry Redknapp. In 2003, Redknapp would win the club promotion to the Premier League.

During his first three years at Portsmouth, it is believed Mandarić invested over £20m in the club, loaning millions of pounds (over £15m by 2003), before, in early 2006, selling 50 per cent of his stake for around £15m to the 29-year-old French-Israeli businessman, Alexandre 'Sacha' Gaydamak. Later on in 2006 Gaydamak junior would reputedly pay Mandarić a further £30m for the other 50 per cent of the club.

Post-Mandarić, Pompey would in 2008 win the FA Cup, spending massively on players in order to do so, before enduring a catastrophic and hopeless decline that would see them drop out of the Premier League, then the Championship, then League 1, while effectively imploding with debts of over £100m, all amid the background of a changing cast of owners.

'What happened at Portsmouth breaks my heart,' Mandarić would say of the club's subsequent plight. '[I]t made me think that whatever I do with my next club, I've got to find the right owner to sell to.'

That next club was Leicester City, bought in early 2007 for a figure thought to be north of £20m. Over the next three years Leicester would be relegated from the Championship, then promoted back, all while working through a host of managers.

Via a Delaware-registered company, Mandarić would loan over £11m to the club as he sought to move them forward, before, in 2009, selling up to a Thai consortium, comprising the owners of the duty-free retailer, King Power; the fee reputed to be £40m (a few years and over £100m of investment later, Leicester would be back in the Premier League, remarkably winning it in 2016). Then, in December 2010, Milan Mandarić bought Sheffield Wednesday.

II

Initially, when he came to the rescue in Sheffield to begin his Owls adventure, Mandarić was supportive of Wednesday manager Alan Irvine. Despite having failed to keep the club in the Championship in 2009/10, after inheriting a relegation situation from his predecessor Brian Laws, Irvine was admired by his new boss. The latter quickly provided his manager with the funds to help improve his League 1 promotion-chasing team, and incoming were the defenders Reda Johnson from Plymouth Argyle, Mark Reynolds of Motherwell and the young striker Gary Madine (all of whom signed for undisclosed fees, but are thought to have cost at least £750,000 in total).

Along with the chairman's support, though, came immediate pressure. Irvine's assistant, Rob Kelly, recalls of the time, 'We knew we had to win straight away. It was quite simple and completely results-orientated. Milan's a winner and that's what he deals in. His track record tells you that if you win he'll stick with you. But it was all still going to take time and we didn't have that.'

A few days before the EGM that would confirm his purchase of the club, Mandarić had been at Hillsborough to witness the 6-2 hammering of Bristol Rovers: a fine beginning to the club's new era. For the following game down at Exeter, however, the Owls lost 5-1, before then losing the next five after that. The last of those, a sorry 5-3 defeat at Peterborough in February 2011, was the final straw for the new owner. His patience had already run out and Irvine was sacked. 'It is unfortunate,' Mandarić would say, 'but this had to take place. We were sliding down the table and now we have to look up and the club has to move forward.' Mandarić was making his mark.

'He gave us a bit of time and a bit of money,' reflects Kelly today, 'but things hadn't quite progressed as he would have liked it. It was right at the start of a big transition for the club. We wanted it to be a successful period. We wanted to move things on quickly. But we needed time to do that, and in the end we didn't really have that time.'

Mandarić would move to replace Irvine with a proper Wednesday man, Gary Megson.

Megson, who had grown up a fan of the club, had watched his father Don, the great Wednesday captain of the 1960s, play hundreds of times in the blue and white, before playing for and captaining the Owls himself, turning out 283 times for the club through the 1980s, battling and driving things on in the middle of the pitch. Then later, as he forged his own managerial career, perhaps most notably taking West Bromwich Albion to the Premier League – twice, he had closely followed the ups and (mostly) downs of the Owls. He knew the club. He cared about the club. Now it was time for him to come home.

'I've been coming here since I was five and I love the place,' Megson would say of Hillsborough. It wouldn't take long for the deal to be done and for Mandarić to get his man.

The brief for new manager Megson for the remaining 20 games of 2010/11 was simple: try, if he could, to get the club out of League 1, perhaps via the play-offs (at that stage Wednesday sat eight points behind the top six). Failing that, at least get building for next season.

In football, the Megson style of play had not been much of a celebrated favourite way – tall and strong sides programmed to win the ball and hit simple, direct passes. But it was a style that had worked for him in the past and it was expected to work for him again at Hillsborough.

Arriving after the January transfer window had closed, during which time Irvine had already brought in a few players, Megson had pretty much to make do with what he had in front of him in terms of playing staff. Results to the end of the season weren't great. As Megson stood watching from the touchline, his suit jacket off and shirt sleeves rolled up, he would manage wins from only about a third of the remaining games, leaving the club well adrift of the play-offs by the end of the campaign. Despite this, however, the signs of promise were just about there. Gradually, Megson's influence was taking hold more and more and for the next season, 2011/12, it was 'bring it on'.

* * * *

Through the summer of 2011, Megson worked to further shape his side with a good amount of upheaval taking place among the playing staff. The likes of Darren Potter, Gary Teale, Richard Hinds and Tommy Spurr left the club; incoming were some good lower-league performers, including the experienced midfielder David Prutton and big centre-back Rob Jones. There was the tough and effective midfield stopper-and-spoiler José Semedo, and the excellent Wolves defender Danny Batth (loaned for the season, having spent time with the Owls the previous year). Early into the season, the promising striker Chris O'Grady would also arrive from Rochdale, along with the creative midfielders Ben Marshall (borrowed from Stoke City) and Chris Lines.

Ahead of the 2011/12 campaign, Wednesday had been made second favourites for the title and promotion (perhaps with good reason as, along with their city and promotion rivals Sheffield United, the Owls would have one of the highest wage bills in the division that season: £8.3m). And Megson, sitting beside his father at the pre-season game against local non-league side Stocksbridge Park Steels, was positive about the season ahead. '[S]pirits were high,' Don Megson would recall. 'Gary was optimistic.'

* * * *

As the season kicked off, early results and performances would give positive indications of how it might play out: four wins, one draw and three defeats. Wednesday were lurking just outside the play-offs on goal difference at this early stage; the second-favourites for the title four points off second place.

For game eight, however, things changed and Wednesday, travelling midweek to Stevenage, were sloppy, calamitous and all over the place in losing 5-1. The result and the performance were not good enough and unfortunately provided fairly early on the first major doubt regarding Megson's ability to get the club out of League 1.

After Stevenage, Wednesday would win four games – happy days. But then, in the next four, not win once. More doubt and more pressure, especially with promotion rivals Charlton, Huddersfield and Sheffield United (now led by former Owl Danny Wilson) all doing well.

The season went on. The dark nights came and the cold crept in. In the game just before Christmas, deep into injury time against Huddersfield at Hillsborough, Wednesday gave up a 4-2 lead to finish 4-4. The Owls were still up there, but it was getting tighter.

Then, in early 2012, came for Milan Mandarić the draining and unwelcome (and for Sheffield Wednesday, potentially destabilising) distraction of a court case involving the Owls' owner and his former Portsmouth manager Harry Redknapp, in which they would face the serious charges of cheating the public revenue.

* * * *

The charges, when they had been made against him two years earlier, had come as a massive shock to Mandarić. And when the case made it to court it would prove a tough few weeks for Mandarić and his fellow defendant Redknapp.

The case related to two payments totalling €295,000 which between 2002 and 2007 had been made by Mandarić to Redknapp's 'Rosie47'-passworded Monaco bank account (the code named after his pet bulldog) – the case coming down to whether the payments, made during each of Redknapp's two spells as Portsmouth manger were employment bonuses (and therefore taxable), or not; and if they were taxable, why had no tax been paid on them?

In court, Mandarić would refer to the payments as investment 'seed' money, given from one friend to another (and therefore not taxable), rather than being anything to do with Redknapp's employment at Portsmouth, arguing that as a rich man who pays taxes, why would he commit a crime to help somebody else avoid a little bit of tax? And after a couple of weeks, after the prosecution had finished its case and the defence had presented theirs, the jury was sent out to decide the fate of Mandarić and Redknapp – the two men waiting nervously as the jury deliberated.

Later, when it had all finished, the Wednesday owner would speak of how in the years and months leading up to the case he had endured tremendous worry and stress; how the time in court was a massively traumatic and draining ordeal; how in all it had been a horrible dream.

Back in the courtroom, when the verdict of not guilty was read out for both Mandarić and Redknapp, emotions were high as the two defendants hugged each other in relief – the horrible dream now over for the pair.

Afterwards it was also learned of how Mandarić had been cleared of tax evasion in *another* case back in the previous October, this one relating to the transfer of former Portsmouth player Eyal Berkovic. The press had been unable to report on the earlier case until the Redknapp–Mandarić trial had been concluded.

Mandarić, hurt that the cases had even been brought against him in the first place, would speak of how he had considered leaving the UK, and of his 'enthusiasm tank… going down to empty'. Who knows how close he had come to making such a decision, and what that would have meant for Sheffield Wednesday – how disrupting it would likely have been to lose their hands-on owner. Thankfully, though, he realised that there was still a big job to be done back north in Sheffield and would soon be back, seemingly invigorated and ready to drive on the Owls. '[W]hen you see those people who are so appreciative and when you see the team is making progress every week and month in every department,' he said, 'you want to stay, to see the team score the goals and finish the job.'

The court cases were over and Mandarić was staying.

Finishing the job seemed to include supporting Gary Megson in signing several new players during the January transfer window. The Derby goalkeeper Stephen Bywater, who had been on loan since September, would be secured on a permanent basis, as would the Spanish defender Miguel Llera, who had been on loan from

Blackpool. Llera in particular would make a significant contribution to the team and their promotion hopes over the remaining months of the season. Bury's Mike Jones, meanwhile, a midfielder, also joined the club.

At the end of January, the Owls sat third in the table, just behind Huddersfield on goal difference and one point ahead of the Blades.

* * * *

Sadly for Megson's Wednesday side, February would bring only one win and three defeats in the league as hopes of an automatic promotion place began to dissipate. Watching the Owls go down to a defeat at Chesterfield, and looking at the league position that the result left them in – third place and five points behind Sheffield United, having played two games more than their city rivals – gave Mandarić much to ponder. Was Megson the man to take Wednesday up?

The manager had been under growing pressure. Results had been bad and there had been reports of 'bad-tempered meetings' between manager and owner. Many were expecting the change to come at some point, especially if Sheffield United could inflict a defeat over their rivals on blue territory in the upcoming city derby, taking place in the last weekend of February.

On the morning of Saturday 26 February 2012, the top end of the League 1 table looked like this:

		P	Pts	GD
1	Charlton Athletic	32	72	36
2	Sheffield United	30	62	29
3	Huddersfield Town	31	58	29
4	Milton Keynes	32	58	27
5	Sheffield Wednesday	32	57	13
6	Carlisle United	31	49	(4)
7	Stevenage	30	48	16

The day after, Sheffield United, Danny Wilson, their prolific Welsh striker Ched Evans and over 5,000 of their supporters travelled over to Hillsborough for the massive derby game.

For Megson's Wednesday, it was win or bust. Lose and the Blades were off and eight points away in the distance. Even a draw would have meant they probably weren't catchable, never mind battling Huddersfield (who sat third) as well.

There were 36,364 packed into the ground that Sunday afternoon and, despite the potentially atmosphere-ruining 1pm kick-off, the crowd was fired up and ready.

The most important Sheffield derby for years would go like this: the Blades missed a chance, or two. Wednesday would not miss theirs; Chris O'Grady striking for 1-0. Megson, that day sporting a tracksuit rather than his usual trousers-and-rolled-up-shirt-sleeves combination, dished out a hug for his goalscorer. Wilson would look on sternly from the side of the pitch, his arms folded tightly. And Wednesday would hang on to win.

The gap between the Owls and the Blades was closed by three vital points.

But then, under-pressure Megson was sacked.

* * * *

Unfortunately for him, ignoring the brilliant derby result, recent form had not quite been good enough and the following Wednesday evening he was shown the door by his chairman.

'It hurts more than any other disappointment I've had in my life,' Megson, the Owl, would say. 'It's my club… I'm gutted that I'm no longer Wednesday's manager.'

'This was a very difficult decision,' Mandarić would say, 'but one that has been taken with the best interests of Sheffield Wednesday at heart.' A decision which, he added, would give the club the 'best chance of achieving the key aim of promotion'.

With the season now in its final third, all that was required now was someone who could achieve that still unlikely objective. Someone who could, say, take the club on a 13-game unbeaten run that ended with promotion. Easy.

* * * *

At the time, Dave Jones was one of the sub-Premier League's strongest managers. In the 1990s he had, arguably, overachieved with Southampton (having earlier raised his profile at Stockport County), before guiding Wolverhampton Wanderers to the top level in 2003. He'd spent over five years trying to do the same with Cardiff City, taking them to an FA Cup Final along the way, before being let go by the Welsh club before he could finish the job. Despite this setback, he was doubtless still considered one of the more highly regarded managers outside of the top division.

Jones was Milan Mandarić's ace up his sleeve.

About a year after leaving Cardiff, Jones, in early March 2012, was appointed Wednesday's third manager under Mandarić. Hopefully, everyone thought, he might be able to help the club catch up to Sheffield United in the automatic promotion places and move Wednesday out of League 1.

Jones's reign would start in grimmest Rochdale in the north-west. That afternoon the new man sat up in the stands beside Mandarić (this was Spotland, Rochdale, where 'up in the stands' meant about five rows up) and surveyed what he had taken on.

The 0-0 result and performance was fitting: industrious with glimpses of superiority, but no thrust or cutting edge. Overall, Jones did not like what he saw. Work would have to be done to build the confidence of the players and tweak the playing style: more five-a-sides in training to build confidence on the ball. They needed to play with pride and be more attacking, fast and adventurous; the ball played into space, with players running in behind to get into pockets of space. '[T]he best form of defence is attack', as Jones would say.

It seemed to work. Over the next two weeks, Wednesday would defeat Bury, Bournemouth and Notts County, and draw with Walsall. The Blades, meanwhile, floundered, dropping seven points over their four games of that same spell. With eight games to go, Wednesday sat only two points behind them.

All of a sudden, Jones's men were right back in it.

Next up were Leyton Orient, down in the capital – 1-0 to Wednesday. Then at home to Preston North End, 2-0. Wilson's Blades had been winning too, though, so the gap remained at two points. The early kick-off away at Huddersfield would offer Wednesday the chance – if they flopped – to stutter and hand some of the ground back to United before they'd even taken a kick. Hopefully, they wouldn't.

For the Owls fans streaming out of Huddersfield station that day, past the statue of a waving Harold Wilson and down past the gasworks to the McAlpine or Galpharm or whatever it was now called stadium, they were in for a treat. On the hour, Miguel Llera, the Spanish defender brought into the club by Gary Megson, lined up a kick and arced it over the wall and into the net for 1-0. A second would be added and the win confirmed; the Terriers' own promotion hopes effectively ended in the process. And the pressure was kept up on the Blades, who would win themselves later that day.

After Huddersfield would come another win, this time over Oldham at Hillsborough, Llera heading in one of the three goals. The following Saturday, a draw at Colchester, Llera again scoring.

Wednesday were ten games unbeaten under Jones – but the Blades had been winning too and extended their lead over the Owls to four points. With only nine points left available for each team, Wednesday's automatic promotion hopes, despite Jones's best efforts, appeared almost to be over.

It couldn't be done now… could it?

* * * *

When the Blades travelled down to franchise club Milton Keynes Dons on 21 April 2012, one day after their Welsh striker Ched Evans had been sentenced to prison for five years for rape, the Sheffield United players took to the pitch appearing to be in some kind of shock, at least according to one observer there that day.

That person, and the 6,000 other fans there, watched amid a muted atmosphere as the former Leeds man Alan Smith scored his first goal for five years to give MK the win.

Meanwhile up in Sheffield, at Hillsborough, Wednesday got a remarkable 95th-minute winner against Carlisle that left them just a solitary point behind the Blades with only two games remaining.

Had United won that day and Wednesday lost at home to Carlisle, promotion would have been theirs. But they didn't. So it wasn't.

The switch between the two Sheffield clubs – one of whom would end up in the automatic promotion places, the other not – would come a week later. It was a glorious day. After Wednesday had gone to Brentford and won again – 2-1; Llera getting another goal – the Blades, playing later, would be held by Stevenage at Bramall Lane. The Owls at last moved ahead of their city rivals and into second position. One point ahead, with one game to go.

'Nothing is decided yet,' said Wilson over at the Lane. 'We're not giving up on anything.'

But the Blades had blown it. Wednesday had pick-pocketed them.

One week later, at home to already-relegated Wycombe Wanderers, all Jones's men had to do was match whatever result the Blades could find down in Exeter.

Twelve games after having taken over at the club – 12 games unbeaten – Jones was on the verge of leading Wednesday, Milan Mandarić's Wednesday, to promotion from League 1.

* * * *

In the week before the great season finale, tickets were being snapped up at a fast rate by the Wednesday fans. When all the seats had been sold for the Kop, North and South Stands, the travelling fans from Wycombe were moved over to the north-west corner stand, so that all of the Leppings Lane end could be given over to Owls fans – 5,000-plus more seats snapped up.

There would be over 38,000 Wednesday fans in the ground that bright sunny day; the biggest gathering of Wednesday fans since the play-off final in Cardiff seven years earlier.

Around Hillsborough that afternoon before kick-off, it was like a derby day with the Blades. The pubs were bursting full and thousands of fans streamed to the ground along surrounding arteries – on the trams along Middlewood Road, in their cars along Penistone Road, through the railway arches down Herries Road, or on feet through the park.

Kick-off approached and the ground filled up. The fans and the noise and the anticipation. Promotion only a couple of hours away.

The Wednesdayites – a sea of them – standing and waiting. On the Kop, the balloons and the inflatables; the beach balls and rubber rings – even some paddling pools. Up and down, and round and round. 'Wednesday's going up, Wednesday's going up', everyone chants. Party time. Here we go.

The Wednesday Boys that day: Bywater, Buxton, Batth, Llera, Beevers, Antonio, Semedo, Lines, Treacy, Madine and Ranger.

Twenty-five minutes in, Michail Antonio (on loan from Reading) slipped through to score. 1-0 to Wednesday. And Hillsborough shook.

The minutes went by and in the distance, 'Shhhhh…' The scoreboard beside the South Stand came to life.

'Oooooh!' went the crowd.

'Exeter 1-0 Blades' read the scoreboard. And Hillsborough roared.

With the Owls winning and the Blades losing, they'd do it now, everyone thought. No danger now.

After the break, another goal for Wednesday: 52 minutes, Nile Ranger heading in. Down in Exeter, the Blades had got it back to 1-1, then led 2-1 (they'd still finish with a draw). But nobody cared. With Wednesday winning, it didn't matter at all.

Back at Hillsborough, the minutes ticked by. Bouncing, cheering, shouting and singing. Then the whistle blew. Over. Finished. Wednesday had won the game, taken the three points: second place in the league was theirs. What had seemed like the unlikeliest of promotions before Jones had arrived at the club had been achieved against all odds.

Thousands ran on to the pitch to swamp and celebrate with the team. There were arms round Jones, the orchestrator of the promotion. Goalscoring specialist Llera was lifted on to shoulders. And for Mandarić, the smiling chairman looking down, it was handshakes all round, his decision to move on Megson and bring in Jones now vindicated.

Job done.

On the evening of 5 May 2012, the very top of the League 1 table looked like this:

		P	Pts	GD
1	Charlton Athletic (P)	46	101	46
2	Sheffield Wednesday (P)	46	93	33
3	Sheffield United	46	90	41

Wednesday were going up. Back to the Championship.

Thank you, Dave Jones. Thank you, Milan Mandarić.

Happy days.

18

Progress

SUMMER 2012. Back in the Championship, the aim for
Wednesday was singular and simple: survive. It was a year to
consolidate. Hold the club's place in the second tier and try
to push on after that.

When he had taken over from Gary Megson and led the Owls
to promotion from League 1, Dave Jones had done it with a group
of players that had been assembled for him. For 2012/13, he would
tweak and improve the group as required, the team becoming more
his own.

Jones's key signing that summer was the former Liverpool
goalkeeper Chris Kirkland. An excellent talent who had once been
capped by England, Kirkland had been hampered considerably
in his career by injury. Jones, though, took a chance and handed
him a two-year contract, crossing his fingers that he might get
through a full season. Other notable changes for 2012/13 included
the signings of centre-halves Anthony Gardner (formerly of
Tottenham Hotspur) and Martin Taylor, West Brom full-back Joe
Mattock and Kieran Lee, a promising midfielder from Oldham
Athletic. They were signed for no fees, while Derby forward Chris
Maguire would cost £200,000; another £750,000 would be paid to
bring in Michail Antonio from Reading following his loan spell
during the promotion run-in of the season just gone.

On the opening day of the campaign, thousands travelled down from Sheffield to fill the Derby County away end, roaring on the team to a comeback draw. Two wins from the next two games meant that consolidation season had got off to a brilliant start.

For 2012/13, though, Wednesday would have, at £11.9m, the third *lowest* wage bill in the Championship, so, perhaps naturally, they were to face tougher times ahead. Struggles and winless runs would come, two significant: no wins from 11 in one; seven defeats in a row in the other. And the season, despite bright beginnings, would become a slog.

But Mandarić didn't panic. Where perhaps before he might have dispensed with his manager during such difficult times – as he had at Portsmouth and Leicester – he now favoured stability over disruption. Jones, with his stern-faced, arms-folded sideline demeanour, was kept on to guide his Owls through. And in the end, holding on, bobbing in and out of the relegation places, Wednesday would be all right.

A few events stood out that season.

One was during the televised Friday night visit of Leeds United, which saw tanked-up Leeds and Wednesday fans create a loud and nasty atmosphere at Hillsborough – broken seats, coins thrown by unruly sections of the crowd, repellent chanting. And after the visitors had equalised, one Leeds lowlife got on to the pitch and shoved Kirkland in the face, causing him to fall over.

Afterwards, former Blades boss Neil Warnock, now the manager of Leeds, would anger Kirkland by making comments about him going down too easily after the shove. Warnock hadn't actually seen the footage and would later apologise, though not before the towering Owls keeper had angrily entered the Leeds dressing room in search of Warnock (before thankfully being restrained).

A more happy occasion was José Semedo Day at Nottingham Forest where, as a tribute to the popular Portuguese midfielder, thousands of masks depicting his face were distributed to many of the travelling Wednesday supporters, to be worn over their faces in the ground, resulting in a weird wall of Semedos looking back at the player from the Wednesday end. 'I remember stepping on to the football pitch in Nottingham and seeing thousands of fans with my face!' Semedo would recall of that day. 'What a sight!... it nearly brought a tear to my face.'

Five years on from a number of its members having been dragged through the sorry club-suing-the-fans episode, it was the online forum Owlstalk that had helped organise the masks day.

By the end of the season, with 16 wins and 58 points earned by Jones's men, a win over Middlesbrough on the last day assured Championship safety. Eighteenth position in consolidation season; four places safe. Job done.

* * * *

Summer 2013. Jones moved to make several more changes to his playing squad, with Burton Albion winger Jacques Maghoma, Manchester City's French defender and former Wednesday loanee Jérémy Hélan, former Hull City defender Kamil Zayatte and the towering Albanian-born striker Atdhe Nuhiu all joining the club. Judging by the fact that hardly anything was spent on those transfers (only Hélan had commanded a fee), it seemed there wasn't a great deal of cash around Hillsborough at the time. Based on the transfer fees paid (or rather not paid), Mandarić's approach to spending appeared to be one of prudence and care as Jones's team would again, it was hoped, make at least some steady progress in the league.

As it turned out, however, Wednesday would have a dismal start to 2013/14, managing no wins from the first 12 games, just about anchoring them to the bottom of the table. So much for pushing on, then. Wednesday couldn't even creep on, it seemed.

It was, said some, admirable how Mandarić persevered with his manager through the poor run. But things had to improve, fast.

Premier League strikers Matty Fryatt (borrowed from Hull) and Connor Wickham (borrowed from Sunderland) would help bring Wednesday their first league win of the season – three goals between them in the five-goal rout against Reading at Hillsborough – yet it would soon go wrong again for the team, with more defeats to follow.

Following the 2-0 loss at Blackpool, Jones would say, 'We're all fighting for our jobs... [but] sacking managers isn't the way forward. I don't have a magic wand... I don't know the lottery numbers and I don't know what my future will be... things can't get any worse.' But they could: he was let go by his chairman.

'The club would like to thank Dave for all of his hard work and wish him well for the future,' a club statement read. For Jones, the man who had brought that wonderful and unlikely promotion in 2011/12, it was the end of the road for him as Owls boss.

Jones's assistant Stuart Gray was put in charge of the team on a temporary basis and had managed to get Wednesday back to winning ways. Mandarić was impressed, decided to stick with him, and eventually would hand him the job of 'head coach' permanently. By the end of the season, Gray would have reversed the Owls' situation, steering them to safety in the league with a respectable 16th-place finish, two better than the previous year.

'We started with something like one win from 18 games,' Gray would reflect on the season. 'But credit to the players for how we have ended the season.'

* * * *

In 2013/14 Wednesday would make a loss of £5.6m, up from the £3.7m loss they had made the season before. The loss would be underpinned by an increase in bank borrowings (up now to £1.4m), input from the owner (according to the club's accounts, up to over £17m by May 2014 via his company UK Football Investments, LLC) and two loans taken against the club's Hillsborough home: £1.5m from the former West Ham United owner Terence Brown (to add to another previous loan of £2m which he, as part of a group, had also made to the club against the ground in October 2012) and around £1.5m reportedly received from the Gibraltar-registered Gol International Ltd., a business controlled by the 'super-agent' Pini Zahavi (who, it is said, had first introduced Mandarić to Sacha Gaydamak, the man he had sold Portsmouth to).

For those who had noticed among the fan base, those latter loans were, potentially, a worrying hark back to darker days of the club carrying around significant borrowings held against their biggest asset – the stadium. Debts that, as the club posted losses, would be difficult to pay back.

Such financial arrangements couldn't go on forever and increasingly the belief among many was that it might only be a matter of time before Mandarić sold up, passed the baton on to another party – hopefully to someone who would have the resources to further progress the club – and moved on, possibly getting a decent reward from his original investment in the process. Indeed, back at the start of the 2013/14 season, he was already making noises of the club then being available to the right buyer. So, when the time did come, to whom would the Owls be sold?

The examples of Portsmouth, who post-Mandarić's ownership spent big, won the FA Cup, before going bust and falling through the levels, and Leicester City, who would receive massive investment from their new Thai owners, taking them back to the Premier League then winning it in 2016, would provide good clues.

While guidance could also be found in the FA's Owners' and Directors' Test, more commonly known as the Fit and Proper Test, and relating regulation, which serves to ensure that 30 per cent-plus controlling shareholders and directors of their clubs are of sound background, have not been disqualified as being a director in the past or been declared bankrupt, or have unspent convictions for dishonesty or corruption either in England or abroad.

In the summer of 2014, it looked as if the time had come, that the buyer had been found, when the news broke of a potential takeover by the Azerbaijani businessman Hafiz Mammadov.

Mammadov was the owner of Baku FC, the major shareholder of RC Lens; he reputedly also held small shareholdings in Atletico Madrid and Porto. Lens and Atletico carried on their shirts the slogan of the Azerbaijan Tourism body, 'Azerbaijan: Land of Fire'.

Mammadov owned the oil exploration and construction industry Baghlan Group, a company supposedly worth hundreds of millions of dollars, which had strong links to Azerbaijan's controversial, autocratic political regime (which was headed by the domineering President Ilhan Aliyev, a man who, in 2012, had been awarded 'Organised Crime and Corruption "Person of the Year"' by The Organised Crime and Corruption Reporting Project). Mammadov, it was rumoured, had 18 bodyguards to protect him.

As his takeover bid for the Owls moved through the Football League ratification process, the fans imagined the riches and new signings that might come ahead of the new season. Yet as the weeks went by and the deal remained unresolved (Mammadov's rumoured arrest in Azerbaijan cited among the speculated, though subsequently denied, reasons for the hold-up), worrying news also emerged of funding difficulties at his French club, RC Lens.

By this point, the Championship season had got under way. The Owls had the 'Land of Fire' logo plastered on their shirts – but no takeover had happened. By September, with no funds provided by Mammadov, the deal collapsed; Mandarić having lost patience and time having run out for the hopeful new owner of the club.

'Unfortunately,' said Mandarić, 'despite working hard with both Mr Mammadov and his representatives since the agreement was signed, he has not been able to meet the obligations. While I hope that Mr Mammadov will very quickly overcome his difficulties in Azerbaijan, I cannot allow this speculation to continue.'

No takeover for now, then. Sheffield Wednesday fans had seen this kind of thing before. Better luck next time.

Hanging on the telephone: Pete McKee, the artist and Wednesday fan who had started out drawing for the *A View from the East Bank* fanzine before moving to the pages of the *Sheffield Telegraph*, where since 1994 he had provided, an amusing and topical take on sporting – mostly footballing – events in the city, would in thick lines make his observations.

PROGRESS

* * * *

When 2014/15 got under way – for Wednesday, down on the coast at Brighton – expectations for the new season weren't too great. Yet thanks to a stunning start, courtesy of Giles Coke's belting curling effort from outside the area for the 1-0 win, hopes started to rise. Later, inspired free transfer goalkeeper Keiren Westwood and Leeds's young cast-off defender Tom Lees (signed for an undisclosed fee) would emerge as stars of the team; Stevie May, a striker signed from St Johnstone, having less of an impact. Popular winger Michail Antonio had been sold to Nottingham Forest for £1.5m.

A decent league position would be firmly held on to through the season and, despite a few moans and groans from the fans about this and that (namely regarding the reserved and not-that-entertaining style of play that had been instilled by Gray), good strides were being made.

Earlier in the season Wednesday had twice travelled to Manchester City, the moneyed reigning champions of the Premier League: first in the League Cup on a warm September night at the Etihad, where they had succumbed 7-0; and again in January in the FA Cup. That day striker Atdhe Nuhiu had put the Owls 1-0 ahead and Wednesdayites dreamed… before hopes were dashed as the equaliser then late, late winner came: 2-1. So close.

Never mind. Both visits had given the travelling Wednesdayites the chance to glimpse City's wealth, provided to them by their super-rich owners: painted breeze blocks on the concourse, popcorn from the food kiosk, big open, perfect pitch and snazzy scoreboard, £100m-and-more of talent in their team. It was a handy, and timely, glimpse of what could be.

19

Next Chapter

IN 2015, this was the story for the city of Sheffield. With the hurt of the city's decline through the 1980s, and the struggle of the 90s, that distinct 'post-industrial identity' still was something that was being strived for. The 'service' sector now employed most of the city's working population – at the universities, in the NHS, retail and professional services and so on. Meanwhile, the old industries that encompassed and surrounded engineering and steel production had transformed so much that only a fraction of their former workforce was now required to reach their current output.

In retail, plans had been afoot for the city centre to grab back the ascendency from the sprawling Meadowhall complex out in the east end of town. However, the long-planned 'Sevenstone' project – a £600m transformation of the main shopping area that would bring high-end retail outlets, car parking and leisure facilities – had been 'credit-crunched' in 2008, leaving Meadowhall, with its popular shops, vast free car parks, motorway access and roof, to dominate for now. Plans for a 'Sevenstone'-type resurrection would plod on, hopefully to one day be realised.

What had been happening in the city centre, though, was its emergence as somewhere that people now wanted to live, with thousands of new flats having been built in the S1 postcode. Even the old and run-down brutalist, now Grade II-listed concrete Park

Hill complex, sitting dominant up on a hill behind the fountains cascading down to the station, was undergoing a glass and yellow-and-orange cladding redevelopment revival.

Tourism remained a focus for the city too, with continual promotion of the satisfactions of Sheffield's surrounding 'Golden Frame' countryside of green hills and trees, which in the summer of 2014 had been glimpsed by millions of television viewers as the Tour de France carnival passed through. Also still being peddled was the notion of Sheffield: Cultural City, what with its growing music festival/massive weekend-long piss-up, Tramlines; its highly regarded documentary festival; things like big poems appearing on the walls of buildings; and the sight of one of the city's greatest recent exports, the Arctic Monkeys (made up of four Wednesday fans) having conquered Glastonbury the summer before.

There was Sheffield: Sport City, too. The World Snooker Championship at the Crucible Theatre; Jess Ennis had won heptathlon gold at London 2012; a rich boxing heritage; the Steelers: Britain's most successful ice-hockey side; plus the thousands of people going to the football, Wednesday at Hillsborough or Sheffield United at Bramall Lane.

The city's two universities brought a student population of over 60,000, without whom Sheffield would be nowhere near as vibrant a place.

Economically, though, Sheffield was not thriving. It had been claimed about a £1.6bn gap had existed between what the city's economy could output (based on the resources available to it; namely, its people) and what it did output. Unemployment had stood at over ten per cent back in the summer of 2014.

And while places like an Advanced Manufacturing Park, where academia met high-technology organisations such as Boeing and Rolls-Royce, and hubs such as the digital businesses base, Electric Works, were helping guide the direction of the city's future economy, much work was still to be done.

* * * *

The same could be said for Sheffield Wednesday. After the Mammadov takeover collapse, Milan Mandarić had still been open to offers for the club, still on the lookout for a potential new buyer, and now, it seemed, following the previous false alarm, the wheels were in motion for a sale to a new man to take over.

The figure who emerged was a Thai businessman. An individual who apparently had been in discussions about making a move for several months. And, happily, unlike before with the Azerbaijani, the deal was able to be completed. A done deal.

For real.

Dejphon Chansiri, from Bangkok, Thailand, was the son of Kraisorn Chansiri, co-founder of the $3bn-plus-turnover Thai Union Group (or the Thai Union Frozen (TUF) Group), 'the world's largest producer of tuna' and owner of the John West brand in the UK.

Appearing in Sheffield seemingly from nowhere, he agreed in early 2015 a £30m-plus purchase of Wednesday from Mandarić. Most of the debts would be cleared, which at May 2014 appeared to comprise the £17m-plus owed to Mandarić's company, UK Football Investments, LLC; £1.4m to the bank; along with the £5m-plus which had been loaned to the club by other parties. And 100 per cent of the club's shareholding would be bought by Chansiri, who before the end of the season would, the 2014/15 accounts suggest, go on to lend a further £4.5m, and invest as new equity another £4m.

The money, so went the reports at the time, would come from his personal funds and not TUF's, the company in which Dejphon seemed to own less than a five per cent shareholding. 'I myself own businesses in real estate and construction in Thailand,' he would explain; companies such as Chansiri Real Estate Co., Ltd. (in which he owned a 25.4 per cent share), Thai Union Properties Co., Ltd. (six per cent) and Geminai & Associate Co., Ltd. (92 per cent). 'I have purchased Sheffield Wednesday Football Club independently through my own funds.' The outgoing Mandarić, meanwhile, would assure everyone how Chansiri 'is absolutely the right person to take Sheffield Wednesday forward'.

At his official, post-Football-League-ratification unveiling, Chansiri would tell a packed press conference all about his plans for the club. 'I believe this club has huge potential,' he would say via a translator. 'I want to get Sheffield Wednesday back in the Premier League and make the supporters of this club proud… I will do the very best within my powers to get this club back where it belongs.'

He would elaborate on how he hoped to achieve this 'in a smart and sustainable manner'. 'There needs to be some investment,' he said, 'but just throwing money at a club is not a guarantee of success.' Indication, perhaps, that a Leicester City-type approach to a Premier League return, where fellow Thai owners the Raksriaksorn family had thrown over £100m of their fortune at the club, would not be the way under Chansiri.

Even before the takeover had been announced, Chansiri helped fund the January 2015 loan signings of Manchester United's Will Keane and Chelsea's Lewis Baker.

After that, but before his unveiling, Wednesday brought in the Romanian striker Sergiu Buş, believed to have cost £375,000 from CSKA Sofia; Manchester United's Belgian youngster Marnick Vermijl, undisclosed fee; Filipe Melo from Portuguese club Moreirense, undisclosed; along with key midfielder Lewis McGugan, brought back on loan following an earlier spell from Watford. Improvements to the club's infrastructure would also be promised. It all suggested positive beginnings for another new era under the new owner.

As for Mandarić, about to leave the club having swooped in to the rescue in 2010, he had some final words. 'I didn't sell the club for the money,' he would say, 'or because I have to leave; I sold it because these people are more aggressive financially and they will do their job.'

Before the Cardiff City game at Hillsborough in early February 2015, when the deal to sell to Chansiri was nearly complete, Mandarić would say farewell to the club and the fans, taking to the pitch just before kick-off. As blue and white placards were held up by fans in the North Stand, spelling out in Serbian the message 'Хвала Milan' (Thank You Milan'), and the crowd gave him a standing ovation, chanting his name, it was goodbye.

'My friends,' he said, 'four years ago I came in front of you and asked you for your support and your trust... [to] make some progress as much as possible on the field and off the field... You responded with [a] very special relationship that I will cherish for a very long time... We always trusted each other... [and] I [will] miss you greatly... I love you. I thank you... God bless you all.'

Goodbye Mr Mandarić.

Хвала Milan.

* * * *

So, as one more chapter had ended in the story of Sheffield Wednesday, another had now begun.

With the thrust of the change of ownership adding to the decent momentum achieved so far in 2014/15, the Owls, by the end of the campaign, would finish 13th in the Championship – a sound achievement, many thought. Chansiri, however, had bigger plans for the club than that; he had spoken of returning Wednesday to the Premier League in the near future, and ahead of 2015/16 got to work putting in place what was needed to help Wednesday achieve that goal.

That summer saw a number of changes on the footballing side. One was the establishment of a new three-man advisory committee that sought to guide Chansiri on footballing matters. One of that committee's members would be the former West Ham and Newcastle manager Glenn Roeder. The committee would later be disbanded, however, when Chansiri felt he had sufficiently learned the ropes.

Then came the more radical move of parting with Wednesday's well-liked head coach, Stuart Gray.

Gray had been in charge of the first team since late 2013 having taken over from Dave Jones and, considering the lack of resources that had been available to him for bringing in new players, many believed he had done a good job – this, despite the football that his team had played through 2014/15 often being a reserved and less than exciting brand: only 16 goals and five wins at Hillsborough that season. Ultimately, then, with Chansiri in search of 'attacking, aggressive football with entertainment for the fans', it was decided that Gray would be moved on.

His replacement would be the relatively unknown – in England at least – Carlos Carvalhal, a well-travelled Portuguese coach with a CV that listed 14 clubs in three different countries, through a period of 17 years.

Few in Sheffield appeared to know who the new man actually was, but encouraging details would soon be learned of him. That he had authored two coaching guides: *Futebol: Um Saber Sobre O Saber Fazer* (available in English as: *Soccer: Developing a Know-How*) and the Portuguese-only *Entre Linhas* (translated as *Between the Lines*).

That he was a friend of José Mourinho. And most of all that he was a hardworking, thoughtful, analytical student of the game. 'I wake up at 7.30am and go to sleep at 10pm every day…' he would say; 'All that time I'm focused on work'; and he had a strong vision of how football should be played – something along the lines of, 'you run, but you run all the time with the ball… Always with the ball'; 'We must play good football.'

The 'Carvalhal Way' chimed with what Chansiri wanted.

To help build his new team, Carvalhal would receive strong support from the owner in the transfer market.

Incoming to Hillsborough that summer would be, in back-to-front order on the pitch: Crystal Palace back-up keeper Lewis Price (free transfer) and right-back Jack Hunt (season-long loan), FC Twente defender Darryl Lachman (undisclosed fee), Frenchman Vincent Sasso (season-long loan from SC Braga), Charlton left-back Rhoys Wiggins (undisclosed fee, believed to be around £750,000), Spanish midfielder Alex Lopez (borrowed for the season from Celta Vigo), wingers Ross Wallace (free transfer from Burnley) and Modou Sougou (also a free after he had departed Marseille), and following his two earlier loan spells with the club the season before, Lewis McGugan, joining from Watford for a reported £300,000.

The Portuguese forwards Marco Matias (aged 26) and Lucas João (21) also arrived from Nacional, their cost thought to be in the region of £1.1m and £2m respectively (though in the era of the undisclosed fee, it is difficult to know how much for sure). Then later, after the season had got going, Watford's feisty Italian under-21 international forward Fernando Forestieri would be signed for a fee believed to be around £3m. He was a terrific capture – skilful, creative, passionate; a true statement of intent from Wednesday. As was the free transfer signing from Crystal Palace of the Scottish international Barry Bannan who brought tremendous quality and passing ability to Wednesday's midfield.

Czech international left-back Daniel Pudil also joined from Watford on a season-long loan, as did Norwich's experienced centre-back Michael Turner. Finally, Turner's Norwich teammate Gary Hooper came in on another loan deal, the Owls supposedly covering the proven and prolific striker's reputed £32,000-per-week wages.

It had been some years since Wednesday had spent such sums in the transfer market on even one player, never mind a group of them. But the new man Carvalhal now had his players in place – the building blocks with which to create his vision of a team.

Making room for the new incomers had been the popular keeper Chris Kirkland; defenders Lewis Buxton, Dejan Kelhar, Kamil Zayatte and Joe Mattock; midfielders Giles Coke, Rhys McCabe and Jacques Maghoma; forward Chris Maguire and striker Gary Madine – all ten released for no fees. Later, striker Stevie May would be sold on to Preston, one disappointing season after arriving from St Johnstone for a fee apparently in the region of £1m. Meanwhile, the £7m sale by Nottingham Forest to West Ham of Michail Antonio would earn Wednesday about £1m in a sell-on fee for the winger that had been sold on the previous summer.

And with that Carvalhal forged his new look Wednesday into a confident, pressing, hardworking, at times classy, prolific, entertaining and, above all, *winning* unit.

Following a tricky opening run, where only one win was found from the first five league games – the highlights of that spell being a 2-0 win over Bristol City, Marco Matias's wonder volley against Leeds at Elland Road, and an excellent performance at eventual champions Burnley, where although the Owls went down 3-1, the football they played was great – the real good stuff was to come.

Games would be won – over Fulham (3-2 at Hillsborough), Brentford (2-1 away) and Preston (3-1 at home), then a good draw at home against Hull City (1-1). Excellent football would be played – Fernando Forestieri hunting down the goals (he'd have ten in the league by the New Year); Barry Bannan, Kieran Lee and Ross Wallace in the midfield pinging the ball around the new levelled-off and smooth, part-artificial Desso pitch (which had been laid that summer to replace the previous bog-like and uneven playing surface). And the table would be climbed. Even Premier League Newcastle United and Arsenal would be knocked out of the League Cup.

For the 3-0 despatch of Arsenal, a glorious and dominant display, 35,065 were there at Hillsborough to see Carvalhal's lads go right from the start full pelt at Arsène Wenger's team. The Owls worked and worked, carried out Carvalhal's plan, passed the ball around with confidence and overwhelmed their top-tier opponents.

Wallace, Lucas João and Sam Hutchinson were on the scoresheet that marvellous night, one that marked a key early staging post for the progress already being made by this emerging Owls side.

After Christmas, following a good run of great wins and top performances, culminating in a 2-0 victory over Leeds at Hillsborough, the entertaining Owls moved into the play-off positions.

Was this really happening?

Certainly, it had been a dramatic transformation. From steady progress in the Championship (avoid relegation; then aim a bit higher), Wednesday had kicked on significantly. The team was looking good. The likes of Forestieri and Carvalhal already loved and idolised. And Wednesday in the play-off places – after so long away, the Premier League and all its riches (at least £100m in television revenue for the team finishing bottom in 2016/17) now able to be properly glimpsed.

For Wednesdayites everywhere this new way of being for the team, and for the club, meant so much.

* * * *

'I'm having a great time,' says Nigel Short outside the Kop, catching up before one game then heading into the ground. 'I turn up now expecting us to win. And it's been a long time since you could think that as a Wednesday fan.

'It was early in the season, at Burnley away, that I started to think this season could be good. We lost [3-1] but the way we played was brilliant I thought. And really it continued since then.'

Of course back between 2006 and 2008 Short had experienced Wednesday trying to sue him for comments he had made online about how his club was being run, at the same time as he was fighting cancer. And as he explains of his experiences today, things are quite different, 'It really is great being a Wednesday fan at the moment,' he says with a smile. 'Certainly it's better than when I was getting sued. These days it's a pleasure to come here.

'And the new owner, Mr Chansiri, seems like he's in it for the long haul. Generally I'd say I'm cautiously optimistic about him. I've seen too much down here over the years to be anything other than that. But he does seem to represent stability, with ambition. And as long as he keeps sending us in the right direction, to me that's great.'

* * * *

At this stage little was still known of Dejphon Chansiri, the man from Bangkok who was funding, and enabling the club's swift progress. He seemed quiet, not too many interviews nor comments from him. But the occasional sights of him standing and smiling on the Hillsborough pitch, or holding a blue and white scarf over his head, showed how much he was enjoying himself.

What was learned of him, though, was how astutely he had worked in the background to quickly push the club on, hopefully to the Premier League. Chansiri had decided to move on Gray and take the perhaps bold step of replacing him with Carvalhal. The team had been invested in significantly (certainly when compared with previous years), though good value had been found in the transfer market. Moves had been made to improve the whole environment at the club both for the players and the supporters – spruced up changing rooms, concourse and corporate facilities; mega new video scoreboard installed between the South and West Stands; the new playing surface. The 'highest-ranking Buddhist in Thailand', Somdej Phra Wannarat, had even been invited over to Sheffield to bless the club.

No doubt, Chansiri had been delivering, appearing to be underpinning much, or most of the financial resources required to do this himself (as opposed to, say, turning to the bank as the club had once done back in its troubled, ever more distancing past).

Although back in the summer a lot of the club's supporters had not reacted well to the new, increased ticket prices which had been introduced where a non-season-ticket-holding adult choosing to sit behind the goal on the Kop that season would now have to pay between £20 and £45 per game to watch Wednesday. For the opening-day game against Bristol City, the price for this ticket would be £39, or £46 to sit along the side of the pitch on the South Stand. The season before, the equivalent price for the first home game of the season had been £25. On average across the 23 home league games that season a walk-up-and-pay-on-the-day, no-membership adult ticket for the Kop would end up costing just over £31, compared to the equivalent average of just over £24 per game the season before. Still, over 14,000 more people would watch football at Hillsborough in 2015/16 than they had the season before; over 25,000 more would sit in the home stands than the previous year, and just under 11,000 less in the away end than the previous year.

January 2016 saw further moves to consolidate the playing squad with the Owls – Chansiri – spending again to make permanent Hunt's loan deal from Crystal Palace (undisclosed fee) and Hooper's from Norwich (£3m believed to be the price for him) – after hitting six goals in the six previous games of his loan spell, Hooper in particular was a much-welcomed permanent signing.

Also joining on loan for the rest of the season was Everton's Republic of Ireland international winger Aiden McGeady and the Aston Villa full-back Joe Bennett, a former Middlesbrough youngster for whom Villa had previously paid £2.75m. Extended contracts would be handed to captain Glenn Loovens, Sam Hutchinson, Barry Bannan and giant striker Atdhe Nuhiu. While out of the door would go Rhoys Wiggins, joining Bournemouth for a reported £200,000, about £500,000 less than the Owls were believed to have paid Charlton for the defender back in the summer; along with the barely-used striker Sergiu Buş; and the never-used defender Darryl Lachman.

Based on all of the reputed, reported and strongly rumoured fees that had been spent, and received by the club so far in 2015/16, net transfer business for Wednesday stood at over £8m (though very possibly more than that). Added to that were the fees paid to other clubs for the loans and the most likely dramatic increase to the club's wage bill.

Of course the club had now to ensure that they complied with the Football League's Financial Fair Play (FFP) rules, which in 2015/16 would allow a club to lose £13m, excluding certain expenditure, such as youth development and infrastructure costs, with transfer embargos to be handed to clubs that did not comply with the regulations, and stipulations applying over how a portion of that amount could be funded – that is, via equity contributions from a benefactor(s).

* * * *

In February, at Birmingham, Carvalhal's men, newly bolstered from the previous month's transfer activity, continued their entertaining upwards drive as at St Andrew's, in the pissing rain, they saw off one of their play-off rivals with a 2-1 scoreline.

That day, Wednesday had trailed, had lost to injury goalkeeper Westwood and midfielder Hutchinson, while Kieran Lee had also pulled out in the warm-up, but with less than 15 minutes remaining they had come back to brilliantly take the win. In the away end the 3,047 travelling Wednesdayites went barmy for each of Hooper's goals.

After the whistle, when the lads celebrated in front of the away end, it was clear that the win meant as much to them as the fans cheering and singing in front of them. That day, that season, those players – *our brothers* – cared. *All in it together until the end.* The Owls sat sixth in the table.

A worrying wobble did come – five without a win, only one goal scored, key man and top scorer with 12 goals for the season, Forestieri, sent off *twice* in those games. But fear not, 'We don't have nerves and think [that] we must achieve this, we must achieve that,' Carvalhal would say. 'We just do what we like to do, play football, try to put quality on the pitch and try to win the games.' And enough winning days would come again.

At Forest, the returning Forestieri drove the dominant and classy 3-0 win. Next, 3-0 at home to Charlton. Then, after Easter at Huddersfield, 1-0 – Bannan, midway through a three-game suspension, celebrating in the away end with the other 3,955 from Sheffield: *All in it together.* Then Blackburn, 2-1 at home. Five points clear in the play-off positions. Who knew how it would end.

* * * *

Friday 15 April 2016 brought the 27th anniversary of the Hillsborough disaster, that tragic day back in 1989 that led to 96 football fans attending the Liverpool v Nottingham Forest FA Cup semi-final, losing their lives at Wednesday's home ground because of the crushing on the Leppings Lane terrace.

Since that day the families of the victims, and the survivors had searched relentlessly for justice. But mostly they had searched without success.

In the immediate aftermath of the disaster there had been the shameful smearing of the Liverpool fans with the Establishment and media combining to wrongly push drunkenness, ticketless-ness and hooliganism as contributory factors to the event – rather than, as Lord Taylor's subsequent report into the disaster would find, because of Wednesday's failure to provide a ground that was safe and Sheffield City Council for failing to provide the ground with an up to date safety certificate, along with, primarily, the police's 'failure to handle the crowd'.

Then there had been the inquest in 1991 in which the jury had returned the verdict of 'accidental death' for the victims, as opposed to unlawful killing. Then came the revelations that over 150 police statements taken in the aftermath of the disaster had subsequently been altered, with comments having being added to help point blame towards the Liverpool fans, and/or parts having been removed which had been unfavourable to South Yorkshire Police. And then the criminal trial of Chief Superintendent David Duckenfield, the man in charge of police operations that day, who in 2000 had avoided by a hung jury a guilty charge of manslaughter.

As the years ticked by, it had seemed like justice would not be found.

But then came the publication of the Independent Hillsborough Panel's new, almost-400-page report that in 2012 reiterated emphatically Lord Taylor's earlier findings that the disaster had not been the fault of the Liverpool fans. But also, that the crushing that day had been foreseeable, that the victims had been subject to significant obstacles to find justice, and tragically how over 40 of those people might have been saved had appropriate action been taken on the day by the various authorities responsible for their safety that day. The report led to the High Court quashing the result of the original inquest, and in 2014 the new inquests into the disaster had begun.

Held in Warrington, Cheshire, the new inquests had heard evidence from hundreds of people relating to the disaster, including relatives of the victims, survivors and emergency-services workers, along with both rank-and-file and top-level police officers. From the latter group had been Duckenfield:

'You breached your duty of care to ensure the safety of the fans, didn't you?' it was put to Duckenfield on one of the days he had stood to give evidence.

'Overall, yes sir,' he replied.

'Your negligence caused the disaster and the deaths of 96 Liverpool fans, didn't it?'

'I wouldn't use the word negligence, sir,' he replied.

But the jury disagreed and in April 2016, in that courtroom in Warrington, Cheshire, more than two years since the inquests had begun, they would return their verdicts:

That each of the 96 victims had in fact been 'unlawfully killed', and that Duckenfield, having breached his duty of care to the dead, was 'responsible for manslaughter by gross negligence'.

That on the day of the disaster, the Liverpool supporters had *not* demonstrated any behaviour which had 'or *may have* caused or contributed to the dangerous situation at the Leppings Lane turnstiles'. But rather, that it was police failings that were, as David Conn would write in *The Guardian*, 'the principal cause of the disaster'.

Also that after the crush had begun to develop errors and omissions in both the police and ambulance service's emergency responses had 'caused or contributed to the loss of lives'.

When the jury was asked if there were any 'features of the design, construction and layout of the stadium which you consider were dangerous or defective and which caused or contributed to the disaster?' the answer was 'Yes'.

When asked 'Was there any error or omission in the safety certification and oversight of Hillsborough stadium that caused or contributed to the disaster?' the answer was 'Yes'.

And when asked 'Was there any error or omission by Sheffield Wednesday FC (and its staff) on 15 April 1989 which *may have* caused or contributed to the dangerous situation that developed at the Leppings Lane turnstiles and in the west terrace?' the answer was 'Yes' too.

On hearing the verdicts, the families and the survivors had cheered and cried in the courtroom. The long, long wait was over. Twenty-seven years on from the disaster, the first moment of justice for the 96 had been found.

At the time of writing, two investigations into possible criminal offences committed by individuals and corporate bodies in the run-up to the disaster, and in its aftermath, were ongoing.

* * * *

Back in Sheffield, with six games of the 2015/16 season to go, Wednesday still sat in the play-off positions but again had wobbled – going down 4-1 at Bristol City, drawing with Ipswich and Milton Keynes at Hillsborough and then away at Derby. With only two games to go, the gap over seventh-placed Cardiff City was down to four points. But Wednesday played them next – lose in the showdown home fixture and the gap would be down to one point with one game left.

After all of Wednesday's hard work for the season, their shot at a return to the Premier League – something few Owls fans would have contemplated only a year or so before, such was the progress that had been made, the entertaining and winning football that they had been given by Carvalhal's men that season – was now under threat.

'We must just focus on the next game, do what we are doing in the quality we have been doing it in,' said Carvalhal calmly before the Cardiff game. And 31,843 would be there at Hillsborough to see it. All three home sides of the stadium full with Wednesdayites for the massive fixture.

In the hour before kick-off the rain had fallen around the stadium as it filled up and the anticipation for the game grew. What it all meant; could mean. Sixteen years since dropping out of the Premier League. The possibility of taking that top six position and having a bash at going all the way.

All the Owls needed was a draw.

Kick-off neared and, as before with the Wycombe League 1 promotion game back at the end of 2011/12, where the inflatables had bouncing around the Kop, the beach balls and the paddling pools were again swirling round and round. 'We're all Wednesday aren't we, We're all Wednesday aren't we?' went the crowd. Loud.

It would be a dominant and classy Wednesday display. The Owls were right back on form as they brushed Cardiff aside with three second-half goals, Hooper bagging two of them with Hillsborough rocking for each.

Three points in the bag. The play-off position secured with a game to spare up their sleeve. The fans, again, jumped and hugged. Top man Carvalhal gave the Kop a wave. And the rain stopped and the sun shone.

A week later, at Wolves, the less-used members of the squad got a run out and Wednesday lost 2-1. But that didn't matter.

		P	Pts	GD
1	Burnley	46	93	37
2	Middlesbrough	46	89	32
3	Brighton and Hove Albion	46	89	30
4	Hull City	46	83	34
5	Derby County	46	78	23
6	Sheffield Wednesday	46	74	21
7	Ipswich Town	46	69	2

Whatever happened next, the future for Wednesday was brighter than it had been for some time before.

The Premier League in sight. The possible return?

Who knew.

Epilogue

Home

SHEFFIELD. 2016. Pre-match build up, a new routine. You walk the long way down the hill, along through Crookes and past your pubs, down by Walkley. You turn the corner and there, laid out in front, is the view ahead and below – the rows of houses stretching out, the factory chimneys and the hills behind them rising.

Further down and left is the ground. Hillsborough. Home. The hub in blue and white. Where it all happens. Where it all happened. Coming into view at the end of the park.

Standing there for a minute, you take it in, before your head drifts to those familiar thoughts of the past.

The thoughts of Wilko's batterers, Atkinson's artists and Francis's Wembley heartbreakers.

Then the thoughts of the decline and the debt. The custodians of our club, the old guard. And of Di Canio, pushing the ref, a moment to push off the club's fall.

The thoughts of how the more you worked through the project, this journey and story of your football club, the more you understood. Understood what happened here in Sheffield, down there at Wednesday.

Standing there, you think of that line from Jim senior's poem, 'These are things I know.'

* * * *

Further down, you walk to Hillsborough corner. Cross over the river and into the pub for the warm-up where you talk of Wednesday with your friends. Happy times now these days. Carvalhal's lads, playing it around on the grass; playing like nothing you have seen from a Wednesday team in years.

You finish up the drinks and follow the tram tracks along... Veering off to the park, snaking your way with the others along the path. Then, up ahead and behind the railings, peeking through the trees at the end, there it is: Hillsborough.

As you walk and get nearer you think of the years in the doldrums and the wilderness. You think of the reprieve of Cardiff 2005 – 40,000 Wednesdayites together for the play-off party. Then you think of the people trying to bring a change at your club – through all of that to here and today, to Chansiri and his money, Carvalhal and the team. A changed football club. Us looking upwards now and not down.

On to Penistone Road, you get the programme at the bridge then, walking on, past the families and the friends, you make your way along for another dose.

HOME

Once more you move through the old brick turnstile of the Kop and climb up the steps to your place. You look around at the ground filling up, then down over the rows and rows that stretch down to the pitch where the Owls are, ready to go.

And the fans, all around you sing, 'We're Sheffield Wednesday, we're on our way back.'

Postscript: Play-offs

13 May 2016. Championship play-offs semi-final, first leg. Hillsborough Stadium, Sheffield. Attendance: 34,260
Sheffield Wednesday 2 Brighton and Hove Albion 0

16 May 2016. Championship play-offs semi-final, second leg. The Amex Stadium, Brighton. Attendance: 27,272
Brighton and Hove Albion 1 Sheffield Wednesday 1 (aggregate 1-3)

28 May 2016. Championship play-offs final. Wembley Stadium, London. Attendance: 70,189
Sheffield Wednesday 0 Hull City 1

Always next year.

Appendix

Sheffield Wednesday – Statistics: 1985–2016

Season	League Tier	Tier	Position	£Turnover	£Profit/ Loss	£Debt*
1985/86	First	1	5th	3.2m	0.4m	0.2m
1986/87	First	1	13th	2.3m	0.2m	0.1m
1987/88	First	1	11th	2.2m	-0.4m	0.6m
1988/89	First	1	15th	2.3m	-0.1m	0.1m
1989/90	First	1	18th (R)	2.8m	-1.7m	1.6m
1990/91	Second	2	3rd (P)	5.9m	0.2m	0.9m
1991/92	First	1	3rd	7.5m	-2.4m	3.3m
1992/93	Premier	1	7th	12.8m	1.4m	1.9m
1993/94	Premier	1	7th	11.9m	-0.2m	1.8m
1994/95	Premier	1	13th	11m	1m	2.6m
1995/96	Premier	1	15th	10m	-2.3m	8.3m
1996/97	Premier	1	7th	14.3m	-3.2m	10.3m
1997/98	Premier	1	16th	16.3m	-4.8m	6.4m
1998/99	Premier	1	12th	19.1m	-9.2m	11.7m
1999/00	Premier	1	19th (R)	18m	-2.6m	16.2m
2000/01	First	2	17th	13.2m	-9.1m	16.3m
2001/02	First	2	20th	18.6m	-0.4m	17.2m
2002/03	First	2	22nd (R)	8.5m	-8.4m	23.6m
2003/04	Second	3	16th	9m	-4.1m	27.1m
2004/05	League 1	3	5th (P)	9.7m	-3m	27.5m
2005/06	Championship	2	19th	11.6m	-0.5m	27m
2006/07	Championship	2	9th	11.3m	1.5m	27.8m
2007/08	Championship	2	16th	12.3m	2.2m	25.8m
2008/09	Championship	2	12th	11.1m	-3.7m	25.6m
2009/10	Championship	2	22nd (R)	13.9m	-3.9m	26.4m
2010/11	League 1	3	15th	9.4m	-5.7m	6.4m
2011/12	League 1	3	2nd (P)	10.9m	-5.2m	9.1m
2012/13	Championship	2	18th	14.9m	-3.7m	13.1m
2013/14	Championship	2	16th	13.9m	-5.6m	23.8m
2014/15	Championship	2	13th	14.9m	-4.4m	5.7m
2015/16	Championship	2	6th	Not available at the time of publication		

*Bank borrowings and other loans (including directors and owner loans)

Sheffield Wednesday – League Position v £Debt

Acknowledgements

WHEN you work for so long on a project like this, it is amazing to discover just how many people are willing to help you out along the way. Whether sitting for an interview or offering their guidance, without their help this book would not have been possible.

When I sent out the outline idea to Paul at Pitch Publishing he was immediately enthusiastic, showed the faith and along with Jane supported me right until the end.

I am grateful of course to those who agreed to give up their time and be interviewed for the project. They were: Dave Allen, Andy Booth, Chris Brunt, Marc Degryse, Simon Donnelly, Trevor Francis, John Gath, Lee Grant, Steve Haslam, Gérard Houllier, Paul Jewell, Rob Kelly (who one bright September afternoon in Nottingham let me sit in Brian Clough's dugout), Darryl Keys, Darko Kovacevic (via Stella Samouilidou at Olympiacos), Mark Lewis, Graham Mackrell, Steve MacLean, Ian McMillan, James O'Connor, David Pleat, Darren Purse, Petter Rudi, Frankie Simek, Trond Egil Soltvedt, Paul Sturrock, Kevin Summerfield, Alan Sykes, Emerson Thome and Howard Wilkinson.

Extra special mentions must go to Daniel Gordon and Nigel Short who each repeatedly gave up their time to meet and talk to me, and to Lee Strafford who for hours and hours in Sheffield again and again took the time out to show me the way.

The following people were also kind enough to help with vital background information: Geoff Atkinson, Philippe Auclair, Narendra Bajarla, Dominique Bartholome (of *L'Equipe*, and *France*

Football), Ian Bason and the Foxes Trust, Matthew Bell, Mihir Bose, Dave Brown, James Corbett, Mark Edwards, Chris Eyre, Professor Chris Gratton, Professor Geoff Green, Nick Harris, Paul Holmes, Graeme Howlett, Phil Hunt at the International Steel Statistics Bureau (for the Sheffield steel output figures), Michael Kendrick, Dan King, Carl Lee, Ken Malley, Michael Morton, Rick Parry, Roger Reade, Richard Riggs and Chris Kitchen at the National Union of Mineworkers (for the miner's strike statistics), Paul Thompson, Rob Sawyer, Patrick Seyd, Matthew Slater, Raymond Sparkes, Rob Tanner, John Williams and Martyn Ziegler.

Gary Armstrong (a Blade), Anthony Clavane, Danny Broderick and my pal James Titterton (another Blade) were there throughout the process to offer their views, but also to help with reviewing part, or all of the text – their input was priceless. When at last the text became almost ready for public consumption, Kate Moore and chief editor Gareth Davis were on hand to expertly whip it into shape.

Trevor Braithwait at Sheffield Wednesday patiently put up with my requests to talk with Milan Mandarić and set up the first meeting. Although in the end a second meeting and full interview never did take place, never mind, it was still nice to meet you both. Olaf Dixon at the League Managers Association put me in touch with several of the club's past managers. And David Coupe kindly provided a long-term lend of his fantastic blue file of newspaper clippings.

Steve Titterton helped to broaden the range of the subject and, along with my friends Chris Olewicz and James Caruth, was there to listen to my ideas and offer some more back in return. In the early days Pat Allison helped with one of the trickier chapters; in the later days Dave Lawson did the same.

Just as I was getting started David Conn, whose work had gotten me into all of this stuff in the first place, was good enough to meet up and buy me lunch. Peter Markie was always there with an enthusiastic ear and a brew. Jim Caruth Senior shared his recollections of good times spent on the Kop and was happy to lend a line from one of his poems. Louis Clay gave up an afternoon to trudge around Hillsborough to take his lovely photos. Pete McKee allowed me to use the Wednesday cartoons (he also gave me an hour to share some of his memories and explain his process) and his manager, Chris Smith, helped find them. Ta lads.

ACKNOWLEDGEMENTS

Some people helped but for various reasons did not wish to be named. Their time and input was just as important and just as appreciated. You know who you are (unless you don't).

Thanks to my family and friends for all of their encouragement and support along this pretty long journey, especially my Dad who for several years has listened to me talking about the whole bloody thing, and my Mum, who is the best.

To anyone else who helped, thank you.

Up Sheffield! Up the Owls!

Bibliography

Books, Journals, Reports and Legal Cases

Sheffield Wednesday

Cowens, Steve and Cronshaw, *Anthony, Divide of the Steel City: Blade Versus Owl* (Pennant Books, 2007)

Croft, Wilf, *Wednesday Till You Die* (Crofty Tenerife, 2008)

Dickinson, Jason, *The Origins of Sheffield Wednesday* (Amberley Publishing, 2015). *One Hundred Years at Hillsborough: 1899-1999* (The Hallamshire Press, 1999)

Dickinson, Jason and Brodie, John, *The Wednesday Boys: A Definitive Who's Who of Sheffield Wednesday Football Club* (Pickard Communications, 2005). *Sheffield Wednesday: The Complete Record* (Derby Books, 2011)

Ellis, Steve, *Hillsborough: A 21-Year Photographic History* (The Hallamshire Press, 1997)

Farnsworth, Keith, *Sheffield Football: A History, Volume I, 1857-1961* (The Hallamshire Press, 1995). *Sheffield Football: A History, Volume II, 1961-1995* (The Hallamshire Press, 1995). *Wednesday Every Day of the Week* (Breedon Books Publishing, 1998). *Wednesday!: The History of Sheffield's Oldest Professional Football Club* (Sheffield City Library, 1982)

Firth, John, *I Hate Football: A Fan's Memoir* (PeakPublish, 2009)

Gordon, Daniel, *A Quarter of Wednesday: A New History of Sheffield Wednesday, 1970-1995* (Wednesday Publishing, 1995). *Blue and White Wizards: The Sheffield Wednesday Dream Team* (Mainstream, 2002)

Johnson, Nick, *Image of Sport: Sheffield Wednesday, 1876-1967* (Tempus Publishing Ltd., 2003).

Kings of Cardiff: A Pictorial Celebration of Sheffield Wednesday's 2004/05 Promotion Campaign (Greenpark Publishing, 2005)

Sparling, Richard A., *The Romance of the Wednesday: 1867-1926* (Desert Island Books, 1997)

Whitworth, Tom and Olewicz, Chris, *20 Legends: Sheffield Wednesday* (Vertical Editions, 2012)

Sheffield and The North

Armitage, Simon, *All Points North* (Viking, 1998)

Beattie, Geoffrey, *Survivors of Steel City: A Portrait of Sheffield* (Chatto & Windus Ltd, 1986)

Bennett, Larry, *Neighbourhood Politics: Chicago and Sheffield* (Garland Publishing, 1997)

Bergmann, Alexander (ed), *Music-City. Sports-City. Leisure-City. A Reader on Different Concepts of Culture, Creative Industries and Urban Regeneration Attempts* (Grin, 2008)

Binfield, Chris et al. (eds.), *The History of the City of Sheffield, Volumes I, II and III, 1843-1993* (Sheffield Academic Press, 1993)

Blunkett, David and Green, Geoff, *Building from the Bottom: The Sheffield Experience* (Fabian Society, 1983)

Collie, Keith, Levitt, David and Till, Jeremy, *Park Hill – Sheffield: in Black and White* (Categorical Books, 2012)

Docherty, Charles, *Steel and Steelworkers: The Sons of Vulcan* (Heinemann Educational Books, 1983)

Fisher, Mark and Owen, Ursula (eds.), *Whose Cities?* (Penguin, 1991)

Fishwick, Nicholas, *From Clegg to Clegg House: The Official Centenary of the Sheffield and Hallamshire Football Association – 1886-1986* (Sheffield and Hallamshire County Football Association, 1986)

Foley, Paul, *The Impact of Major Events: A Case Study of the World Student Games and Sheffield* (Department of Town and Regional Planning, Faculty of Architectural Studies, The University of Sheffield, 1991)

Griffiths, Paul, *The Five Weirs Walk* (The Hallamshire Press, 1999)

Hampton, William, *Democracy and Community: A Study of Politics in Sheffield* (Oxford University Press, 1970)

Harman, Ruth and Minnis, John, *Pevsner Architectural Guides: Sheffield* (Yale University Press, 2004)

Hartley, Jean, Kelly, John and Nicholson, Nigel, *Steel Strike: A Case Study in Industrial Relations* (Batsford Academic and Educational Ltd., 1983)

Hattersley, Roy, *A Yorkshire Boyhood* (Chatto & Windus, 1983). *Between Ourselves* (Pan Books, 1994). *Goodbye to Yorkshire* (Littlehampton Books Services, 1976). *Who Goes Home? Scenes from a Political Life* (Abacus, 1995)

Hey, David, *A History of Sheffield* (Carnegie Publishing Ltd., updated 2010)

Hey, David, Olive, Martin and Liddament, Martin, *Forging the Valley* (Sheffield Academic Press, 1997)

Hinds, Barry, *Looks and Smiles* (Michael Joseph, 1981)

Hinds, Barry, Howard, Russell, Mangan, Michael, and Dave, Sheasby, *Threads and other Sheffield Plays (Sheffield Academic Press, 1990)*

Horton, Bob, *Living in Sheffield: 1,000 Years of Change* (The Breedon Books Publishing Company Limited, 1999)

Howse, Geoffrey, *A Photographic History of Sheffield Steel* (Sutton Publishing Ltd., 2001)

Jackson, Bernard with Wardle, Tony, *The Battle for Orgreave* (Vanson Wardle Production Ltd., 1986)

Judd, Dennis and Parkinson, Michael (eds.), *Leadership and Urban Regeneration* (Sage Publications, 1990)

Lee, Carl, *Home: A Personal Geography of Sheffield* (Fou Fou Publishing, 2009)

McKee, Pete, *22 Views of Sheffield* (Pete McKee, 2009). *The Joy of Sheffield* (Pete McKee, 2013)

McMillan, Ian, *Neither Nowt Nor Summat: In Search of the Meaning of Yorkshire* (Ebury Press, 2015)

Peace, David, *GB84* (Faber and Faber 2003)

Pevsner, Nikolaus and Radcliffe, Enid, *The Buildings of England – Yorkshire: The West Riding* (Penguin, 1967)

Pollard, Sidney and Holmes, Colin (eds.), *Essays in the Economic and Social History of South Yorkshire* (South Yorkshire County Council, Recreation, Culture and Health Department, 1976)

Price, David, *Sheffield Troublemakers: Rebels and Radicals in Sheffield History* (Phillimore & Co. Ltd, 2008)

Pybus, Sylvia, *'Damned Bad Place, Sheffield': An Anthology of Writing About Sheffield Through the Ages* (Sheffield Academic Press, 1994)

Russell, Dave, *Looking North: Northern England and the National Imagination* (Manchester University Press, 2004).

Sheffield: City on the Move (Sheffield Corporation, 1972)

Smith, Martin, *The Great Flood: How Sheffield, Rotherham, Barnsley, Doncaster, Chesterfield and Worksop Survived the Summer Showers of 2007* (At Heart Publications, 2007).

State of Sheffield Report (Sheffield Executive Board, 2014; 2015; 2016)

Sutton, G.W., *The World Student Games: Report of the District Auditor* (District Audit Service, 1992)

Taylor, Ian, Evans, Karen and Fraser, Penny, *A Tale of Two Cities: Global change, local feeling and everyday life in the North of England – A Study of Manchester and Sheffield* (Routledge, 1996)

Tuffrey, Peter, *Sheffield Flats: Park Hill and Hyde Park – Hope, Eye-Sore, Heritage* (Fonthill Media Ltd., 2013). *Yorkshire People and Coal* (Amberley Publishing, 2012)

Vickers, J. Edward, *A Popular History of Sheffield* (EP Publishing Limited, 1978)

Wainwright, Martin, *True North* (Guardian Books, 2010)

Warman, C. R., *Sheffield: Emerging City* (The City Engineer and Surveyor and Town Planning Officer, Sheffield, 1969)

Westergaard, John, Noble, Iain and Walker, Alan, *After Redundancy: The experience of Economic Insecurity* (Polity Press, 1989)

Autobiography/Biography

Ashton, Joe, *Red Rose Blues: The Story of a Good Labour Man* (Macmillan, 2000)

Atkinson, Ron, *The Manager* (deCoubertin Books Ltd., 2016). *Big Ron: A Different Ball Game* (Andre Deutsch, 1998)

Auclair, Philippe, *Cantona: The Rebel Who Would be King* (Macmillan, 2009)

Biggs, Alan, *Confessions of a Football Reporter: Another Biggs at Large* (Vertical Editions, 2011)

Blunkett, David, *The Blunkett Tapes: My Life in the Bear Pit* (Bloomsbury, 2006)

Blunkett, David with MacCormick, Alex, *On a Clear Day* (Michael O'Mara Books Limited, 2002)

Bullen, Lee with Biggs, Alan, *No Bull: The Lee Bullen Story* (Vertical Editions, 2013)

Charlton, Jack, *Jack Charlton: The Autobiography* (Partridge Press, 1996)

Coe, Seb, *Running My Life: The Autobiography* (Hodder & Stoughton, 2012)

Cooper, Andrew, *Eric Taylor: A Biography* (A. Cooper Publications, 2011)

Crace, Jon, *Harry's Games: Inside the mind of Harry Redknapp* (Constable, 2013)

Davies, David, *FA Confidential: Sex, Drugs and Penalties – The Inside Story of English Football* (Simon & Schuster, 2008)

De Bilde, Gilles and Raes, Frank, *Gilles: Mijn Verhall* [My Story] (Van Halewyck, 2004)

Dennis, John and Murray, Matthew, *John Dennis: The Oakwell Years: It Was Sometimes Like Watching Brazil…* (Wharncliffe Books, 2012)

Di Canio, Paolo with Marcotti, Gabriele, *Paolo Di Canio: The Autobiography* (Collins Willow, 2000)

Di Canio, Paolo, *Il Ritorno: Un Anno Vissuto Pericolosamente* [The Return: A Year Lived Dangerously] (Baldini Castoldi Dalai, 2005)

Dooley, Derek and Farnsworth, Keith, *Dooley* (The Hallamshire Press, 2000)

Ferguson, Alex with McIlvanney, Hugh, *Managing My Life: My Autobiography* (Hodder and Stoughton, 1999)

Francis, Trevor with Miller, David, *The World to Play For* (Sidgwick and Jackson Ltd., 1982)

Graham, George with Giller, Norman, *George Graham: The Glory and the Grief* (Andre Deutsch Ltd., 1995)

Harkes, John, *Captain for Life: And Other Temporary Assignments* (Gale Cengage, 1999)

Hughes, Rob with Francis, Trevor, *Trevor Francis: Anatomy of a £1 million Player* (World's Work Ltd., 1980)

BIBLIOGRAPHY

Jones, Dave with Warshaw, Andrew, *No Smoke, No Fire: The Autobiography of Dave Jones* (Pitch Publishing, 2011)

Kelly, Graham with Harris, Bob, *Sweet FA* (CollinsWillow, 1999)

Kelly, Stephen F., *Gerard Houllier: The Biography* (Virgin Books, 2004)

Laws, Brian with Biggs, Alan, *Laws of the Jungle: Surviving Football's Monkey Business* (Vertical Editions, 2012)

McMillan, Ian, *Talking Myself Home: My Life in Verses* (John Murray Publishers, 2008)

Megson, Don with Olewicz, Chris, *Don Megson: A Life in Football* (Vertical Editions, 2014)

Redknapp, Harry and Samuel, Martin, *Always Managing: My Autobiography* (Ebury Press, 2013)

Sawyer, Rob, *Harry Catterick: The Untold Story of a Football Great* (deCoubertin Books Ltd., 2014)

Semedo, José and Kotadia, Sam, *Win the Day: Courage, Positive Thinking and the Warrior Spirit* (Mindsport Ltd., 2015)

Srnicek, Pavel with Scott, Will, *Pavel is a Geordie* (Mojo Risin' Publishing, 2015)

Stein, Mel, *Chris Waddle: The Authorised Biography* (Simon and Schuster, 1997)

Sterland, Mel with Johnson, Nick, *Boozing, Betting & Brawling: The Autobiography of Mel Sterland* (Green Umbrella, 2008)

Sturrock, Paul with Duddy, Charlie and Rundo, Peter, *Forward Thinking: The Paul Sturrock Story* (Mainstream, 1989)

Sturrock, Paul, *Luggy: The Autobiography of Paul Sturrock* (Pitch Publishing, 2015)

Warnock, Neil, *The Gaffer: The Trials and Tribulations of a Football Manager* (Headline, 2013)

Warnock, Neil with Holt, Oliver, *Made in Sheffield: My Story* (Hodder & Stoughton, 2007)

Wilkinson, Howard with Walker, David, *Managing to Succeed: My Life in Football Management* (Mainstream, 1992)

Woolnough, Brian, *Ken Bates: My Chelsea Dream* (Virgin Books, 1998)

Yorath, Terry with Grahame, Lloyd, *Hard Man, Hard Knocks* (Celluloid, 2004)

Football, General/Other

Arlott, John, *Concerning Soccer* (Longmans, Green and Co, 1952)

Armstrong, Gary, *Football Hooligans: Knowing the Score* (Berg, 1998)

Armstrong, Gary with Garrett, John, *Sheffield United FC: The Biography* (The Hallamshire Press, updated 2008)

Bell, Matthew and Armstrong, Gary, *Fit and Proper? Conflicts of Conscience in an English Football Club* (Peakpublish, 2010)

Bose, Mihir, *Game Changer: How the English Premier League Came to Dominate the World* (Marshall Cavendish, 2012)

Bower, Tom, *Broken Dreams: Vanity, Greed and the Souring of British Football* (Simon & Schuster, updated 2007)

Carvalhal, Carlos, Lage, Bruno and João Mário Oliveira, *Futebol: Um Saber Sobre O Saber Fazer* [Soccer: Developing a Know-How] (Prime Books, 2014)

Carvalhal, Carlos, *Entre Linhas* [Between the Lines] (Prime Books, 2014)

Clavane, Anthony, *A Yorkshire Tragedy* (Riverrun, 2016). *Promised Land: A Northern Love Story* (Yellow Jersey Press, 2010)

Conn, David, *The Beautiful Game? Searching for the Soul of Football* (Yellow Jersey Press, 2005). *The Football Business: Fair Game in the '90s?* (Mainstream, 1997). *Richer Than God: Manchester City, Modern Football and Growing Up* (Quercus, 2012)

Deloitte & Touche: Annual Review of Finance (various years)

Dobson, Stephen and Goddard, John, *The Economics of Football: Second Edition* (Cambridge University Press, 2011)

Dobson, Nigel, Holliday, Simon and Gratton, Chris, *Football Came Home: The Economic Impact of Euro '96* (The Leisure Industries Research Centre: Sheffield, 1997).

The FA and Premier League's Commission of Inquiry (FAPL) Report (1997)

Foot, John, *Calcio: A History of Italian Football* (Fourth Estate, 2006)

Fynn, Alex and Guest, Lynton, *Out of Time: Why Football Isn't Working* (Simon & Schuster, 1994)

Goldblatt, David, *The Ball is Round: A Global History of Football* (Viking, 2006). *The Game of Our Lives: The Meaning and Making of English Football* (Viking, 2014)

Hodkinson, Mark, *Life at the Top: A Brief Taste of the Big-time for Barnsley Football Club* (Queen Anne Press, 1998)

BIBLIOGRAPHY

House of Commons, Culture, Media and Sport Committee, *2018 World Cup Bid, Sixth Report of Session 2010-12* (HMSO, 2011). *Football Governance Report, Seventh Report of Session 2010-12, Volumes I and II* (HMSO, 2011). *Oral Evidence: Sir Dave Richards, Richard Scudamore, Brian Lee, Dennis Strudwick* (HMSO, 2011)

Hopcraft, Arthur, *The Football Man* (Collins, 1968)

Inglis, Simon, *Football Grounds of Britain, Third Edition* (Collins Willow, 1996). *League Football – and the Men Who Made It* (Willow, 1988)

Kuper, Simon and Szymanski, Stefan, *Why England Lose: And other Curious Football Phenomenon Explained* (Harper Collins, 2009)

Lansdown, Harry and Spillius, Alex (eds.), *Saturday's Boys: The Football Experience* (Willow Books, 1990)

Lovejoy, Joe, *Glory, Goals and Greed: 20 Years of the Premier League* (Mainstream, 2011)

Lyttle, Richard B., *Soccer Fever: A Year with the San Jose Earthquakes* (Doubleday & Company, Inc., 1977)

McMillan, Ian, *It's Just Like Watching Brazil: A Premiership Season in Verse* (Yorkshire Art Circus, 1999)

Plenderleith, Ian, *Rock 'n' Roll Soccer: The Short Life and Fast Times of the North American Soccer League* (Icon, 2014)

Reng, Ronald, *The Keeper of Dreams* (Yellow Jersey Press, 2004)

Ruhn, Christov (ed.), *Le Foot: The Legends of French Football* (Abacus, 2000)

Russell, Dave, *Football and the English* (Carnegie Publishing, 1997)

Singh, Gary, *The San Jose Earthquakes: A Seismic Soccer Legacy* (The History Press, 2015)

Szymanski, Stefan, *Football Economics and Policy: 1* (Pelgrave Macmillan, 2010)

Tomas, Jason, *Soccer Czars: A Searing Insight into the Private and Professional Lives of the Tycoons Running the Big Clubs and British Football* (Mainstream, 1996)

Tomkins, Paul, Riley, Graeme and Fulcher, Gary, *Pay As You Play: The True Price of Success in the Premier League Era* (GPRF Publishing, 2010)

Tossell, David, *Playing for Uncle Sam: The Brits' Story of the North American Soccer League* (Mainstream, 2003)

Ward, Andrew and Williams, John, *Football Nation: 60 Years of the Beautiful Game* (Bloomsbury, 2009)

Wangerin, David, *Soccer in a Football World* (When Saturday Comes Books Ltd., 2006)

Williams, John, Perkins, Sean, *Ticket Pricing, Football Business, and 'Excluded' Football Fans: Research on the 'New Economics' of Football Match Attendance in England* (Sir Norman Chester Centre for Football Research, 1998)

Wilson, Jonathan, *Inverting the Pyramid: The History of Football Tactics* (Orion, 2008)

Winner, David, *Those Feet: An Intimate History of English Football* (Bloomsbury, 2005)

Young, Percy M., *Football in Sheffield* (Stanley Paul, 1962)

Hillsborough Disaster

Hillsborough: The Report of the Hillsborough Independent Panel (HMSO, 2012)

The Hillsborough Stadium Disaster: Inquiry by Lord Justice Taylor: Interim Report (HMSO, 1989)

Scraton, Phil, *Hillsborough: The Truth* (Mainstream, updated 2016)

Taylor, Rogan and Ward, Andrew, Newburn, Tim (eds.), *The Day of the Hillsborough Disaster: A Narrative Account* (Liverpool University Press, 1995)

Tempany, Adrian, *And the Sun Shines Now: How Hillsborough and the Premier League Changed Britain* (Faber and Faber, 2016)

Saloon-Bar Moanings (Suing the Fans)

Norwich Pharmacal Co v Customs and Excise Commissioners [1974] AC 133 (HL)

Rogers, Kevin, 'Bloggers beware!', *New Law Journal*, 157 (1718-19), 2007

Rowbottom, Jacob, 'To rant, vent and converse: protecting low level digital speech', *Cambridge Law Journal*, 71 (2), 355-383, 2012

Sheffield Wednesday Football Club Ltd v Hargreaves [2007] EWHC 2375 (QB)

Short, Nigel, *Nigel 1 – Cancer 0: The Online Ramblings of a Cancer Survivor* (The Solopreneur Publishing Company Ltd., 2013)

Other

Birchall, Johnston, *Co-op: The People's Business* (Manchester University Press, 1994)

Caruth, James, *The Death of Narrative* (*Smith Doorstop* Books, 2014)

Gratton, Chris and Henry, Ian P. (eds.), *Sport in the City: The Role of Sport in Economic and Social Regeneration* (Routledge, 2001)

Gratton, Chris and Taylor, Peter, *Governance and the Economics of Sport* (Longman, 1991)

Hatherley, Owen, *A Guide to the New Ruins of Great Britain* (Verso, 2012). *Militant Modernism* (0 Books, 2008)

Jones, Owen, *The Establishment: And How They Get Away With It* (Allen Lane, 2014)

Lampe, John R., *Yugoslavia as History: Twice there was a Country* (Cambridge University Press, 1996) .

Little Global Cities: Novi Sad (Kerber Verlag, 2012)

MacCurrach, Robert, *In the Bend of the River: Finding Vojvodina* (Book Stream, 2010)

MacGregor Marshall, Andrew, *A Kingdom in Crisis: Thailand's Struggle for Democracy in the 20-First Century* (Zed Books, 2015)

Orwell, George, *The Road to Wigan Pier* (Victor Gollancz, 1937)

Priestley, J. B., *English Journey* (William Heinemann Ltd., 1934)

Scraton, Phil, *The State of the Police* (Pluto Press Limited, 1985)

Shepherd, Ben, *Terror in the Balkans: German Armies and Partizan Warfare* (Harvard University Press, 2012)

Thorpe, Nick, *The Danube: A Journey Upriver from the Black Sea to the Black Forest* (Yale University Press, 2013)

Turner, Alwyn W., *A Classless Society: Britain in the 1990s* (Aurum Press Ltd., 2013). *Rejoice! Rejoice! Britain in the 1980s* (Aurum Press Ltd., 2010)

Wilson, Duncan, *Tito's Yugoslavia* (Cambridge University Press, 1979)

Zirin, Dave, *Bad Sports: How Owners Are Ruining the Games We Love* (Scriber, 2010)

Magazines and Newspapers

Daily Mail
Daily Mirror
Daily Telegraph
FC Business
Financial Times
FourFourTwo
France Football (France)
Green 'Un
Guardian
The Independent
L'Equipe (France)
The Mail on Sunday
News of the World
New York Times (United States)
The Observer
Sheffield Independent
Sheffield Morning Telegraph
Sheffield Star
Sheffield Telegraph
Sports Illustrated (United States)
The Sunday Times
The Times
The Wall Street Journal (United States)
When Saturday Comes
Yorkshire Post

Fanzines

A View from the East Bank
Just Another Wednesday

Websites

adrianbullock.com (The Sheffield Wednesday Archive)
bbc.co.uk
britishpathe.com
hillsboroughinquests.independent.gov.uk
insideworldfootball.com

BIBLIOGRAPHY

owlstalk.co.uk
sportingintelligence.com
swfc.co.uk
swissramble.blogspot.com

Other

Various club programmes, publications and company accounts,
videos and DVDs.

About The Author

Tom Whitworth's work has appeared in, among other publications, *When Saturday Comes* and *FC Business*. A Sheffield Wednesday fan, he lives in Sheffield, up one of its many hills.